FIONA STANFORD

DON'T SAY GOODBYE

Our Heroes and the Families they Leave Behind

HODDER

First published in Great Britain in 2011 by Hodder & Stoughton
An Hachette UK company

First published in paperback in 2011

1

ISBN 978 1 444 71636 8
eBook ISBN 978 1 444 71637 5

Typeset in Plantin Light by Hewer Text UK Ltd, Edinburgh

Printed and bound by CPI Group (UK), Croydon, CR0 4YY

Hodder & Stoughton policy is to use papers that are natural, renewable
and recyclable products and made from wood grown in sustainable forests.
The logging and manufacturing processes are expected to conform
to the environmental regulations of the country of origin.

Hodder & Stoughton Ltd
338 Euston Road
London NW1 3BH

www.hodder.co.uk

40% of the author's net profits from sales of this edition will be donated to charity.*

Foreword

CLARENCE HOUSE

I was enormously touched to have been asked by Fiona Stanford to write a foreword for *Don't Say Goodbye*. I am full of admiration for Fiona's unshakeable determination to produce this most moving of books.

As Colonel of the Welsh Guards and as a father of two serving officers, I know only too well the hugely significant role the families of our soldiers play in supporting their loved ones. They are very much an integral part of our proud Regiment and I am incredibly pleased that their often underestimated support has been highlighted in this important book.

In a small way I have experienced what it is like to be 'behind the scenes.' I do know something about the worry, the hope, the desire to see their safe return, yet knowing that their role is crucial and backing them in their decision to fight for our country. In such a position, and as a parent, my condolences for those who have lost their loved ones are deeply heartfelt. By raising funds for the bereaved, the wounded and their families, *Don't Say Goodbye* will play a part in doing all we can, in turn, to support them.

In recognizing this devotion on the home front, given so selflessly not only by the Welsh Guards families but, by the wider military community, I hope the nation as a whole will join me in thanking them and in acknowledging the vital part they play in supporting the Armed Forces.

Introduction

During the summer of 2009, seven men from the 1st Battalion Welsh Guards were killed in action while on operations in Helmand Province, Afghanistan. One of these men was the Commanding Officer, Lieutenant Colonel Rupert Thorneloe, who died instantly when his vehicle drove over a roadside bomb. Every death is one too many, but this incident particularly shook me because Rupert's wife Sally is a friend of mine.

My husband Richard handed over command of the Battalion to Rupert just before the Welsh Guards deployed to Afghanistan, and they knew each other well. Rupert was a lovely man – a wonderful husband and father, and an excellent soldier. He epitomised the essence of a small, family regiment by his loyalty, hard work and sense of duty. Since Richard and I married in 1995, my life has become very much a part of this close-knit 'family'. I know at first hand the agonies suffered by the families of those men who are away fighting. And when Rupert was killed, I knew that it could so easily have been Richard.

I went to Rupert's funeral and watched as his coffin, draped with the Union Jack, bearing white roses, his forage cap and ceremonial sword, was carried up the steps and into the Guards Chapel in London. Inside the Chapel I looked around at the other wives, most of whom had husbands who were still away fighting in Afghanistan and who were living with the daily torment that they might be next to receive the 'knock on the door'. Seeing the utter despair in their eyes was heart-breaking. They were filled with grief and sadness but also with the hope that their own time bomb would not explode, taking their husbands away – every Army wife's ultimate nightmare. The relief that it had not happened yet, combined with the guilt at the awareness that another wife, mother, and family's life had been plunged into darkness, played havoc with their emotions, as it had done so many times with mine. I felt so lucky. Richard was out in Iraq at the time, which was no longer as dangerous a place as Afghanistan was proving to be. The fighting in Afghanistan is said to have been the fiercest and most intense since the Second World War so I felt that Richard was comparatively safe living and working with the Iraqi Army in Basra.

Sally had the rest of her life to face without her husband, and their children without their father. Standing in the Chapel, I realised that I wanted to tell the story; Sally's story, the story of the six other Welsh Guardsmen who had been killed that summer, the stories of all the thousands of families left behind when their loved ones go off to fight, and my own story, as an Army wife living an Army lifestyle. I felt that the least I could do was to honour Rupert's death with a tribute to him, to his six comrades and to the many other servicemen and women who have been killed while serving their country in Afghanistan. It was a chance to perpetuate, in a small way, the memories of these men and women and to honour the sacrifices made by them and their families. It would recognise not only the contribution made by the wounded and the Battalion as a whole but also the support given by their families behind the scenes. The story focuses on the Welsh Guards, but it reflects that of every family in the Army, Navy and Air Force.

As I stood in the Chapel, full of sadness and acutely aware of the grief and anxiety that was overwhelming my friends, I realised that as well as writing a memorial, I wanted to bridge the gulf in experience between Army families and the civilian population. Although public support for service personnel on operations overseas is usually significant and, thankfully, growing, the public can rarely empathise with the challenges faced by the families, let alone their way of life. The overseas service lifestyle is sometimes perceived as a glamorous whirlwind of balls and exotic postings, but these are few and far between nowadays. During the two world wars whole nations suffered vast numbers of casualties and deaths. There was hardly a soul untouched by the effects of war and conscription meant that there was no choice but to fight. Nowadays, National Service is a thing of the past and the Armed Forces has shrunk to such an extent that very few people are exposed to even a taste of military life. The British Army is smaller than it has been since the 1800s, yet it is stretched to its limits; to put its size into perspective, it would only just fill Wembley Stadium. The pressure on the Armed Forces for the numbers involved is greater than ever. Average tours are six months, but taking pre-deployment training into account the real time spent away is usually at least nine. British senior officers are now doing tours that last a year. How do relationships manage to survive the inevitable separations unscathed? Many don't.

I wanted to show this human face of the support behind the scenes that allows the Armed Forces to do its job, which it does on behalf of all of us. The conflict in Afghanistan is ongoing and undeniably contentious, but whatever the reasons for or against our involvement in the war, the bottom line is that members of our own Armed Forces are out there, doing their best and in order to do this effectively they need both moral and physical support from their families at home. After all, a happy and supportive home life makes for a contented, focused and loyal serviceman or woman. The media coverage and sympathy shown to the families when their loved ones are repatriated or when they are wounded is a testament to the empathy demonstrated by the general public, and the money raised for the growing number of military charities also shows how much public support there is. Nevertheless, Armed Forces families are usually out of the limelight – until the worst happens.

It was at the funerals in the summer of 2009, when I was confronted with the ultimate price paid by the Welsh Guardsmen who died and by the grief of their families, that I understood that writing this book was not just a good idea, it was a necessity.

I want to tell the story of the people left behind.

Despite the anguish felt by those left at home during the Afghanistan tour, one overwhelmingly positive aspect of the situation was the strength the families gained from each other and the lifelong friendships that were formed. Experiences like these are what make Army life unique, and are incredibly valuable. When laughter overcomes tears it becomes a cherished privilege; family time and the family unit become sacred and life is appreciated and valued. Nothing is taken for granted. I wanted to describe these positives as well as the challenges, and to focus on the camaraderie among the families, particularly the women. They support their men in their chosen career, frequently shelving their own careers to do so; they live a nomadic existence, as do their children, despite sometimes yearning for a safer, more settled and 'normal' life. They are truly the backbone of the Armed Forces. Camaraderie is a word that is too often attributed only to the men, but it develops among the women into a strong community spirit; something that is frequently absent in busy lives lived in different circumstances.

The expression 'Army wife' is dreaded by all the wives I know and is often a synonym for a fearsome, organising woman. It conjures up the image of an expert flower arranger who can whip up dinner parties at a moment's notice. Things have changed, thank goodness, although we do need to be adaptable, organised and capable of being independent. Flower arranging is not a requirement; flexibility is.

Wives, mothers and 'sweethearts' have of course been keeping the home fires burning while their men have been at war for generations, but times have changed and are still changing. Warfare has developed from an agreed rendezvous on a battlefield, often watched from high ground by the wives (and camp followers) themselves, through to trench warfare, and on to conflict with the unknown enemy of the modern terrorist. Communication has also changed; we now live in the age of rolling news, presented very graphically. 'No news is good news' was all that families had to go on in the past, when letters and messages could take months to arrive. Now we have instant texting, email, video links with Skype and live satellite reports delivered to our own homes. Sometimes I think this is a mixed blessing. Of course it is wonderful to be able to know more and faster in an emergency, and a joy to speak to your husband when he is away, but in warfare, circumstances are always unpredictable, so communication is still patchy. Many times I have wished for a respite from the images from places of conflict when Richard has been deployed there and we have been unable to speak.

The one constant throughout the ages is human emotion. The wife left to tend the home when her husband fought at Agincourt must have experienced the same worry, the same questions from her children and the same fear of bad news as today's modern wife trying to hold down a busy job before collecting the children from school, while wondering whether last night's mobile phone conversation with her husband on operations in Afghanistan was their last. In fact, no matter what her nationality, culture or creed, or indeed whether the war's cause is just or not, the wife of a fighting soldier will have experienced the very same anxieties and sentiments right down the ages to the present day.

This is the story of the unsung heroines and families on the modern day home front. Many of the people I spoke to when I was writing this book were already my friends, but some I only met while researching it. Asking someone who does not know me personally to talk to me about their most private thoughts and painful emotions felt like a huge responsibility, and I feel very fortunate to have been entrusted with it. Somehow, though, the bond that unites us, that of belonging to the wider Army family, has allowed the families to whom I have talked to reveal their innermost feelings, special memories and emotions. I am eternally grateful to them. This is my attempt to sing their song, to show their contribution to the vital role their men play and to explain their reasons and feelings to those who ask 'How do you do it?'

Proceeds raised from this book will be donated to the Welsh Guards Afghanistan Appeal, the Regiment's own charity set up to help its bereaved families and those wounded in the conflict, plus the families who support them.*

Dedicated to the seven men from the Welsh Guards killed in action in Afghanistan in 2009:

Tobie Fasfous 28th April
Mark Evison 12th May
Sean Birchall 19th June
Rupert Thorneloe 1st July
Dane Elson 5th July
John Brackpool 9th July
Christopher King 22nd July

We will remember them all, their families and the many who were injured.

To Richard, Oliver and Annabel, for your love and support.

Contents

I

'Why Did I Marry a Soldier?'

4 July 1994; Adam and Eve pillars, summit of Tryfan, Snowdonia, North Wales.

'Will you marry me?'

Richard and I had climbed Tryfan, one of our favourite mountains in North Wales, on a clear but blustery summer afternoon, the air still fresh after the morning's rain. The view over to the neighbouring Glyders and the Carneddau across the Ogwen Valley was breathtaking and the serene beauty of Llyn Ogwen was stunning. We had the summit to ourselves and had scrambled up to the very highest point. After all, you cannot climb this particular mountain without also scaling the two seven foot standing stone monoliths on the summit, named Adam and Eve. I don't know which is which, but I do know that they are four feet apart and that when jumping from one to the other there is a three thousand foot drop to the base of the mountain.

'Yes,' I replied, raising my voice above the gusts of wind. I didn't need to pluck up courage to make that four-foot jump; the adrenaline was already running high. We both stood up simultaneously, leaped across to the other standing stone, laughed and then Richard jumped back to mine. Those who do the jump are said to have made the 'Leap of Faith'. It was doubly appropriate for us at that moment, which, in keeping with the date, we jokingly nicknamed the 'end of independence day'.

Richard asked for 'permission' to get married, twice; the first time, as a token of respect, from my father and the second, according to Army tradition, from his own senior officer. At the time he was just taking over a role as ADC (Aide de Camp) to General Charles (now General The Lord Guthrie) in the Ministry of Defence (MOD). When he plucked up the courage to ask my father, on a glorious summer's day in my parents' garden, my mother very nearly dropped the tray of tea and cake she was carrying to the table in her excitement. The following week, he asked his senior officer. This is also a formality nowadays, but it goes back to the times when any officer below the rank of Captain was not considered to be earning enough to support a wife. It gave the senior officer the chance to give permission, or not, as the case may have been. Coincidentally, the officer Richard was taking over from had just become engaged as well and had, ten minutes beforehand, asked General Charles if he could 'have permission' to get married. 'Of course, and congratulations,' was the gist of the reply. Richard, oblivious to the fact that General Charles had just been asked this question, took a deep breath and knocked on the same door to ask whether he could get married. General Charles's face was one of astonishment and surprise as the second question was 'popped' hot on the heels of the first. 'What?' he replied, 'to each other?'

We had met in 1985 when we were both eighteen, on a British Schools Exploring Society expedition to Alaska. That was my first big adventure after leaving school in Buckinghamshire, where I had spent most of my teenage years. When I got back from the wilds of Alaska I headed for London, to begin my nursing training at St Thomas' Hospital and Richard began his officer training at the Royal Military Academy (RMA) Sandhurst. We would see each other frequently and we had a lot of fun, but our relationship was firmly 'just friends'. In fact, we had a mutually beneficial arrangement: Richard would provide friends for the nurses' parties, and I the nurses for the Sandhurst and young officers' functions. Although we kept in touch, we were often in different parts of the world; either he was away with the Army, or I was off travelling and nursing overseas, in Australia and Chile.

Finally, in 1993, we realised what we had, right under our noses. He had volunteered for, and passed, the US Ranger course, a very gruelling sixty-eight days of starvation, sleep deprivation and making decisions on an empty stomach. Afterwards, I flew out to Washington to see him. Having not recognised him at the airport, looking as he did – emaciated and with his head shaved – I spent the next week watching him eat as if each meal were his last. On one occasion he ate a whole duck in a Chinese restaurant, head and all; even the waiter was impressed. By the end of the trip, during which we drove from Washington to New York, the Shenandoah Valley, the Blue Ridge Mountains and Pennsylvania, we realised that it was time to make a few decisions together. We were engaged, on Tryfan, six months later.

The following year was spent in the whirlwind that inevitably goes with planning a wedding. My mother took to it willingly and worked all hours to ensure that it was all we had ever wished for. The only thing she could not plan was the June weather and it rained solidly all day until the guests departed, at which point the sun finally shone over the distant Malvern Hills.

After an idyllic honeymoon we moved into our first quarter in London to embark on married life. Unfortunately, we were forced to confront harsh reality almost immediately. Within two weeks of our returning from honeymoon my mother was taken ill, and after a long and agonising eight months she died. Two weeks later my maternal grandmother died, and two weeks after that we set off on our first overseas posting in the Sultanate of Oman. I was nine weeks pregnant with our first child and had visions of giving birth behind a sand dune. This turbulent first year of our marriage was a true test of solidarity; during this time I had worn a white wedding dress and two black mourning suits, had packed all our belongings into Military Forces Overseas boxes and said goodbye to the family and friends on whom I had leant so heavily over the past few bitter-sweet months.

Our nomadic lifestyle had begun, and where could be more appropriate than among the Bedu of the Wahiba Sands. Oman was an adventure and in some ways just what I needed after the sadness of the previous few months, but to begin with it was almost too much too soon. I was catapulted into a different culture and knew nobody other than Richard as the posting was away from the Battalion itself. It was an unreal existence for me and from my little bubble I could almost convince myself that my mother had not died. Visiting family and friends were a vital link to the life I had left behind, even though we were meeting new friends in Oman and making the most of our exciting surroundings. I missed my mother terribly in those first few months, but never so much as when the baby arrived. A good mother/daughter relationship is one of the most precious things a first-time mum can have, valued all the more in its absence; I craved having her there to advise, help and coo over a new baby as only a grandmother can.

Richard's parents visited for two weeks and were staying with us when Oliver was born, and their support was invaluable. Without a daughter of her own, Richard's mother Jane was only too happy to stand in and offer me support, but was tactful enough to avoid trying to 'replace' my own mother. My sister Kate also came out from England for two weeks when Oliver was six weeks old, leaving her own two small boys with her husband. It did not start well: her flight came into Muscat at 2 a.m. and, being exhausted new parents, we decided to set our alarm and snatch a few hours sleep before-hand. Unfortunately we slept through it and woke suddenly to Oliver crying at 3 a.m., to realise that Kate had been wait-ing patiently at the airport for an hour without our phone number. Thankfully she was not at all upset; the sense of adventure and freedom she suddenly discovered outweighed any disgruntlement.

Her visit did me the world of good; we had a chance to bond as never before in our adult lives. We went to the camel races, visited forts, snorkelled with turtles and shopped in the souks. Kate even got up in the night to help with nappy changing. She threw herself into the spirit of adventure, sleeping in the open desert with the rest of our party when we took Oliver on his first camping trip. Oliver and I had it easy in a zipped tent but it was not big enough for two people and a travel cot, so Kate was outside. Given that she has a phobia of snakes, this was an amazing achievement for her; seeing the snake tracks in the sand the following morning at least proved to her that she could overcome it.

Without Richard's understanding and support to help me through, I would not be telling the tale of our Army life now. Oman was a very special time for us. He was always there to listen, to comfort and to laugh with me, and that laid the foun-dations for our future. We had no television, only a radio, and we would tune into the World Service frequently. The nursery rhyme 'Rock a bye baby' will always take me straight back to the signature tune for the start of the broadcast. The laughter and the tears of our first two years of marriage set the seal on our relationship and we felt ready to face anything else that fate may throw at us, together. I had no expectations other than to enter this brave new world of Army life as a team.

Given my own life choices, my mother had been the perfect role model for me. She supported my father in all his decisions as he made his way in his long and highly successful police career, even at her own cost. My family lived in a world where public service was considered a serious matter and we all knew that there were sacrifices to be made. Sadly, she never lived to see him receive his knighthood and his life peerage in recognition of his devotion to duty. The longest I have lived anywhere in my life was in Nottinghamshire from the age of six to thirteen. I know my mother loved living there, and the wrench of moving to Buckinghamshire (relative suburbia for her) was tough. At the same time my sister was leaving home and my brother Simon joined the police force himself. Suddenly, as the only child left at home the bond between my mother and me grew very strong and I realised for the first time just how much she had supported my father over the years. She never moaned about the upheavals or having to leave her friends, and always made the best of any situation, for all of our sakes. I have a lot to thank her for, if only I could do so. It was this bedrock of constancy and loyalty in an ever-changing life that gave me the confidence to approach an Army marriage with my eyes wide open.

So, when I made my vows, I promised loyalty not only to Richard but also, indirectly, to the Welsh Guards. From that day on, my life was to be dictated by the ensuing postings, their locations and the opportunities and constraints imposed by them. Getting married is one of the biggest decisions in anyone's life; marrying a soldier means you share your marriage with the Army and must take on the 'baggage', warts and all.

I have asked many of my friends from the Battalion to give me their thoughts on the complexities of marrying into the Army. Over and over again I have heard that the driving force behind the decision to commit to a soldier was the same as it is for any woman to any man – love, and a desire to spend the rest of their lives with someone, to have a family and grow old together. This is my answer to the question 'How do you cope with being married to a soldier?' I cope because I have chosen to and because Richard is my soulmate, so I am very very motivated. But despite all that, it is certainly true that there are other things to consider aside from love, such as a commitment to a whole new way of life.

Annabel Lewis, whose husband Mark is a Major in the Welsh Guards, writes:

'A forthcoming tour often speeds up a proposal, which then inevitably leads to a lone engagement or spending the first six months of marriage alone. When your boyfriend's in the Forces, deciding to get married is not a simple "yes" or "no" answer to the question, "Do I love him/can I spend the rest of my life with him?" The question is also "Can I be happy without my own home for the next thirty years, can I move house every couple of years, do I want to live apart from him to have my children at home or will my children go to boarding school so I can follow my husband around?" These questions are virtually impossible to answer, not least for a woman in her twenties who has been living an independent life in her own home with her own friends and money.'

Another friend, Alice, was engaged to Major Giles Harris while he was a Company Commander with the Welsh Guards in Afghanistan in the summer of 2009 and her relationship was put to the test before their wedding day, which was set for a few weeks after the Battalion's return. Some would say that planning a wedding without a fiancé at hand might have its advantages, but Alice was doing so with a cloud of anguish hanging over her. To organise such a momentous occasion while wondering whether Giles would make it back in one piece could be construed as tempting fate, but Alice was determined that a positive outlook was the only way to deal with the situation. She relied heavily on the friendships she made while Giles was in Afghanistan. Alice describes the circle of friends who would pull each other through:

'*We used to have twice-monthly girly nights out, usually in Battersea. They started with five of us after my friend Alannah texted me to suggest getting together, and I then invited three other friends whose boyfriends were away with the Battalion. That first night, we sat in 'The Lavender' pub and chatted over a bottle of wine. It was about two weeks into the tour. After about an hour one of the girls and I got a text informing us that someone from the Battalion had been killed. It was the first text we received, the first time it all became very real. We sat there in shock unsure of the protocol – could it be one of ours? Of course it wasn't – we wouldn't have got that text if it was – but my mind was not func-tioning properly. By the time the tour finished there could be up to twenty of us meeting up in various pubs around Battersea.*

Alannah was an amazing friend to me when Giles was away. My other, non-Army girlfriends, while brilliant, didn't really understand. One of my big things was that I needed to be busy most nights and I hated it when people cancelled on me. One after-noon, having been looking forward to seeing a couple of girlfriends, one emailed me saying that they both had last-minute dates that night. Great for them, but obviously not so good for me, who wasn't on the dating scene! Of course, I called Alannah in tears, who very quickly told me that she would be my date for that night, and we went out for supper. It was great to have that kind of support.

In fact, Giles, and Alannah's boyfriend Speedy [Andrew Speed, a Major in the Scots Guards who was deployed with the Welsh Guards to Afghanistan] *went back to Helmand from R and R* [Rest and Recuperation leave] *together. Alannah and I waved them off at Brize Norton, and then went to a local pub, 'The Trout', to chat about our two weeks with the boys and cheer each other up. It was 11.30 in the morning when the waitress asked us what we wanted. I ordered a very large glass of white wine, to which Alannah said, "I suppose I'll just have a tequila shot." Goodness knows what the waitress thought, but she brought them, and they helped.*'

Alice looks back on her wedding and its preparations with immense relief that she and Giles were lucky enough to be able to see it through. The hardships of being engaged while Giles was deployed in Afghanistan had laid the foundations for absolute commitment, and the conviction that they had made the right choice.

'Since I got married I wake up every morning feeling hugely lucky that my husband is lying next to me. Up to two months before the wedding, I remember feeling that I was incapable of getting truly excited. Don't get me wrong – I cooed over the dress, read hundreds of readings and chose two, decided on the invitation list and booked the honeymoon. But until I knew Giles was safely landed in the UK, I couldn't get truly and rip-roaringly excited – it was still a "what if" situation.

When I walked down that aisle I knew that I had made the right decision. I had thought about this man every moment from the time he left, even when I was at work, or out with my friends, or trying to get to sleep, he was in my thoughts. I knew, without a doubt, that I wanted to marry him. I also felt very relaxed about the wedding itself – as long as he was there on the day, and I was there, then it would be wonderful, everything else a bonus. I don't know many women who are put in a position where they learn to appreciate their other half in quite the same way, because of that fear that he might be taken away from you.

Organising the wedding was certainly a challenge, though. Deciding on the invitation list over a fuzzy phone line to Afghanistan while being cut off at regular intervals was frustrating but goodness knows how surreal it must have been for him, having to discuss hymns and flowers, while sitting on a dusty vehicle in the back of beyond! An image I will never forget was having the church rehearsal with my husband-to-be standing next to me in desert combats, the best man next to him also in combats and the person marrying us (the padre from the tour) also in combats, having come from a memorial service.

It has been a life-changing experience, one where I feel I have come out a stronger and better person. I'm more relaxed about life and more appreciative of the wonderful family, friends and husband I have. I've also made new friends who have been in the same situation to laugh and cry with. I am lucky – other wives, fiancés and girlfriends in the Regiment and outside it have not been as fortunate and I will always remember that – but my husband came home, and I hope I'll always feel as blessed.'

Michelle Bowen's introduction to her husband Alun (now a Capt) in the summer of 1987 is the stuff of fairy tales. Alun was present at the wedding of Dai Matthews, a fellow Guardsman, as one of the Guard of Honour (the line of six Guardsmen standing either side of the church door, through which the bride and groom walk as they emerge from the church after the wedding service). Michelle had been invited as a guest of the bride, Tracey, and tells the tale of how they met:

'At the end of the service, during which the majority of the Guard of Honour were in the local pub across the road, the traditional throwing of the bouquet took place. Alun watched as the beautiful flowers sailed through the summer air and towards him. Thankfully they missed and landed in my hands as I was standing immediately to the left of him. Until that point neither of us had noticed each other's presence (well not true really as Alun was resplendent in a smart red tunic and big furry hat ... how could he not be noticed?) but as I caught the flowers Alun mentioned that it was lucky and that I would clearly be married next ...'

The romance continued after the catching of the bouquet. On 29 February 1988 Michelle decided to take the initiative, taking advantage of the leap year tradition of women being allowed to propose on this date. Either that or she may have had to wait another four years:

> *'We were sitting in a small café in Cardiff when I popped the question out of the blue in a jovial fashion but had a surprise when I received a positive reply. This was, however, followed by a proper proposal by Alun after he bought the ring. He turned and shouted "catch", throwing the ring at me, in keeping with the bouquet incident!'*

The wedding, in July 1990, went smoothly, disguising several calamities that had happened in the run-up. A 'play' fight between Alun and one of his pageboys on the way to his stag night resulted in a Friday evening visit to the casualty department of a busy Cardiff hospital to glue the gash in Alun's head. On the morning of the big day Michelle unpacked the three boxes containing the wedding cake to find that a horde of ants had invaded them. (Thankfully a hairdryer set to cool and blown frantically removed the ants, and the guests were never any the wiser.)

Then the saga of Alun's best drill boots, highly polished and ready for him to wear with his ceremonial uniform, which were hijacked by his best man the night before. Michelle explained:

> *'When Alun knelt for the marriage to be blessed, a "Mutley" laugh boomed out around the small church. My father, seated at the front, had spotted a large "HE" on the left boot and an equally large "LP" on the right boot . . . you get the idea.'*

Once the couple is through the challenges of the engagement and the wedding itself, real life arrives, in the shape of Army accommodation. Impressions of the first allocated married quarter are very lasting: it is a memorable time for all newlyweds. For those who had previously lived in their own homes it may come as a shock to no longer be in control of where they live.

An unmarried serviceman or -woman is allocated a room 'in barracks' which is on the Battalion's base, or camp; the location dependent upon where it is posted at the time. This is where the Battalion headquarters are situated, behind the wire, where security is tightly controlled by a guardroom entrance and a patrolled perimeter fence.

A married quarter is a house provided by the Army for married couples and their children. Sometimes these quarters are on the base, but more often they are outside the wire on a 'patch' as close to the Battalion's base as possible and among other identical or similar Army houses. The size of the quarter is allocated by rank for officers but by family size for Non Commisioned Officers (NCOs). In certain circumstances single-parent service personnel are also entitled to a quarter. Rent is deducted from the serviceman or woman's salary to pay for lodgings.

Although every room in a quarter is painted in the safe but predictable shade of magnolia, occupants may change the colour scheme as long as they paint it back to magnolia when they hand the quarter over again.

Army issue curtains have improved over recent years, from the hessian shades of beige, to the slightly more acceptable floral patterns, but still they may not be everybody's cup of tea. Waking up to their busy swirly patterns with the sun streaming through from behind them usually gives me the same sensation as waking up with a thick hangover, and certainly makes an existing hangover worse. They are also unlined, so many people buy or make their own. Putting in lots of rugs is another quick trick for personalising the space. Some people have been known to buy 'fake' fireplaces to surround the gas or electric fires to give a room a focal point, as there are few open fires with their own mantelpieces left. As far as the garden goes, moving with outdoor pots is the answer unless you want to spend a year planting up a garden, only to move before you have a chance to see it blossom.

Our own first married quarter was a ground-floor flat in West Hampstead with a communal play area for children but no garden, where we lived for eight months before being posted to Oman. Although our wedding presents had set us up nicely, we had not put any furniture on the list and only possessed a hat stand and a laundry basket of our own; the rest belonged to the MOD.

My first impression, far from the fairytale newlyweds' 'Rose Cottage', was of the iron shutters across the windows, which we were advised to lock every time we left the flat unattended. The bedhead had bedside tables built into it so that every cup of tea spilt as soon as you sat on the edge, and the dining-room chairs were covered in black fake leather. Nonetheless, it was home and we were very proud of it.

We had been allowed to move our few belongings into the flat just before we were married, so that there would be somewhere already set up when we returned from our honeymoon. I had been to the flat a few times, but nothing prepared me for how I would feel arriving at our marital home for the first time as a wife.

Suitcase in hand with its 'going away' outfit inside, I paused in the street outside the entrance to our new home. Strangers passing by must surely have known we had just got married: didn't we have it written all over our faces? I was certain that no other newly married couple could ever have been, nor ever would be, on such a high as we were. In my daze, I had not realised that Richard was speaking to me, and taking my case from my hands while guiding me in through the outer door and into the communal entrance hall.

'Sorry? What was that?' I asked, surprised that I had somehow arrived in front of our own door without realising it.

'I said, romance hasn't died yet.'

'Oh no, course not. What are you talking about, the wedding?'

'No, this,' he replied, and before I had time to prepare, he had scooped me up, pushed open the front door, carried me over the threshold and kicked the door shut, blocking out the world outside.

Surprisingly for a block of six or so flats occupied by likeminded Army personnel, people seemed to keep themselves to themselves and as I was working locally I did not have the opportunity to bump into people during the day. One evening I decided to introduce myself to our neighbours. They were all pleasant enough and seemed to have their own busy lives, which was no big surprise in London, but no one seemed to know the occupants on the ground floor across the entrance hall from us. These elusive people clearly existed because their door was sometimes ajar, although when I approached it was always quickly shut. I was disappointed: this was not the welcome committee I had expected. I had thought all Army wives would be only too pleased to introduce themselves, if only out of nosiness. Nevertheless, I knocked on the door a few times in anticipation, but nobody ever answered. Eventually I decided that they must be doing a John Lennon and Yoko Ono thing, were probably on honeymoon and not receiving visitors, so I left them in peace.

It was not until one evening a couple of weeks later, when I was starting to resent the fact that our own honeymoon had not been as long as theirs, that I was alerted by a commotion from the direction of their flat.

I heard an urgent hammering on their door, followed by commands of 'If you don't open up we'll be forced to break in.'

I rushed to bolt the front door, unable to resist a peep through the spy hole at the same time. Unfortunately, it was slightly out of line with their door, so all I could see were the elbows of men in Army uniform. At least I knew we didn't have burglars on our hands, but I decided to make use of our security measures and hastily drew the shutters, and locked them for good measure. Muffled conversations then ensued along the lines of 'You have no right' and 'We have every right, this is MOD property,' followed by the slamming of interior doors and finally, the external front door. Then silence. I felt as though I had been nothing but a 'curtain twitcher' after that, and slightly foolish that I was now barricaded into my own flat for no reason, so let down the metaphorical drawbridge again and had a look around outside. No evidence of forced entry, and a closed front door over the corridor. It was as though nothing untoward had ever occurred.

It transpired through Richard's investigations the follow-ing day that the Army had been alerted to some squatters in the building who, thinking they were on to a good thing, had not appreciated that an Army quarter is patrolled by armed Military Police who can be an imposing sight. Having been confronted, the squatters had fled, tails between their legs, and I was only sorry that I never did get a good look at them before they went. I doubt the 'march out' inspection, now called a 'move out' inspection, when the quarter is inspected for clean-liness on handover to a new occupant, was up to standard when they vacated the property.

Catrina Campbell is married to Andrew, a WO2 (Warrant Officer Class Two) in the Welsh Guards. I first met her while mucking out stables for the Household Cavalry horses in Pirbright, Surrey, the old Guards' Depot and training centre, during our posting to Aldershot in 2000. We became good friends through our mutual wish to have some 'me time' while our children were at nursery, though we were both actually terrified of the huge horses – they were the 'naughty' ones who didn't behave in London for the Trooping of the Colour and who shied at every piece of flapping tarpaulin and at every gunshot, which was unfortunate, as the Pirbright ranges were next to the stables.

Catrina told me that her first married posting was to Ballykelly in County Londonderry, Northern Ireland in the thick of the Troubles with the Irish Republican Army (IRA), who wanted independence from the United Kingdom, and the Loyalists who wanted Northern Ireland to remain part of the UK. It was rather a baptism of fire for a new bride:

'*I married Andy in February 1992 and two months later we were travelling to Ballykelly to begin our new life. This was to be our home for the next two and half years. I can remember feeling nervous and excited all at the same time. All I knew about the area was what I had seen on the news, as the area had been in the thick of the terrorist fighting for twenty three years.*

We arrived in Stranraer [in Dumfries and Galloway, southwest Scotland] *for the crossing to Larne. There were quite a few families travelling to the camp the same day; once we had arrived in Northern Ireland it was like wacky races driving through the lanes at night as everyone was trying to be the first to get to Ballykelly (although none of us had a clue where we were going).*

Our first quarter was a two bedroomed semi-detached house in Shackleton Drive – we had a Parkray coal fireplace. This contraption heated all our water and radiators but we had to make sure that we kept it lit at all times. If I never see a Parkray again it will be too soon. The camp was just like any ordinary housing estate apart from the fact that it was surrounded by a twelve-foot-high fence with barbed wire across the top.

All the quarters were "behind the wire" and there was a Guardroom and a Sanger, which was a fortified building positioned at the entrance. Each time you left and entered the camp you would need to show your ID card. We also had a community centre, "NAAFI" [Naval, Army and Air Force Institute] shop and post room on camp. The community centre was the hub of our lives as most of the wives didn't work and every morning we would go there to meet for a coffee and chat. Due to the terrorist risk your post was delivered to a central post room. After a few weeks I managed to get myself a job handing out the post. The girls I worked with made me feel very welcome and introduced me to lots of the wives.

One of my best memories would be standing in our back garden the day our husbands were returning from operations. I would listen to the sound of the Chinooks bringing them home and at one point they would pass right over our quarter three or four at a time. Even now when I hear or see a Chinook it takes me back to the garden of my first quarter all those years ago. There were some great characters who made my time bearable in Ballykelly and who gave me great support as a new wife.'

There is something about being on a 'patch' surrounded by other quarters. When you are new, people are on the lookout for who their new neighbours are going to be. There might be a day of 'Oh you are the people who have moved into the so-and-sos' old house', which always makes you feel there are boots to fill and expectations to live up to. But soon, you become the real occupants and hardly ever have to go around introducing yourself – apart, that is, from our experience in Hampstead. Whether out of curiosity or kindness, there will always be people knocking on the door, introducing themselves and offering to take the children for you while you unpack. Somehow, despite not knowing them from Adam, you always feel comfortable in letting them do so. It is the unwritten trust that goes with the territory. For a newly married wife, this can seem intrusive, or it can be exactly what is needed when she is suddenly without her own friends and family. The 'intrusion' is usually accepted for what it is very quickly: pure good will.

One friend told me a story about the time she was new to a patch in Germany and was suffering from a dreadful bout of flu. She arrived looking and feeling like nothing on earth. The first thing her neighbours did was to introduce themselves, help her unpack, take the children for tea and offer her their cold remedies, because she had packed hers at the bottom of goodness knows which box.

Sue Miles met Martyn in 1979, when he was a Lance Corporal. He deployed on the Falklands Conflict with the Welsh Guards in 1982 and worked his way up through the ranks, becoming Regimental Sergeant Major of the Battalion. He is now a Major and they have a wealth of experiences from over the years to talk about. They came to stay for the weekend to help me with stories for the book and 'swung the lantern' into the small hours over food and glasses of wine:

> *'I met Martyn in Guildford (my home town) whilst he was posted to Pirbright. He asked me to marry him two weeks after our first date. We were both nineteen years old. Two months later he went to Northern Ireland for a four-month tour; this was my first taste of what Army life was going to be like!!*
>
> *We married in August 1981, two years after our engagement, had one week for a honeymoon, then Martyn went off to Kenya on exercise for seven weeks. During his time away I was notified that a married quarter had become available on Pirbright camp and I moved in with the help of some of my family. Martyn returned from Kenya and had to ask "one of the boys" the whereabouts of his married quarter, as he had been away whilst I moved in. Quite amusing for him as he had to knock at the door.'*

Karen and Nicholas Mott (he is known to the Battalion as Nicky, but not to his mother) were also at the weekend gathering with us. Getting them together with the Miles was very entertaining. Their stories went back a long way. They have been married since 1987 when Nicky was a Guardsman. He, too, had been deployed to the Falklands Conflict shortly after joining the Welsh Guards, and since then he has worked his way up through the ranks to reach Regimental Sergeant Major at the Infantry Training Centre Catterick and has subsequently been successful on commissioning from the ranks; he is currently in the rank of Major. When they first became engaged Karen had no intention of moving around the world in quarters; she had wanted to stay with her family in Ellesmere Port, Cheshire:

'We met at school at the age of eleven. I never thought I would be able to adapt to Army life coming from such a large and very close family. When we first got engaged I thought: "Well, I'm not going with you." Initially, Nicky was going to leave the Army at my request but I could tell his heart wasn't in this decision. He suggested I visit his brother Billy who was in Army quarters in Pirbright to experience some "patch life". After a weekend of socialising I loved the idea, and it put a completely different light on the situation. Twelve months later I found myself married and off to Hohne in West Germany.

My family was upset when I left because no one else had gone away from home before but after that Mum and Dad visited us everywhere except in Northern Ireland. They wouldn't go there as they were too afraid, having heard so much about the violence, but my nan paid for my sister to visit us so she could tell them exactly what it was like. She reported back that it wasn't as bad as they imagined so after that they were a bit happier about us living there.'

Hohne base is on the original site of Belsen, the Nazi concentration camp from the Second World War in which thousands of Jews were executed. It is about two miles long and half a mile wide. The present-day barracks are the same ones used by the SS during the war and look out directly onto the barbed wire that surrounds the old concentration camp, now a memorial site. Mounds the size of football pitches mark the sites of the original huts where the Jews were housed. It is thought that under the floor of the present NAAFI was a mosaic of a swastika and that there was a Nazi eagle above the door, both of which had been chipped away to reveal some of the design underneath. Some of the quarters, too, had the traces of the eagle or swastika where they had been removed and had left a stain underneath. Considering that many men in the Battalion had been fighting in the Falklands only four years previously, the posting to Hohne for five years was not a location conducive to psychological recovery.

The purpose of a NATO presence in Germany after the Second World War was to defend it from the threat of invasion by the Soviet Union. The camp was roughly an hour's drive from the border of the German Democratic Republic, or East Germany, the socialist state established in 1949 in the Soviet zone of occupied Germany where electrified and fortified wire and minefields divided East from West. At German reunification in October 1990 East Germany was integrated into the Federal Republic of Germany (then called West Germany), so a NATO military presence is no longer considered as vital as it was. Consequently the British Army have been pulling troops out of Germany over the last few years and the Welsh Guards has not been posted to Germany since 1988.

After supper, Karen described her experiences in Hohne. Her start to married life and new beginnings was set in such contradictory surroundings, with its haunting reminders of past tragedies and human suffering:

'In Hohne I would get up early in the mornings to go to work with other wives to earn a wage to support the earnings of a Guardsman. We were trying to pay off a sofa we had bought and needed to build up possessions for our new home. My job involved working for the local council in areas such as Belsen Camp where thousands of Jews are buried in mass graves. It was really eerie and had a very strange atmosphere. Even though there were plenty of trees around, there was no birdsong at all on Belsen whereas a few miles away there would be.'

These extraordinary reports of there being no birdsong in Belsen are widespread. Richard has often reflected on this himself, since he spent a year over there during his first posting with the Welsh Guards before we were married. It is as if nature itself has declared Belsen a no-go zone, a place so scarred with suffering and misery that natural instinct forbids its habitation.

Looking back on twenty-three years of married life, Karen firmly believes that the reason her relationship with Nicky has been so strong is because they have not always had their own extended family to call upon in hours of need; they just had to get on with it and sort out any problems they had themselves. Although she comes from a large and close-knit family who would always be there for her, the fact that she and Nicky, away from home, have had to rely on each other as a team has made their marriage stronger. Even when Nicky goes away on tours they still regard themselves as being 'in it together', having both decided that this was the way of life they wanted, and this has made them recognise each other's role in the team. From paying off their first sofa to buying their own house fifteen years later, they have supported each other through the good times and the bad.

Those outside the Army often ask how we, as wives and girl-friends, cope with our lifestyle, and frequently comment that they could never be an Army wife themselves. They question how we can willingly send our men off to conflicts knowing that they may not come back. The fact is that they probably could and would cope if they ever fell in love with a soldier and decided to support him in his chosen career. When we meet our partners they are often already doing the job they love and all we can do is to support them in that, just as the wife of a policeman or doctor marries into their husband's way of life. The difference with a military career is that the families are bound up with its lifestyle, especially if they live in quarters, to the extent that having any sort of independent existence becomes virtually impossible. The alternative would be to ask the husband or partner to leave the military, which does happen of course, but obviously they might not be happy doing something other than their military vocation. Inevitably, some situations test even the most dedicated and there is no knowing how relationships will cope until they are put to the test.

As ninety-five per cent of the Guardsmen are Welsh, their girlfriends and wives often come from their home towns. In some cases, this means that a newly married wife may have been plucked from the Welsh Valleys where her family has lived within a few miles, or streets, of each other for generations, and placed in her first married quarter in the anonymity of Central London or Aldershot. Many families speak Welsh at home and for them, the language and culture shock can be enormous. Homesickness is a new and upsetting experience for them on top of a totally new way of life.

Nowadays, in a thirty-six-month period, a British soldier will spend on average seven and a half months away from home on exercise and training courses in preparation for an operational tour, and will then spend six months on the tour itself. During this time the families are also moved between postings; for the Welsh Guards once every two to two and a half years. The Welsh Guards now rotates between Hounslow, from where the men will do ceremonial duties in London for the duration of their posting, and Aldershot, from where the Battalion will prepare and deploy on operations.

If a new wife marries just before one of these six-month tours she can be left alone, and very scared. In these situations most new wives would choose to go back to their families for the duration. If she does come from an area such as the Welsh Valleys, where she has grown up surrounded by family, extended family and friends, the community spirit in these places is still very much alive and often provides all the support she needs when without her husband.

There are many ways of coping, but the ultimate test presents itself when the men are away in direct combat and there is a very real possibility of their being wounded or killed. Despite the advances in communication and the changes in warfare over the centuries, the one constant is that of human sentiment; the raw emotion, constant worry and feeling of helplessness that those at home experience must have been the same ever since men first went away to fight.

Stacey Merritt-Webb's husband Darren is a Lance Sergeant in the Welsh Guards. Her raw emotion can be seen in the journal she wrote when he was in Afghanistan. At times she found the separation too much to bear, as is summed up in one of her comments:

> *'No one understands the constant ache in my heart, I miss him so much. Why did I marry a soldier?'*

Although the speed of modern communication is a far cry from the 'snail mail' of days past, letter writing remains a favourite way of sharing news and imparting feelings. The anticipation of receiving a letter and the pleasure in taking it away to read and reread in private is a rare treat in these days of fast emails and quick texts.

Margaret Antelme is married to Charles (Charlie), the present Commanding Officer of the Welsh Guards, who took over from Rupert Thorneloe after he was tragically killed in Afghanistan. At the time, Margaret had only known Charlie for three months while he had been in London working at the MOD.

Margaret comes from a family with a long tradition of service in the American military. Both sets of her grandparents were in the Army and her parents grew up in army quarters all over the US and Europe, where they met at the age of twelve. Her uncle also joined the Army. Her aunt, Jan, has endured being at home for her husband's multiple year-long deployments during her twenty-eight-year marriage to a US Army Officer. Margaret tells of her aunt's advice to her when Charlie went to Afghanistan:

> *'She told me it was crucial to stay "connected" to a husband in the Army. Through the years, connection had become invariably easier gradually evolving from the "MARS" grams and letters, to mobile phones and email.* [MARS stood for Military Affiliated Radio System, which was the only form of communication for US Forces before mobile phones.] *When you are apart for long periods of time, one cannot predict events that will change you during those absences, so finding ways to keep this connection is her advice to all Army wives during deployments. Jan said to me in a letter:*
>
> *"Find ways to live each day together even when apart. Just as our soldiers plan their military campaigns, I began planning to ensure we remained "in touch" and launched our military campaign. In putting together my husband's mail kit (for his use), I purchased stationery and pastel envelopes. I stamped and*

addressed each envelope for him and provided mailing labels for our children and his parents as well. I packed it all in waterproof bags and told him all I needed was a periodic short note letting me know he was okay. My mail kit consisted of 4X6 cards and envelopes. Each day, I sat in the rocking chairs on our front porch and wrote a short note so he remained up to date on "our life" back home. Friends made a few good-natured jokes about my mailing campaign, but it was important to us as a couple. Two weeks leave out of twelve months does not a relationship make . . . I treasured every pastel envelope encased letter that arrived in my mail. And when the 3rd Infantry Division returned, several of his comrades told me that upon their arrival in Baghdad, and his unit's assignment to a specific section of the city (i.e., more permanent quarters), they saw the stack of letters on Will's desk. We've kept those letters and someday I'll share those, along with our emails, with our children."'

Margaret welcomed this advice from her aunt, and acted on it:

'No matter how much we have resolved to using modern forms of communication, there is nothing more powerful than receiving a handwritten note. I decided to send Charlie at least one parcel a week with small things that reminded him of London and our life here together. He unexpectedly proposed the week he returned from Afghanistan. Although it is a different year, a different war, and a different country, the women of my family have all shared the same experiences in the Army, and it is these experiences which continue to unite us as a family. Even with technology and better forms of communication, nothing can change the emotions one feels when a loved one goes off to war for an indefinite amount of time. I feel fortunate to have had such amazing advice, which I hope will give other wives the stability to survive a first deployment in these unpredictable times.'

While researching old letters written during the Second World War by wives and sweethearts whose loved ones were fighting overseas, I was struck by the similarity of the sentiment to that of the wives and girlfriends who have contributed to this book.

One letter caught my attention in particular, as I sifted through the countless piles of letters held in the Imperial War Museum in London. There were so many, most of which I assumed were sent to the museum from relatives who were clearing out attics after their parents or grandparents had died. In the end I had to just pick a handful at random. The one that caught my eye was written by Elizabeth Belsey in 1940 during an air raid at her home in Keston, Kent, to her husband, who served with the Royal Artillery between 1940 and 1943. Their first baby, Charlotte, was born just before the Dunkirk Evacuation and was four months old when the letter was written. During daylight raids, Elizabeth used to push her in her Moses basket under the kitchen table or underneath the stairs. I discovered this extra information when, in writing to the Imperial War Museum for permission to use the letter, I received a reply from Mrs Belsey herself, who is now ninety-eight years old.

'*Tues Sept 3rd 1940:*

My precious love,

The sirens have sounded, so I pass this morning's raid by beginning a letter to you . . . It is a year today since war broke out. How well I remember sitting on the terrace at Lulworth, hearing the news come through, and travelling back to London in great heat, and you kissing me across the platform barrier in Waterloo. It seems such a long, long time ago, such a long, long time since we had a home together in Hayes. I wonder if we ever shall again.

Oh Darling, you don't know how I miss you and want you every moment of the day . . . when you had disappeared, I put your bicycle away and went and sat on the terrace steps, where I had just been sitting with you before, and watched the sun fade from the trees, and tried to compose myself. I felt the same as I used to feel as a child when homesick in someone else's home ... there is nothing to compare with the desolation and misery it causes. (Please don't be unhappy when you read this; I feel better when I write it down, so you must discount this overflow and not let it distress you). I wanted to cry every time I saw anything that reminded me of you, such as your turnips or your trousers or even the piece of chocolate you bought me by the ponds. (I have eaten it now, and it was very nice) ...

Now the all-clear is sounding pleasantly across the country, and nothing unpleasant has reached us.

Nothing is too high a price to pay for the privilege of having you and being loved by you. I cannot calculate the sum of the happiness I have derived from you since I first knew you.

... I must stop writing like this, for it does nothing to cheer you up, or me either.'

I telephoned Mrs Belsey to ask about her life during this time. She had been astonished to read the letter again after so many years. She told me that her husband was involved in anti-aircraft and was among the earliest people to use radar. He was frequently away on 'gun sights' all over the country, testing the anti-aircraft equipment, while Elizabeth dealt with the frequent air raids at home along the south coast of Britain; they were both dealing with their own forms of danger. In 1943 he was commissioned and transferred to the infantry in the Queen's Royal Regiment, with whom he served until he was demobilised a year after the war in Europe. He actually saw no active service until the Normandy landings in 1944, in which he was wounded:

'After five days in Normandy, he was shot through the hip, invalided home, and spent eight weeks in plaster from the armpit to the

ankle. He hated it. Then after many weeks of leave he spent the rest of the war defusing unexploded mines and cleaning up after the departure of the Americans.

After the bombing of Biggin Hill airport, my mother's large house not far away was taken over by the RAF to help rehouse their personnel, and we all had to get out. We spent the rest of the war in a remote village called Hilton, between Cambridge and Huntingdon, where no bombs fell. We spent about as tranquil a war after that as was possible. Here, I had two more children and some years later, a fourth, so I was never called up for any war work.

My husband died ten years ago and my eldest daughter had her seventieth birthday in April 2010. The war seems a very long time ago and sometimes I wonder whether it was really I who went through it.'

Why, then, do we marry our soldiers, and how do we live with it? Why do we enter this life when we know we will be separated from them, moved around, wrenched apart from our friends and messed about with our jobs, not to mention the disruption caused to our children? The obvious answer would be that we do it for love. But this needs more of an explanation. Perhaps it can be summed up by Kathleen Salusbury, whose husband Jules is a Major in the Welsh Guards, in her reply to the statement: 'I don't know how you do it. I couldn't be married to a soldier.'

'I never find it hard to come up with reasons for my ability to cope, even though I would agree with Mae West's observation that, "A woman in love couldn't be reasonable or she wouldn't be in love". So, aside from the fact that I absolutely love my husband, my response is, "My husband loves his job". But this only answers why I do it – being asked to contribute to Don't Say Goodbye *has made me properly think about the "how".*

And this is because of support from friends and family and the support and understanding of the "Regimental family" and wider "Army family".

I was initially reluctant to embrace being an "Army wife", not realising what a supportive and rewarding network it allowed me to be part of. Other Army wives and Army families have done many little things for my family and me on many occasions, and ultimately this is what makes an unreasonable life, possible. There is a point to the pomp and circumstance, the coffee mornings, the book clubs, the identical houses, the dinners, the parties, and the wretched fancy dress! It creates a common bond, a community spirit and an understanding that makes what could be a lonely existence actually quite fun.'

Pari Spencer Smith is married to Tom, a Captain in the Welsh Guards. She explained how she found the strength to support him in his chosen career:

'One of my colleagues told me there was no way she would be strong enough to deal with a boyfriend or husband who was sent to a war zone – never mind not seeing them for six months, bar two weeks R and R. Now there's a strange phenomenon. Not seeing each other for four months, then attempting to get to know each other again, with things just getting back to normal by the end of two weeks and then he's shipped back. Oh well . . . I suppose two weeks in six months is better than no weeks.'

Reflecting on the poignancy of Tom's excitement before going out to Afghanistan, Pari also said:

'I sometimes felt like Tom didn't realise how much his absence was going to affect me. He had an air of excitement which I didn't really share and I couldn't understand why he was excited to be leaving me on my own for six months. Of course as expected some men were more apprehensive than others, but on the whole most

were looking forward to the chance to put into practice all the training they had carried out and to do some "real" soldiering.

I think most people think I'm either very brave or a little mad – married to Tom who's almost never around. But we are best friends and we love each other very, very much. I could not imagine my life without Tom and the Army is part of him. Tom wouldn't be himself if he didn't have the Army. I would never wish him to sacrifice his career because I didn't approve only to end up unhappy in another job that he did not want to do.'

Although I did not analyse it at the time, when I married Richard I effectively took an oath of loyalty to Queen and country by default. Expecting wives to look at 'the bigger picture' before they have any experience of it can be a big ask. All we can do is be open to advice, learn from it at every opportunity and, above all, learn how to look after our friends because at some point, we will all need each other. Occasionally though, we do still question things, especially in our low moments. I have done it many times, only to berate myself afterwards by telling myself that I knew what I was getting into. I think this is perhaps what many people in civilian life feel: that the partners of service-men and -women knew what they were signing up for. But in reality, nobody can really prepare you for the whole package that comes with being an Army wife. Sometimes, despite the network of support and the couple's own best efforts, the pressure is simply too much and some marriages do fail, as in everyday life. But divorce rates at Non Commissioned Officer level for the British Army stand at the national average, and divorce rates at Officer level are just below the national average. There are no statistics to suggest that the British Army way of life leads to an increase in marriage breakdowns.

When I married Richard I took comfort from knowing first hand that a good marriage and a great family life were possible, even in difficult circumstances. My own parents had shown me that. Perhaps my thirst for adventure lured me, or perhaps I just wanted to be with Richard no matter what the cost. But ultimately I gambled that our relationship would prove strong enough to weather the strains of separation and the demands of living within an organisation that is bigger than any of its constituent parts or people. I have always known the Army was his life, ever since I saw him pass out of Sandhurst. The Army still is his life, but for the last fifteen years, he has made career decisions based on a consideration for me and the children as well. Luckily, there has never been a moment in which he has had to decide between the Army or his family. We have miraculously managed to make the two work as a symbiotic partnership, each surviving with the support of the other. How? I am still not sure. He has always supported me wholeheartedly and unconditionally. His understanding and appreciation of 'the other side of the coin' has helped to keep us together through thick and thin. One thing is for certain: we could not have done it without the love we built our marriage on, but neither could we have done it without the support that comes from being part of the wider Army family.

2

You're in the Army Now

Making our way down from the summit of Tryfan after Richard proposed felt like walking on air; the conversation was full of plans for the future and the exciting life we had ahead of us together.

'So, we'll have one of those romantic military weddings and you'll look gorgeous in your tunic. All the girls will go weak at the knees.'

There was a silence, then the reply:

'I won't be wearing it though; traditionally officers wear morning dress not tunic.'

'Well, the wedding's off then,' I replied.

Richard looked crestfallen, poor chap. I couldn't bear to torture him any more.

'I'm only joking; devastated, but still joking, and where on earth did that idea come from anyway? Obviously a man.'

This was not my first experience of the quirks of Army tradition. I had been exposed to some of the more bizarre rituals and language when Richard and I were dating. The Guards' Officers have a unique way of impressing a new girlfriend: by asking her to lunch at St James's Palace. There are always three officers on guard: a Major, a Captain and a Lieutenant or Second Lieutenant. When they are on duty they cannot leave the premises, but it is quite acceptable for them to invite guests over for lunch. While I was doing my nursing training in London, Richard invited me to lunch when he was on guard; it was certainly a welcome change from the hospital canteen.

At one point during the gathering, Richard turned to the Major on duty, who was recently married, and asked in a very nonchalant manner,

'So, have you lit your dragon yet?'

'No, not yet,' the Major replied between mouthfuls of smoked salmon, 'but I will when we have the right kind of smoker to stay.'

I remember that the table fell silent, as we bemused guests waited for an explanation. Maybe this was not the benign, sophisticated lunch we thought we had been invited to.

Looking up, the Major realised that the civilians were totally lost. He and Richard were talking in another language, about another tradition. It turned out that on the marriage of an officer, the Officers' Mess give him a silver Welsh Dragon cigar lighter with a wick coming from the mouth and the body filled with lighter fuel. The base is always engraved with the date of the wedding (but excludes the name of the wife for some bizarre reason). 'Lighting the Dragon' means using the lighter for the first time. We guests heaved a sigh of relief, but there were plenty more of these confusing moments to come; all part of the alien lifestyle and made more complex by the fact that every regiment has its own unique quirks.

New surroundings and constant moves are the obvious challenges to Army life, but for a new wife, being thrust into an environment with its own language and customs is another. Any new wife unused to the jargon in the Army must learn a whole new vocabulary. Military abbreviations are a minefield and any wife who dares to use them runs the risk of getting severely unstuck. Remembering acronyms is rather like memorising a French phrase while on holiday only to receive a rapid torrent of unintelligible French in reply. There are also many contradictions: the Colonel of the Regiment is usually a General, but in the case of the Welsh Guards it is the Prince of Wales; the Regimental Lieutenant Colonel is actually a Colonel, a Brigadier or a General and the Drum Major is, in fact, anything from a Sergeant to a Warrant Officer Class One. Also, the Commanding Officer is often referred to as, for example, Colonel Richard by the Officers, or Colonel Stanford by the Non Commissioned Officers, even though he would be a Lieutenant Colonel.

Once, Richard came home from work to tell me that he was 'Captain of the Week'. My excited reply was 'Oh, that's lovely, well done.' At the time, Oliver had just started nursery, so the award of 'Star of the Week', and its associated achievements, was uppermost in my mind. Richard looked at me in disbelief and with vague pity in his voice replied, 'It's not a prize, or a treat; it means it is my turn to be the Duty Officer on camp,' despite the fact that he was a Major.

This does much to confuse someone who is desperately trying to work it all out. It can help to know the order of ranks sometimes, although I have muddled along quite well in my ignorant bliss at times. To make matters worse, the Guards Regiments have their own ranks for the Non Commissioned Officers (those who are not officers); they are the only regiments whose 'Privates' are called 'Guardsmen' and whose Corporals are called Lance Sergeants. It gets more complicated, but I do not intend this book to become a dictionary for the lost and bewildered.

In the Welsh Guards, the Guardsmen are all referred to by number, which can look to the newcomer highly impersonal, especially in a small regiment which prides itself on being a close-knit 'family'. However, when one considers the fact that on a nominal roll for a Company of one hundred men there could be only about five surnames, such as Jones, Jenkins, Williams, Lewis and Evans, it is not surprising to learn that to avoid confusion they must be referred to by the last two numbers of their

Army number instead: for example "Jones fifty two" and so on. Having a number in this context becomes more personal than a name, and often becomes a type of Christian name in itself.

Shortly after he joined the Battalion, Richard recalls talking to a Guardsman's mother who referred affectionately to her own son as 'Sixteen', his number, rather than his name. When he asked her if she always called him by number she replied that she did, even at home. Such is the close-knit nature of the Battalion that this man, who had since retired after serving for twenty-two years to become a bus driver in Llanelli, volunteered to rejoin the Welsh Guards for the operational tour of Afghanistan in 2009.

For most Army families, there is much less glitz and glamour than there used to be. Extravagant balls, dinners and functions are very much the exception in military life nowadays, rather than the rule. Generally speaking, if a Battalion is posted away from the UK to a place such as Germany or Cyprus, the social life tends to be a little more lively, as it is less realistic for Army families to visit family and friends in the UK at weekends. If a family is UK-based, however, social functions are often fewer; for one, the Mess bills, the costs charged to an individual for social functions, become too high.

The concept of the Army Mess can be quite an enigma to those outside the Forces. For a start, 'Mess' is the name for a meeting place, rather than its more obvious definition. A Mess frequently includes a sitting area and a dining area and Corporals, Sergeants and Officers each have their own; they are divided into ranks not because each rank wants to be dissociated from the other, but to provide an area for each group to relax amongst themselves to have a degree of privacy, away from the more formal chain of command that is prevalent during working hours.

My old friend Bev Evans has been married to her husband Gareth, a Colour Sergeant in the Welsh Guards, for fifteen years. She is a fellow 'Nightingale Nurse,' as we both trained at St Thomas' Hospital, although we did not know each other at this time, and she went on to join the Queen Alexandra's Royal Army Nursing Corps. She describes the peculiarities of Army tradition in her 'Ridiculous Rules of the Sergeants' (Sgts) Mess', which tells of wardrobe etiquette and of a 'typical' evening at a Sergeants' Mess function. Incidentally, the rules in the Officers' Mess are far more lenient!

Rule 1
Dresses below the knee

The dress code of the Mess states that 'cocktail' dresses are the order of dress for us ladies. In the world of real people 'cocktail' implies a shortish party frock. In the Sgts Mess you can reveal as much as you like up top but if you <u>dare</u> to have a millimetre of chiffon above your patella the RSM (Regimental Sergeant Major) will not be responsible for his actions.

Rule 2
The wearing of trousers

The wearing of trousers by ladies in the Mess causes Mess members a great deal of anguish. They haven't quite reconciled themselves to the fact that women are actually serving in the Army, wearing trousers every day and that there have been many Parliamentary Acts relating to the rights of us ladies. The wearing of trousers is a privilege granted only by the RSM. Pease, please someone tell him 'TROUSERS ARE BELOW THE KNEE!' – I think his relief will be immense!

Rule 3
Drink will be taken at a Mess 'Do'

Men must arrive in their 'best bib and tucker' (Mess Dress) all trussed up like chickens with the shiniest of shoes. Within two hours everyone will be soaked in beer and dripping with cheap wine, patting each other on the back and telling each other how great they are. A few hours later the patting turns into something slightly more robust and my husband will inevitably disappear, telling me that he is 'The Negotiator'. This can only mean one thing. He is about to make a bad situation worse.

Rule 4
Silly dancing is obligatory

As the evening progresses it is the rule of the Sgts Mess for ladies to perform 'embarrassing Mummy dancing'. Most Mess members turn into Disco Divas and give 'Dirty Dancing' a run for its money. Some, on the other hand, believe themselves to be 'Ginger and Fred' – otherwise known as 'Binger and Dread'. My husband falls into this category and likes to whiz any unsuspecting lady on his radar around the dance floor, with mixed results.

And finally:

Subtlety is not a useful weapon at a Mess do

Getting the man of your dreams away from the bar at the twilight of the evening's proceedings is often an issue. The ladies have feet on fire from all that 'embarrassing Mummy dancing'; their mascara has run and the lip gloss has turned to lip matte. The men stand at the bar talking nonsense but looking intensely interested in each other's slurring and salivations. So what is a girl to do? She takes Rule 4 to heart, hoists her regulation 'below the knee dress' above her knees and prepares to move. No longer 'embarrassing' but 'stupendous'. Guaranteed to persuade her man to come home.

It certainly took me a while to get used to the ceremonial side of Army life, an aspect that comes with being married to a member of the Household Division. The Household Division consists of two Household Cavalry Regiments (the Lifeguards and the Blues and Royals) and five Guards Regiments (Grenadier, Coldstream, Scots, Irish, and Welsh). By definition, they guard the Royal Household, but they are also highly trained for combat situations. Every two to three years they rotate on public duties, which involve guarding Buckingham Palace, Windsor Castle and the Tower of London. During this time they also take turns to troop their own Regimental Colour (regimental flag) on the Queen's Birthday Parade. If there is a Royal wedding, funeral or state function they are also on public duties, lining the route, acting as the bearer party or providing a Regimental Band.

Consequently, we possibly have more official functions to attend than other military personnel and families. Add in the Welsh Guards' own ceremonies, such as the St David's Day parade every year, the annual Regimental Remembrance Sunday service, annual summer balls, charity dinners, the Presentation of New Colours every ten years, the Prince of Wales' Company Review every ten to fifteen years, the Falklands commemoration rugby match, and the list gets longer.

When I was a new wife, in fact even for years afterwards, it was all a bit of a mystery, but fortunately, by the time Richard was commanding the Battalion and it was the Welsh Guards' year to troop their own Colour, I had got the hang of most things. As the Commanding Officer, he was required to be the 'Field Officer in Brigade Waiting'; in other words, he was the Officer on horseback giving the commands to five hundred Guardsmen. By then, he was a seasoned hand, since the previous year he had also been asked to step in for the Coldstream Guards, whose Commanding Officer was unable to participate. He received news for that first 'Troop' while he was in Bosnia, and thought it must have been a wind up, as he had no experience of riding, let alone controlling a horse on Horse

Guards Parade in front of the Queen and millions of television viewers around the world and had never even been on the Queen's Birthday Parade before. When he had finally been convinced that this was, in fact, serious, he had to learn to ride, straight away, with only three months to go before the event.

What better way to learn than on Lipizzaner horses? It would seem that this venerable, highly schooled breed would be perfect; the only problem was that they had not been ridden for several years and were perhaps not best pleased at being pressed back into service. Picking up that Richard was a novice, the stallions would simply lower their shoulders and tip him off into the deepest, muddiest puddles they could find and then canter off onto the horizon.

Not to be deterred, and with an intensive crash course in Hyde Park Barracks when he returned from his tour, Richard was as ready as he was ever going to be. I would test him on his memory of the commands late into the night, but without the band 'on cue' it didn't exactly make any sense to me, and probably not to him either. The saving grace was his horse, Berniston, who had done many Birthday Parades before, and would perform the routine perfectly, so long as she did not get a little bored and throw in a few tricks.

As with an amazing musical, when the performance on the night runs so smoothly that the actors and dancers make it look like the simplest thing in the world, it is easy to forget how much preparation goes into making something run so effortlessly. For five weeks solid, the Battalion lived, breathed and slept their drill for the big day. On yet another early morning rehearsal in Pirbright Barracks Richard decided to spice it up a little for the men and invited a mystery guest to join them. The Guardsmen were a little surprised to find someone among them who appeared to know so little about marching and drill, but did not realise just how little until the guest stopped, admitted defeat, took off the bearskin, shook her long hair loose and announced that she was, in fact, not only female, but a Welsh kindred spirit: the singer Charlotte Church had joined them 'just for fun'. A little light-hearted humour did much to keep the men's morale up.

So, the first Troop went very well, and Richard breathed a sigh of relief that he had not joined the 'Empty Saddle Club', a (thankfully) rare group of officers who had had the misfortune to be unseated on parade.

As it happened, the Queen's Birthday Parade 2007 occurred on the same day as the Falklands commemoration rugby match at the Harlequins' home ground, 'The Stoop', to honour the twenty-fifth anniversary of the Falklands Conflict. Richard had been invited along and Oliver had been asked to be a 'mascot' and to walk onto the pitch with the players. This, of course, was a great honour, especially as Oliver idolised rugby, having started playing at the age of six at Llantwit Major Rugby Club when we were posted to St Athan. However, it did mean that we had to bolt our lunch after the Birthday Parade and drive over to the rugby ground in time for the opening ceremony. We made it just in time for Oliver to change into the Welsh Guards kit provided for him, along with his name on the back of the shirt. He stood on the pitch of 'The Stoop' and sang both the Welsh and the British national anthems accompanied by the band of the Royal Marines. There followed a short service of remembrance and a hymn before kick-off. Oliver spent the rest of the match retrieving the ball from the side every time it was kicked into touch. Adding to the special nature of the occasion was the fact that 'The Stoop' had been the home ground of his Uncle Simon, who used to play for Harlequins in the early 90s, so the family tradition was continued, in a sense anyway. What a day that was for our family; we did not come back down to earth for weeks.

Then, in 2008, Richard was required to Troop the Colour a second time. This was not without its dramas behind the scenes, such as the two officers who got stuck in a newly repaired lift in Wellington Barracks just before they were required on parade, only being rescued in the nick of time.

While I watched the parade with the children I turned to our nine-year-old daughter Annabel and asked her, 'How come Daddy can tell five hundred men to do something and they do it, and yet when he asks you to do something, you don't?' To which she replied, quite matter of fact, 'Because they're all men, and I'm a girl.' Oh, of course, silly me.

There is nothing like your children to bring you down to earth. I can recall one St David's Day parade in Aldershot in 2001 when, on a bitter 1st March, we huddled together to watch the spectacle. The Prince of Wales, as Colonel of the Welsh Guards, presented the 'leeks' (small handmade button-holes, the symbol of the Welsh Guards cap badge) to the men and then stood on a dais to give his address. As he did so, Oliver suddenly piped up, 'Mummy, is that Prince Charles, the very small man?' I replied that it was, but that he wasn't so very small really. To which Oliver said, 'He must be small because he has to stand on a box to see everybody.'

The Royal Family, due to their unique connection with the Household Division, is always very keen to meet its Guards Regiments whenever possible. The Prince of Wales has his own personal Company in the Welsh Guards: the Prince of Wales' Company of about one hundred men. Every ten to fifteen years he invites them and all their families to a private ceremony where he reviews this Company. We were lucky enough to coincide with one of these, which was held in the gardens of Clarence House, and it was a great honour for so many families to be introduced to Prince Charles. He ensured that he spoke to every family and Guardsman present, over a cup of tea on the lawn. I remember him commenting to Oliver that he must get his blond hair from his father, but then looking at Richard and adding, 'Except, of course, without the white bits around the temples.'

When Her Majesty The Queen Mother died on 30 March 2002 we were living on Upavon Camp on Salisbury Plain. It was a clear Saturday spring morning and I had taken the children, who were four and six years old at the time, onto Salisbury Plain for a picnic and to fly a kite while Richard took his turn on duty in the casualty and compassionate cell, a duty which came round once every six months or so. The purpose of it was to receive calls to implement the return of servicemen and -women on exercise, tours or overseas postings if they had to return to the UK on compassionate grounds, if for example, there was a fatality or serious incident with a member of their close family. He was studying for some exams at the time and expected the day to be a quiet one so he could fit in some revision. How wrong he was:

> *'When I received the casualty notification signal that the Queen Mother had died I must have been one of the first people in the Army to find out. From my position in the compassionate cell, I had to contact personnel who were on overseas postings and exercises, to return to the UK for the Lying in State and funeral arrangements.'*

The Household Division was to take the lead to stand guard for the Lying in State. This included Richard and would involve standing vigil on the catafalque (a raised platform on which the closed coffin rested, draped in the Royal Standard as her Majesty lay in state). Other vigils were performed by the Gentlemen at Arms and members of the Royal Family themselves, including Prince Charles, Prince Edward, Prince William and Prince Harry on the evening before the funeral.

When the news of Her Majesty's death was announced, the BBC's coverage centred on how few people were reacting to the news, but this proved to be completely wrong as there followed mass public tributes and endless queues for the public to pay their respects in Westminster Hall, at all times of the day and night. Richard wrote a journal of the part he took in this historic occasion:

> 'On 4th April, over one hundred Guards officers gathered outside Westminster Hall for the recce [reconnaissance] of their duties within. It was a great gathering of many old friends but when we got inside we were suddenly struck by the atmosphere and grandeur of the building, and of the significance of our task.
>
> The following day we had a rehearsal in Chelsea Barracks. One and a half hours of rehearsing the mechanics of changeover on the catafalque in Chelsea Barracks gym. The catafalque was the same one used in rehearsing the vigil for George VI which had been tucked away and stored in Chelsea Barracks for over 50 years.
>
> We were bussed up to Westminster Hall from Wellington Barracks at 0430 hours on 6th April, where we entered behind the scenes by a turret door. I was on the first "stag" at 0600hrs taking over from the Scots Guards'.

Each 'stag' consisted of twenty minutes' vigil, one officer standing at each corner of the catafalque in full ceremonial tunic and bearskin, sword drawn and pointed downwards, with head bowed and a black armband on the left arm as a sign of mourning.

> 'There were six of us on each team: four were around the coffin, in seniority order with the most senior at the right foot then left foot, left shoulder right shoulder. The fifth man was posted on the balcony at the West Door in case one on vigil felt "unwell" and

the sixth was behind the scenes to take over from the one on the balcony. Each man had to stand with his head bowed, while the fifth officer stood to attention on the balcony. This may sound like an easy enough task, but twenty minutes wearing a bearskin, balanced with head bowed, takes its toll.

From the Welsh Guards alone men had come from far and wide to stand vigil: six came back from Bosnia, one from Germany and two returned from terminal leave before leaving the Army. Lt Col Andrew Ford was in charge of the Welsh Guards at the vigil; he had to come out and to tap his sword to signal the changeover.

I was rather nervous, more about the time we had to stand still with our heads bowed rather than the drill. The Hall was closed between 0600–0800 for cleaning so there wasn't much to look at for the first stag except to count the holes in the flagstones and the number of steps, and to listen to the sound of the cleaners who were busy dusting and sweeping. At one point, one of the vergers changing the candles managed to fall off the catafalque, luckily I didn't see as it would have been hard not to laugh, poor chap. However, the changeover seemed to go well and the twenty minutes was just right; long enough to begin to feel the aches and pains, to soak up the atmosphere but not so long as to be unbearable.

Once the public started to come through at 0800 it was impressive to see so many people who had queued for so long and were so respectful. Many made the sign of the cross, some in tears; there were people from all walks of life, from nuns to punks. One little boy was convinced that we were not real and his mother whispered to the policeman on duty, asking if they could wait to see us changeover so he could see us move, which he did. Otherwise, everyone was silent; the silent majority were literally and figuratively represented in force.

On reflection it was a true honour to have stood vigil at the Queen Mother's Lying in State and to have witnessed at first hand the huge numbers of people filing past the coffin paying their

*last respects to a much revered, admired and well loved lady. It
was one of the most moving and serene State Ceremonial events
that I have done and I am honoured to have had the chance to
do it.'*

The Queen Mother's funeral was not the only occasion
when I felt a particular connection to events because of the
involvement of the Welsh Guards. When Diana, Princess of
Wales tragically died of injuries sustained in a car crash in a
Parisian tunnel on 31 August 1997, her death plunged Britain
into a week of unprecedented mourning. It fell to the Welsh
Guards to have the honour of providing a bearer party for her
coffin at the funeral. Their duty was to escort her coffin from
Kensington Palace to Westminster Abbey, carry it up the aisle
of the Abbey to the altar and then, after the service, back again
to the west doors and onto the hearse. This would then take
it to Althorp in Northamptonshire, the home of the Spencer
family, where she was buried on an island on the estate.

We were in Oman at the time of the Princess's death but
our friend Richard Williams was a Captain with the Welsh
Guards and, as Adjutant, was called back from operations in
Northern Ireland to command the bearer party. With a week
to practise, he was faced with a nerve-racking task that would
be watched by an estimated two and a half billion people
on televisions worldwide. It was quite surreal to see him on
a friend's television from Oman as we watched the service.
We had not seen him since our wedding two years previously
when he had been in charge of the Guard of Honour, ensuring
that the Guardsmen changed into their ceremonial uniforms
of tunics and bearskins at a nearby hotel beforehand, arrived
at the right church to line the path either side of our exit from
the service, and were suitably supplied with sustenance at the
reception afterwards. And then there he was, walking down the

aisle of Westminster Abbey. He and his wife Sarah, and their two daughters, now live only a few miles from us in Salisbury and Richard was only too happy to tell his story of the honour he was asked to fulfil for the Princess:

There are two strands to the professional life of a Guardsman – the ceremonial duties performed in red tunic and bearskin on one side and the deployment on operations on another. It can be a challenge to maintain them, especially when combined with all the tension of being a husband and parent as well. Sometimes they collide in spectacular fashion.

For me it happened in 1997 when I awoke in the drizzle of a South Armagh morning to hear of the tragic death of Diana, Princess of Wales in a tunnel in Paris. Before long we were put on notice to swap the beauty of Northern Ireland's most troubled rural community, for the most solemn of soldierly duties: bearing the coffin of royalty in a state funeral. The Welsh Guards were to form the twelve-man bearer party for Diana's coffin in the centre of one of the most emotionally charged vortexes of public grief seen in the nation's history. We needed to do a good job, to help everyone say goodbye – properly.

We had barely arrived at Chelsea Barracks before we were fitted back into our tunics and began to practise. Rehearsal followed briefing, followed recce, followed uniform fitting and kit cleaning. No one knew what to expect and personal time was low on the list. A few stolen moments with long missed family were possible for some, I saw Sarah, my wife of six months, for an hour or two, but for most it was just a question of getting through the endless rehearsals. These led to a certain amount of suffering, especially the debilitating red-raw shoulders; skin rubbed off by the awkward weight of a 600lb dummy coffin, mimicking the lead-lined version of the real thing. Someone had the idea that a field dressing under the tunic over the offending sore would provide padding and protection; it worked a treat.

Before long we were in the minibus on the way to Kensington Palace. It was a thoughtful and sombre journey. Everyone was visibly moved when we first saw the coffin: the simple lilies and the card to "Mummy". There were thoughts of our own losses, of missed friends, of family to whom we did not have time to say goodbye. Swallow; "Remember what we rehearsed, that this is real, this is important", I told myself. The calm and dignity of the domestic staff in the palace contrasted with the audible grief of the crowds lining the route and the near hysterical wails of the mourners. I worried that the thrown flowers would spook the horses pulling the gun carriage.

Before long we were in Westminster Abbey; an inward nod from us all to the Tomb of the Unknown Warrior. We stepped in slow unison on beeswax polished boots up the aisle, one hundred and fifty metes long, as the congregation (and the world) sang the National Anthem. The sound of our nailed drill boots squeaked and echoed along the last few meters to the chancel in the silence that followed. We placed the coffin on the catafalque. The rock star presence of so many celebrities only added to a sense of dislocation. Sarah sat next to Ralph Lauren and the Emmanuels during the service and was understandably self-conscious in her borrowed black dress and hat. I knew she was somewhere in the congregation and I missed her; I'd barely seen her since we got married.

Then it was time to leave the Abbey for the cloisters. We marched past the mourning personalities and the visibly shaken members of the Royal Family for a short break and to watch the service on CCTV. I was very conscious of the need to stay focussed on the job and, as befits Guardsmen, to do it well. We had to see the coffin safely into the hearse and on its way to Althorp. We made our final journey with the coffin back down the aisle to the doors of Westminster Abbey, to the sublime Taverner music sung by the choir. Then the one minute silence.

Saying goodbye to loved ones is one of the most important things we do in our lives and what we had just done mattered. The tunics, bearskins, gold and polish hide the fighting soldiers beneath who can, when asked, go from the killing fields of Afghanistan to rub shoulders with princes and fashion designers. Soldiers so often represent everything that we believe to be honourable and right about our nation. They did so when they performed that most solemn duty, on behalf of a mourning nation, of saying farewell. I'd like to think that on that warm late summer's day we helped, in a small way, to enable everyone to say goodbye.'

Not only the British public, but a staggering estimated *one third* of the world's entire population, must have seemed ironically peaceful from heaven's perspective on that day, particularly during the minute's silence. This is something I always think about when the nation respects the fallen during the two-minute silence on Remembrance Day; that fleeting, yet so moving moment of silence in what seems to me an impressive example of mass telepathy is surely a snapshot of how the world would be if we could find lasting peace. If only we could always remember how comforting that feeling is.

There are happy occasions in the ceremonial side of Army life, as well as sad ones. In 2008, after the Colonel's Review, which is the second formal Birthday Parade rehearsal the week before the official Trooping the Colour, the Battalion held its summer ball in the grounds of Wellington Barracks. When in London, this is the Batallion's base, although many of the families live in quarters around the capital. Situated opposite Buckingham Palace, where for hundreds of years the Guard Mount has marched over the road to change the Guard at Buckingham Palace, 'Welly B' is the perfect Central London location.

The theme of the summer ball was 'Days of the Raj' and the costumes were very impressive. The transformation was incredible, from the daytime attire of tunics and bearskins for the Guardsmen and summer dresses and large hats for the ladies. The evening's costumes of pith helmets, polo kit, saris, long gloves and parasols – not to mention the belly dancer outfits – were like a behind the scenes change of costume in a West End theatre, and the guests all embraced the theatrical spirit with great enthusiasm.

There was not an elephant available in the whole of London, so instead a camel was acquired to be on hand for rides on the parade square. An albino python patiently wrapped itself around the neck of anyone willing, and fire-eaters performed for the guests.

For such a spectacle to occur in full view of the summer tourists was clearly a bonus, as they gathered outside the railings like visitors to a zoo. I suppose it was a zoo really. After dinner entertainment consisted of high-harness trampolines and Velcro flies, which were brave things to attempt after a large meal; but the freedom of bouncing high enough to see Buckingham Palace floodlit on a balmy summer evening and the night lights in Green Park and on the 'London Eye' was worth the churning stomach. Drummers from the Battalion gave a display in the dark with illuminated drumsticks; their speed and skill made everyone proud to be a part of such a unique gathering. These men are not part of the Regimental Band, who are musicians first and soldiers second; The Corps of Drums are machine gunners when on operations and drummers for ceremonial occasions. One of them, Drummer Leach, was deployed to Afghanistan the following spring and tragically lost his leg when hit by an IED (Improvised Explosive Device).

Some of our guests, who had seen Richard with the Battalion on Horse Guards Parade earlier in the day, did in fact think that this was a normal existence for us. Perhaps it was, but when we returned to everyday life it all seemed like a far-off, glamorous whirlwind. Within a few months the Battalion would be brought down to earth while on operations in Afghanistan, the families would be living on a knife-edge of worry and the parties, the pomp and the limelight would all seem like another, faraway world.

3

The Army Family

'Camaraderie' is a word often used in connection with soldiers to describe the results of the bonding that takes place on the battlefield. It sums up the mutual support and trust that develop from sharing a common experience, often one of hardship and extreme stress. It also encompasses the feeling that only those who have endured similar adversity can truly understand. It is not just the men who develop a strong spirit of camaraderie, though. For all the same reasons, the women left at home frequently form similar bonds; friendships often become stronger when women in the same situations share and empathise over such intense emotions. These emotions can be a vital part of coping with the separations from husbands and partners who are sent away on operations; separations that are inevitably fraught with anxiety and pressure. All the women share the endless worry, the sleepless nights and the times of abject fear triggered by constant news bulletins and publicity.

The sinking feeling when a husband leaves to go on exercise, or worse, an operational tour, is hard to describe. As he waves goodbye, the desperation to be in a different situation and the desire to claw back the inevitable separation can be overwhelming. To then turn back, look the children in the eye, tell them it will all be OK and get on with the daily routine is a tough ask. Often the only consolation is to visit or phone a friend in the same position.

The morning I said goodbye to Richard when, as Commanding Officer, he went away with the Welsh Guards to Bosnia for six months will stay with me always. We were hugely excited at finally owning our own house, in a village near Salisbury, but it did mean that while Richard was away I would be without the support network that comes from living on a patch with other Army families nearby. Luckily, I had caring neighbours, the Vicar opposite and an ex-Army officer next door. Richard was, relatively speaking, lucky with this tour; it was the last one to the area, a peacekeeping mission, and the Battalion would be metaphorically 'turning the lights out' when they left. Still, the first of a seemingly never-ending eternity of days is always a difficult one and highly emotional.

I need not have worried. I dropped the children off at school, hard in itself as they were also feeling very down and returned home but before I had time to dwell on the situation, the doorbell rang. I was not sure for a moment whether to answer it; I certainly was not in the mood for socialising: but I did. The Rectory was opposite us at the end of a small cul-de-sac, and it was Margaret Staples, the Vicar's wife, who was standing on the doorstep. She came in and gave me a hug. That was all I needed to set the waterworks going, but after a good cry and the cup of coffee she made for me, I felt ready to face the world. It was an act of friendship and compassion that I will never forget.

During that autumn the Vicar himself, John, also arrived on the doorstep with a bag of spring bulbs and a bulb planter. He asked if the children and I would like to plant some daffodils outside our house so that they would be coming up when Richard arrived back. Thoughtfully, he had anticipated that this would give us all a goal to aim for and sure enough, when the tips showed through the following spring, the days really did start to race towards Richard's homecoming.

The psychological games I have played to try to find the easiest way around a separation are numerous. After a few years of trying different methods I have reached the conclusion that the countdown to 'D-Day' is often harder to deal with than the 'count-up' to the day when they return; the former is negative, the latter positive. And the time in between comes with its own gremlins, especially when the men have a very real chance of getting wounded or killed in action. Then, there is constant worry as well as separation to deal with. Many people find that keeping busy is the answer, but being too busy results in a gradual physical and mental wearing down that is often not obvious until the pressure is lifted and it becomes clear just how tired and stressed an Army wife may have been.

As well as the closeness of the Army family, for many wives of the Welsh Guards there is also a stability that comes from their extended family back in Wales. Many Guardsmen and their partners traditionally come from very close-knit communities that have been supporting each other for generations. The traditional Welsh matriarchal 'Mam' likes to have her family around her and her family is her life. For her daughter to marry a soldier, and for the young wife to be plucked from the security of her family to live in Aldershot, Germany or any other alien environment, and then find herself alone when her husband goes on an operational tour, can be a very daunting prospect for both the wife and the wife's mother and other family members. Even with people from home backgrounds that are not as close-knit as these, though, the nomadic Army lifestyle, exciting and romantic as it may have sounded, often comes as a shock.

Of course, this situation can happen the world over whenever a soldier's career takes him to different locations. One German wife I knew, who lived on Upavon Camp at the same time as us, had recently married a British soldier, having met him while he was posted to Germany. She could hardly string a sentence together in English, but she found herself living in Wiltshire with a new baby. Upavon Camp is not everybody's cup of tea; it is isolated, being on a very windswept corner of Salisbury Plain, and is 'behind the wire', which means that the whole camp, including the quarters, is surrounded by a patrolled perimeter fence and every visitor has to sign in and out through the Guardroom entrance. Needless to say, this newly married wife was rather miserable, but to give her credit she stuck it out. We would get together for coffee at each other's houses and although conversation was strained (my schoolgirl German left a lot to be desired), we muddled through and I hope she felt less isolated as a result.

The 'acid test' of patch life is whether or not you can get on with everybody on a daily basis. This is quite a lot to ask when the Army represents such a cross section of people, backgrounds, cultures and points of view. There will always be some people who turn into lifelong friends and others who remain acquaintances. The common ground is the lifestyle we all share through our husbands' jobs, and people bond through the teamwork and empathy that being part of the Army family requires.

Some of the Welsh Guards' postings have been abroad, when the whole Battalion has relocated with its wives and children, meaning that extended families in the UK have generally been too far away for wives to visit frequently. When these situations occur, the decision has to be made whether to relocate with the Battalion or stay with family in their home towns; there are no half measures. Being posted to Hohne in Germany or Ballykelly in Northern Ireland in the past has meant that the community spirit on camp has been much greater. On these postings the wives totally depended on each other for support, as weekends away with families was less commonplace.

My friend Sue Miles has very fond memories of the way the wives all pulled together when she and her husband were in Ireland, although she admitted that it was a true test of strength for all concerned:

'We moved twice in six months and landed in Northern Ireland in 1992 – the married quarters were spread out – we had officers quarters at one end, next to them we had "senior ranks quarters" (this was where we were housed). On the same side of the road we then had an estate of "other ranks quarters" and finally, over the road was the largest estate of "other ranks quarters".

I only mention all this background because actually each Company from within the Battalion came into its own for "bringing the wives together" [a Company consists of around one hundred men, made up of three Platoons of thirty men]. *We decided to hold "open house" for the wives of our own Company to have coffee mornings. We moved these meetings around from house to house, irrespective of our husbands' ranks. We were all wives in the same position – our husbands were away every other month and home (Wales & England) seemed like a long way away. Some wives needed extra support such as some of the newlyweds who were not coping with the distance from home. For some, this involved a car journey, ferry and an eight-hour drive so they, not surprisingly felt very cut off from their families. Others could not drive at all and would not be able to afford a flight. We were all very aware that our husbands were doing a vital job and needed to be able to concentrate on that, rather than worrying about whether or not the wife was falling apart at home. So supporting each other and making life as enjoyable as possible was important. We arranged outings for ourselves and the children, trips to the zoo, crystal factories, ice skating and numerous other activities.*

We came home from Northern Ireland on the advance party as we were posted to RMA [Royal Military Academy] *Sandhurst. I felt unusually a little "bereft" at this time because whilst I have*

always been able to cope with being "alone" on various differ-
ent postings, going from Northern Ireland where all us girls were
supporting each other to an individual posting once again was a
bit of a shock to the system. I was lucky as Sandhurst is quite close
to Guildford so it wasn't as if I was too far from my family and
where I called "home".'

Karen Mott also had similar experiences in Northern Ireland.

'*At times, particularly when the boys are away for any length*
of time on operations, camaraderie amongst the wives naturally
kicks in as we're all in the same predicament. In Northern Ireland
my husband Nicky was away for three weeks out of four and often
at short notice while on his week off. There would always be some
form of event for the wives, like a barbecue or Sunday lunch which
helped to keep our morale high.

I will never forget the support I received from the other wives
while we were in Ballykelly on one very sad occasion for our
family. Nicky is one of three brothers and all of them were in
the Welsh Guards at the time. His nephew, Stephen, was tragi-
cally killed when he was knocked off his bicycle in a road traf-
fic accident back at home in Ellesmere Port. Once we had been
given this tragic news, the Families Officer offered his support
and put travel arrangements in place to get us all back home for
his funeral.

Many of the other wives on camp came around in a shot giving
their support and doing whatever they could. We buried Stephen
on Christmas Eve, but when I returned to Ballykelly Christmas
had to continue for the sake of the children. We arrived home to
find that all the preparations for Christmas lunch had been done
and decorations had been put up by friends on the patch. This
was what the closeness and understanding of living on camp was
like.'

I know from personal experience that living away from close family and old friends can lead to extra reliance on the Army family. Our posting to St Athan, Vale of Glamorgan, in 2003–4 was difficult for me, although I did not realise the toll it was taking until we moved on almost two years later. During this time Richard was away for over ten months, an absence that included a six-month and a three-month operational tour and several exercises away from home. The Army quarters were either side of the large RAF base that the Welsh Guards were sharing at the time, although it was by no means at full capacity and there were many empty quarters. Only the wives who came from South Wales and the Cardiff area had family close by, and for those from North Wales the journey was still at least four hours by car. My father had remarried after my mother's death and he and my step-mother Alison were living in Worcestershire, Richard's parents in Suffolk, and the rest of our family was spread out across England.

The women back on the patch coped with being far from our families by organising plenty of wives' outings and events. My other saving grace was enrolling onto a creative writing course in which I immersed myself, dreaming up poems and prose while walking along the vast windswept beaches after dropping the children off at school while our dog chased seagulls, his favourite pastime.

I would sometimes also walk these beaches with friends such as Catrina Campbell and Bev Evans. The opportunity for long conversations on our dog walks gave us the chance to share our concerns and support each other while our husbands were away.

During this posting, with our children aged four and six, I found the separations very difficult. Luckily I had an old school friend, Penny Jenkins, who lived in the Rhondda Valley, and I used to see her occasionally. She and her husband would invite us to stay on their smallholding; the children loved it and we always came home with pork, lamb or pheasant for the freezer. My family visited when they could, but at the time both my paternal grandparents were very ill, so my father and Alison were understandably tied up for much of the time visiting them. Then both my grandparents died within three weeks of each other. As they were not Richard's immediate next of kin, he was not given compassionate leave to attend their funerals while on an operational tour of duty. They were both in their nineties and lived in East Anglia, a six-hour journey for me, so I had not been able to visit as often as I would have liked. One of my lasting memories was of long evening conversations I used to have with my grandfather, who liked to phone after Nan had gone to bed as, during the day, she usually had the monopoly on phone calls. Howling winds used to whistle through our quarter; it was exposed to coastal gales and on one particularly cold winter's night, curled up in front of the fire talking to Pop on the phone I mentioned that I was reluctant to go upstairs to bed as it was so cold.

'Haven't you got an electric blanket my girl?' Pop asked, to which I replied that I hadn't.

A few days later, a cheque arrived in the post from him, with a note to go and buy one and a comment: 'Without a husband, this should keep you warm.' I only saw him once more after that, in Peterborough Hospital a few days before he died. After this, my grandmother took to her bed and never got up again. She pined for him so much after nearly seventy years of marriage that I firmly believe that when she died three weeks later it was of a broken heart.

The pressure I was under at this time was compounded by the demands of a young family – and the children missed Richard terribly – but it was not until he returned in

April and we immediately moved to Salisbury that I began to notice that my hair was thinning rapidly. Within four months I had lost eighty per cent of it. I was just about to start my 'Return to Nursing' course at Salisbury Hospital so I felt that I had to resort to wearing a wig, which I did for the next six months.

After numerous tests I was told that there were no medical problems and that it must be due to stress. It was an unlucky way for stress to express itself and although I was not the only one to have been under pressure I did wonder if I was the only one who was losing my hair, but at least it grew back just as thick as ever and all was well; if my stress had come out in a stomach ulcer or I had been put on antidepressants, as wives often are, I might have had recurrences for years. In my case I could at least have a bit of fun too; I bought a wig in a totally different style to my natural hair. Wigs are extremely realistic these days, so the only giveaway was that it was a bit too perfect. I have never been one to style my hair for hours each day, so I had it cut into less of a 'salon' look, which made all the difference. That posting was probably the toughest for me, simply because there was so much going on in my personal life, but I have no doubt that without those long walks on the beach with Catrina and the laughs I shared with her and Bev, the impact of the stress would have been even worse.

As well as the informal network of friends for support, every Battalion has a Welfare Office to look after the wellbeing of the men and their families when the Battalion is in camp, and that of the families when the men are deployed on operations. It is a crucial link between the families and the Battalion when the men are on operations, and a vital means of support. The Welfare staff are handpicked from across the ranks so that the families have a range of people to talk to, and wherever possible now includes two female Non Commissioned Officers for the duration of an operational tour.

I have mentioned the compassionate cell where Richard was on duty when the Queen Mother died. All families are issued with a compassionate leave card to enable them to call the number of the compassionate cell should serving soldiers need to be called back urgently to the UK, or should the families themselves need to return to the UK in an emergency from an overseas posting. A good friend of mine, Victoria Turner, had reason to be especially thankful for this facility as well as to her community of Army wives. She currently lives in Riyadh, Saudi Arabia, where her husband Jonathan is serving for two years. We met on the playground of Netheravon C of E Primary School on the edge of Salisbury Plain, on our return from St Athan in 2005. It was Oliver's second time at the same school so, for once, he had some familiar faces in his class. Victoria had just moved from Canada and our children were in the same classes together; we and our children have been firm friends ever since.

Victoria says:

While we were posted to Germany, the phone rang unexpectedly in the middle of the night. It was my father telling me that my sister Veronica, who was living in Portugal, was seriously ill with Lymes disease and could I please try to get to the hospital. This was an occasion to use the compassionate leave/travel from overseas card that was in my wallet but I never expected to need. In that moment of crisis and panic, when the world is spinning at a hundred miles an hour, the Desk Officer looking after all the arrangements was amazing. I will never know his name but thank him for the speed at which he managed to arrange a flight to repatriate me with my family, within hours.

I arrived just in time to say goodbye to her, before she died.

*It was the most shocking experience; I had not even known
that she was ill. Following her funeral I returned to Germany.
At that moment the world felt like it had stopped revolving
and I wanted to get off. But this was not what my friends
in Germany would allow. With constant visits, pop-in-the-
oven family meals, sympathy cards with wise words or just a
simple hug, I was not on my own; they rallied round and got
me through it. I will be forever thankful to them for being there
when I needed them.'*

Although there are systems in place to support all British
Army families in emergency situations, the everyday duties
of the Welfare Officers range from organising outings for the
families to providing support when their needs are greatest.
I have had my own, admittedly less heartrending, opportunities to appreciate the work of the Welfare Officers; they
have provided support for the families when the Battalion
has been deployed, helping us to feel connected to each
other and to what was going on. While we were in St Athan,
the Welfare Officer was Nicky Mott, Karen's husband and
a Captain at the time. He is one of three brothers who have
all served in the Battalion together, all of them reaching
the highest Non Commissioned rank of Warrant Officer
Class One.

The Battalion was in Iraq at the time and the Welfare Office
organised a wives' Christmas party held in the Corporals'
Mess at St Athan. It was a formal dinner, followed by a disco
with entertainment provided by a stand-up comic in drag. I
had felt a bit nervous about going. I think the anxieties I was
feeling in St Athan had got the better of me, and I was apprehensive about being the wife of the Second in Command in
the company of many women who I didn't know. I had dith-
ered for ages over what to wear and felt uncomfortable when

I arrived and realised I was looking far too formal compared with all the other wives, who were appropriately dressed for an evening of dance and entertainment. At the end of the dinner I was asked by Nicky to stand up and thank the Mess staff for laying on a superb meal. I did not mind doing this in the least, but it did single me out when I had intended to mingle for the evening without being encumbered by the unofficial rank that attaches itself to wives on more formal occasions, labelling her as 'wife of'.

Anyway, speech over, we all headed for the bar and the rest of the evening's entertainment. As soon as the stand-up comic spotted me in the audience, looking like a schoolgirl who had forgotten her games kit, he began to criticise my choice of clothes and my 'posh' name and singled me out for the duration of the act. When I refused to tell him my husband's rank he assumed he must be the Sergeant Major, so there I let it rest; I did not intend to pour petrol on an already roaring fire. When the jokes started to wear thin I had a face to match my equally bright skirt, despite desperately trying to smile. Although my efforts to enjoy the evening were painful, I was heartened by the friends around me; these were my 'minders', the likes of Bev and Catrina, who fiercely supported me and were touchingly moved by my embarrassment.

The finale to this episode came at the following year's Halloween party for the children, again at St Athan, when the adults were also invited to join in the fun by going in fancy dress. I dutifully disguised myself as a witch, with as many black clothes as I could muster (to make up for my lack of black clothing at the Christmas disco), my hair back-combed and my eyes rimmed in heavy black makeup. Oliver and Annabel were dubious about their mother looking so embarrassing but I stuck to my guns. When I turned up there were very few wives who had done the same. This time they were the ones in the bright clothes and I was all in black. I felt very awkward at first for being the mug who had turned up in fancy dress, but I was met with approving comments from many of the same wives who had accompanied me to the Christmas dinner. They were genuinely impressed, or perhaps sympathetic, that I had made so much effort. Anyway, I left on a high, feeling that I had done a better job of fitting in with the spirit of the party, despite the fact that I was, again, the odd one out on the dress front. At least this time there was no drag artist.

For me the most memorable events are the 'Combat Wives' weekends. My first was while in St Athan, and was again organised by Nicky Mott. Intended as a taster of what our husbands endure on exercise, the weekend introduced us to drill, shelter building, ration packs, observation, stalking, command tasks, rifle shooting and 'tabbing' (learning to alternate running and walking with a full pack). We had all borrowed our husband's 'bergens' (rucksacks) and I could not understand why my pack seemed heavier than everyone else's until, well into the second day, Nicky asked me to empty it out only to find that Richard had left two bulletproof breastplates in the bottom compartment. Richard claims it was an oversight, but the fact that I had mentioned to him previously that we wives should experience the 'real thing' undergone by our husbands did give me my doubts. However, we felt we had miraculously discovered the truth when, after night navigation, we were led back to our 'bivvies' (bivouacs) to find a bonfire, trestle tables dressed with white tablecloths, wine and fish and chips. The 'real thing' was finally revealed.

Bev Evans describes one of the last tasks of the weekend, when we had arrived back at camp from the training area:

> *'After a not so good night's sleep we arose and had to pack up our kit. My previous experience in the Army, some ten years before,*

made this easy for me although at this stage I must point out that my skills as a soldier had been questionable!

We were driven back to St Athan RAF base and set on our next task. A two-mile "run" across the airfield to the Corporals' Mess, where our husbands and children waited to welcome us back:

"Oh well," I thought "I may not be 'Best Drill and Turnout', but I'm not that bad at the old fitness." Then I remembered ... Fiona was with us! The woman with the longest legs in NATO.

Catrina then piped up:

"Well, I've been to the gym every day."

My confidence was dented ... but not shattered.

"Mmm," I thought, " so my legs are not as long as Fiona's and I can't remember the last time I went to the gym but I've walked up and down the hill into St Athan village pushing a pushchair more than once – and I'm on the skinny side; perhaps the wind will take me."

Off we went ... I had a quick look behind. Not bad; not at the back, but not at the front though ... not yet.

I began to feel my competitive edge breaking through. The once familiar surge of adrenaline and jelly legs came upon me.

I was overtaking people ... I was winning!

"Must be the wind," I thought.

About halfway round I was striding out in front. I had found my stride. My breathing was controlled, my pace steady. I felt a momentary sensation of smugness.

Then I saw her ... catching me up. Yes, it was indeed, Fiona "The Legs" Stanford!!!

I remember calling to her: "Come on Fi, catch me up!" Did I mean that? ... Probably not. What I really meant was: "Fiona! Stop, your shoelace is undone," or "Fiona, slow down, we are near the end you won't catch me because I am going to win. Yes that's right, win, win. Win!"

*I picked up my pace, thinking that I had come this far and I
had to keep going.*

*The end was in sight. Fiona was catching me. I belted forward
to perform an Olympic-style sprint finish, despite the heavy boots.
I became oblivious to the competition. I was lost in my own potential glory.*

"Ye . . . ssss, I'd done it. I'd won! Yippeeeee!"

*Fiona came in very close behind and I gushed genuine praise,
driven by my adrenaline-fuelled moment of exhilaration.*

I turned, feeling ten foot tall, invincible, fantastic!

*Nicky Mott said: "Firing range next Bev. Looking forward to
it?"*

*My moment had gone . . . Shooting . . . I knew I was doomed to
failure at that one.*

Bev modestly fails to mention that she also won the shooting competition. Richard laughs at Bev's description of me
as 'Legs Stanford' since running is definitely not one of my
fortés and he himself is, more appropriately, known in the
Battalion as 'Crazy Legs'. I am only pleased that he was not
running with us, as he is rather a taskmaster when it comes
to fitness.

While it is certainly true that a large part of the bonding
process between the wives happens because we are thrown
together in difficult circumstances, it also occurs when
opportunities arise to get to know each other at leisure. In my
experience, this is when the foundations for lasting friendships
are built and will never be rocked. There is no doubt that the
events organised by the Welfare Office while the Battalion is
away are an invaluable contribution to family morale. There
is just nothing quite as good for bonding as being able to
laugh together as well as cry together. Sometimes, though,
laughs are the last thing on anyone's mind.

The Welfare Officer while the Battalion was in Afghanistan during the summer of 2009 was Captain Darren Pridmore, who had a very demanding task ahead of him during such a difficult time for the families, especially for those who lost loved ones. Before deployment to Afghanistan Darren organised a Families' Day to encourage wives to meet each other and to understand more about what the Battalion would be doing in Afghanistan. The Prince of Wales as the Colonel of the Regiment, and Camilla, Duchess of Cornwall, came along to show their support and to meet as many of the men and families as possible.

Pari Spencer Smith, whose husband is a Captain in the Welsh Guards, described her impressions of the Families' Day:

> *'Families' Day was really useful in preparing us for the reality of deployment. I remember sitting in the briefing by Captain Pridmore and Padre Morgan thinking "This is all so irrelevant, I'm well prepared – my Tommy will be fine". Of course, no matter how much you try to convince yourself that your husband will come back safely, there is always a niggle of doubt in the back of your mind. You never really know what will happen, and in some ways you can never really prepare yourself. I personally think it's silly to think about what could happen – almost tempting fate. But there's no doubt that knowing more about the practicalities of what equipment the men would be using and what training they'd undertaken helped to bring it all home to us.'*

There is a certain amount of government allowance allocated for families' welfare during operational tours, but much of the funding comes from the Regiment's small amount of charitable money. The Welsh Guards' 'SWAGs' (Service Wives and Girlfriends) also organise fundraising events of their own to boost the kitty.

Darren told me about the range of activities he had organised for the families while the Battalion was away in Afghanistan, including Thorpe Park, Chessington, Poultons Park and Bournemouth beach. They had barbecues and Sunday lunches every month, with live bands and DJs, face painting and bouncy castles. Twenty-eight families were booked in to a holiday park for a week in Hastings during the Whitsun bank holiday. The wives also went to a *Big Brother* live eviction and were invited to dinner with Lady Dannatt, wife of the last Chief of the General Staff. One of the highlights was the visit to the Prince of Wales' home at Highgrove in Gloucestershire. Prince Charles kindly cleared the diary on three consecutive weekdays for the Welsh Guards' wives to have a private tour of the gardens followed by tea.

When I was talking to the wives during this time, the overriding sentiment that came up over and over again was gratitude for the friendships that were formed and strengthened back in camp. Many women described these friendships as 'lifelong', an amazingly strong and positive outcome from a very challenging six months. It makes sense that emotions should be very strong, though. The experience of deployment is absolutely gruelling for everyone, and of course, even before the nightmare of having their men sent away on operations, the wives and girlfriends had been apart from their loved ones for months; pre-tour training involved three months in Belize, six weeks in Germany and ten weeks on courses and exercises in the eighteen months between returning from Bosnia and deploying to Afghanistan.

One of the lasting friendships made during this time was that between Stacey Merritt-Webb and Laura Fuller. Stacey wrote in her journal:

> 'Really glad I've met Laura, what a pal she is turning out to be. I think her friendship is a large part of the reason I'm still sane. We are so similar in thoughts it's spooky, someone up there is looking after me by making sure we met. I've made a friend forever.'

Stacey told me how she met Laura just before their husbands deployed:

'We met at the deployment Family Day on camp before the men went to Afghan. We'd both had babies shortly before the men left so we were on maternity leave at the same time. We met up every week and walked to a coffee shop in North Camp for a catch-up and we would stop at the post office, so we could post our men a box of goodies and letters.

Just before my birthday we attempted a quiet night out, but while sitting at table drinking our drinks, both our phones bleeped – we had received a text informing us of a death, we didn't really need to say anything to each other, we knew the night was over and we walked home. That was our first and last night out during the tour. After that, whenever we received a group text informing us that a Welsh Guard had died, we would phone each other to make sure that it wasn't one another's husbands then we would walk round to camp at the first opportunity and lay some flowers together. It was so emotional; we shed many tears together.

But we cheered each other up whenever we could. On my birthday Laura brought me some flowers and a cake, as she knew Darren couldn't. We let off some steam and went to Thorpe Park, leaving the children with grandparents and acted like kids for the day – which was fantastic.

Laura was there whatever time of the day or night, and knowing that she was going through the same as me, knowing that she would understand my fears and concerns, knowing that I could say anything to her made such a difference and I will forever be grateful to her. I know in 2012 when we have to go through this living hell again, she will be there for me.'

Another typical example of the way the wives pulled together during the Welsh Guards' tour to Afghanistan was on Marlo's birthday, which fell while her husband, Major Henry Bettinson, was away with the Battalion. Living in quarters in Aldershot she was surrounded by others in the same situation, but as her birthday drew closer she longed for some family time, and the chance to speak to Henry. As she is Australian, her own family are on the other side of the world, so support from friends was vital to her:

'Henry had already missed Harry's second birthday and then Camilla's first birthday during this tour alone, then my birthday was coming up without him as well. No one really knew about it except one other wife, Rebecca Gallimore, whose husband was also in Afghanistan. The day arrived, and I had invited a few people over for morning tea anyway. I hadn't told them it was my birthday, but unknown to me, Beccy and another friend, Denise Bevan, had spread the word.

We had a system to avoid unnecessary panics about who might be knocking on the door. All of us lived in fear of getting the official visit with bad news, so I'd asked my friends to knock on the kitchen window when they came round, instead. I heard the tap and opened the front door:

"Happy birthday!" came the greeting from Beccy, with a huge smile on her face. She had arrived with a cake and candles and had even bought presents for my own children to give me; she had involved Harry in wrapping them up, so that he could surprise me on the day.

Then other friends arrived with gifts. Their children were dressed up in party clothes and even Sally Thorneloe popped in with a present (it was after Rupert had died). I had to stop the tears welling up; this selfless act of friendship in the midst of her own overwhelming grief was so touching; I cannot express how much it meant to me.

I have to say that even though my husband was away and I was on edge the whole time, the sun was shining and it was one of *the happiest, loveliest birthdays I've ever had – and to top things off – I got a call from Henry who hadn't been able to speak to me in over two weeks!'*

Spontaneous acts of friendship like this can gel a community of Army wives and girlfriends for ever. Such was the support that Marlo and Beccy gave each other during those fraught six months that Beccy is now Godmother to Marlo and Henry's third child, George, who was born nine months and two days after Henry's return from Afghanistan.

Bev Evans told me about receiving the news that her husband Gareth was to be posted to Afghanistan in 2007. At the time he was serving away from the Battalion and attached to the 1st Battalion Worcester and Sherwood Foresters Regiment (which has since become the Mercian Regiment). She had relaxed in the assumption that they were on a posting where he was unlikely to be sent on an operational tour, but occasionally these things take us unexpectedly. Sometimes particular skills are needed elsewhere and Gareth was in the end required to deploy with the Welsh Guards Mortar Platoon.

'When Gareth was called up to go to Afghanistan the first time, shock would have been an understatement. When he came home and told me I can remember a sense of panic like a great tidal wave rising from my toes into my throat. I wanted to stamp and shout like a two-year-old in a tantrum.

"Why? Why? Why?! Why you?" I hollered. "It just isn't fair!" Then the words that are now part of Evans family history were uttered (or should I say bellowed):

"I can't believe I'm being left to look after the dog … your bloody dog!"

Rosie, our black Labrador, was at that time a six-month-old puppy. Gareth had campaigned for months to have a dog. My persistent "no" gradually turned into a "yes", mainly because we were on a posting that meant he was unlikely to go away. Oh, the irony of it all.

As it transpired she became a godsend during that tour. Together with some very good friends and our daughters Kathryn and Rachel we more than managed to get through it.

As for Gareth; he thought my extreme reaction was due to him going to a dangerous part of the world, fighting for his country and putting his life on the line . . . Well, maybe it was, just a bit.'

The dog may have been the outlet, and a very valid reason for feeling 'put upon', but underneath all this was the genuine anguish at her husband's leaving for a very dangerous destination. Bev's sense of humour always understates a crisis.

By the time the Battalion deployed to Afghanistan in 2009, Karen and Nicky Mott were living in their own house in Yorkshire. Karen explained the difference for her between living on a camp, as they had done in Northern Ireland and many other places, and being away from the patch when the men are on operations:

'The big advantage of living on the patch is getting news immediately and at first hand. There is also the fact that the other wives have a full understanding of what is going on. During Nicky's last two deployments to both Iraq and Afghanistan, I felt totally detached from the Battalion and was living amongst a community that had little understanding of what it was like being married to a soldier on operations. Although I have a large family to call upon, the lack of understanding of what it's like having your husband away in dangerous surroundings does not register the same as it does with the wives on the patch.'

Though of course they were as supportive as they could be, Karen's own parents do not have an Army background, so she did not want to worry them with her concerns. However, Nicky's family is strongly connected to the Army; his brothers Billy and Jonathan would phone Karen on a regular basis, as did other family members, but his brothers had a better understanding of what Karen would be going through, so communication between them was very open.

Leanne Peters told me her reasons for preferring to live on the patch. She had a particularly stressful time when she lived off camp during the Battalion's deployment to Iraq in 2004. Leanne gave birth to their first child while her husband Steven, now a Sergeant, was away in Iraq, and soon afterwards she developed Obsessive Compulsive Disorder. Although Leanne had a strong support network of friends and family at home, the stress of giving birth to her first child while Steven was away fighting in Iraq manifested itself in the disorder. She had not appreciated that the Welsh Guards Welfare Office would have been able to help, on or off the camp, and became increasingly affected by the condition for the next two years, trying to cope without help. She was obsessed by counting the number of times she would perform a task, repeatedly checked that she had turned the gas off and was constantly washing her hands. When Steven returned from Iraq he only had two weeks' leave before commencing a course in Brecon for another three months; it was a very long nine months for her.

Eventually she did seek help through cognitive therapy with a clinical psychologist, and fortunately she has now recovered, but Leanne stressed to me that she would not wish anybody to suffer in silence as she did. In hindsight, she felt that living off camp had been a mistake for her as a new bride, as it meant that she missed out on the support of other wives. During the tour in Afghanistan Leanne threw herself into organising outings and running the coffee mornings for the wives in

Aldershot. The support she now gives, and receives, on camp has made all the difference, and she now has some 'lifelong friends' as she puts it:

'On the patch, at least there are no rumours; we can talk to each other and pick each other up when we are feeling down. I did have a few dramas while Steven was away; three hospital trips in six weeks, but thankfully my friends were there for me at the drop of a hat. The first time I broke my nose, the second time my son flew out the back door and gave himself concussion and the third time my daughter pulled a ligament in her knee. If not for my friends I would have been a nervous wreck, and this would have been no good for Steven, knowing I was falling apart while he was so far away.

The experiences and upheaval we go through are so surreal, that you end up building up a big emotional shield for yourself to help deal with this lifestyle, but at the end of the day it is worth it. It makes you a better person – the best you can be.

I am proud to be married to a Guardsman and he loves his job. It's his passion and all he knows in life; he joined when he was sixteen. Seeing Steven in Trooping the Colour has to be a highlight of life in the Welsh Guards – I was just so proud of him. One thing's for sure though – we never plan for the future, we take one day at a time as in this life you never know what is around the corner'.

Where do those stand who are not married to their partners? Girlfriends, in particular, often feel out on a limb when their boyfriends are away. Without the right to live in a married quarter, they are frequently off camp and therefore detached from the Welsh Guards' 'family.' Many of the Welsh girlfriends also live at home in Wales. Nowadays, too, more women have their own careers and may own their own homes prior to getting married. Independence is a coveted and often well

earned position and, more than ever, the careers of both partners must be considered equally prior to compromising either
situation. Faced with the prospect of losing both career and
established home if one partner decides to 'marry into' the
Army, a couple may well decide that living in married quarters
and moving so frequently is not for them.

The MOD has recently entitled servicemen and -women
in civil partnerships to receive all the same rights as married
couples; they are now able to live in married quarters and are
entitled to receive the same allowances. However, the MOD
does not, and never has, recognised any form of 'common law'
marriage for those in a long-term relationship, either hetero-
sexual or homosexual.

Despite not being able to live on a patch, there is no reason
why a girlfriend or fiancée should not become part of the
'Regimental family' once she gets to know some of the other
wives and girlfriends, and her status should not affect the
camaraderie between them all. Alannah McDonald, wrote to
me describing her feelings about their farewell and the camaraderie she came to depend on while her boyfriend 'Speedy'
was away:

*'Our goodbye did not go entirely to plan. One always has a perfect
idea of what it could be like but as I stood on the platform watching the train approach at speed I panicked. I gave him a hug
and a kiss and without thinking I stupidly said "right, bugger
off then you, I'll speak to you later." With those parting words I
quickly boarded my train bound for London. It was only when I
arrived home that I kicked myself and the tears raised their ugly
head. How lucky I was to have something so special that made
saying goodbye so hard. Looking back on that moment now we
both laugh. However, at the time it was a brief and tearless goodbye which in some ways was exactly how we both wanted it to be.*

Being inexperienced in the world of Army tours nothing could have prepared me for the emotional rollercoaster I was about to embark upon ... As a girlfriend rather than a wife there is the worry of being left out of the loop as you are not next of kin.

I was lucky enough to have met a few other girls before the tour began. After a few weeks I got in touch with one of the girls to arrange to meet for a drink and it was the best thing I ever did. Alice's reply was very friendly and she seemed keen to meet mentioning a few other girls that we could also invite along. She was pleased for the support herself, since she was trying to organise her wedding while her fiancé was away with the Battalion. From that day on, bonds were firmly formed and our group grew rapidly in size, becoming our monthly lifeline. Emotions that we often encountered generally surfaced during these get-togethers and we quickly realised that we shared the same paranoid anxieties on a daily basis ... We became a team, and we stuck together through the laughter, and the saddest of moments.

Afghanistan was tough for our men in a way in which one cannot possibly comprehend but it was also tough for the ones left behind ... What I will say is that an Army tour has the ability to test the limits in any relationship. When separated for that amount of time as a couple you begin to appreciate one another more than ever before and I am incredibly thankful to have gone through the experience. I received valuable support from the most unexpected circles and I have gained some firm friends whom I value greatly. My mother has always told me that the Army is one big family and I always assumed that that was only the case if you were married to someone in it – how wrong I was. The support network has been phenomenal, I am deeply touched by it and I will never forget it.'

Pari Spencer Smith used to travel down from Oxford on a regular basis to join the girls:

'We all went to immense effort while our men were away to actually get together and have supper, enjoy each other's company and
tell each other our woes and worries over a glass of wine. I felt an
overwhelming need to be with people who understood and who
were going through the same thing.'

Charlie Antelme was chosen to take over as Commanding
Officer when Rupert Thorneloe was killed. At the time,
Margaret suddenly found herself in the role of the girlfriend
at home, with just days to prepare for his departure:

'Within days, [of receiving the news] *the suits were put away
and there was newly issued desert kit all over the living room. It
only really struck me then that he was a soldier and off to fight
in a very dangerous war. I was only twenty-five years old, and
had absolutely no idea what would lie ahead for us. Although it
was 2010, I felt like I had been taken back to 1941 and remembered my grandmother, Jessie Grimsley, telling stories of sending
my grandfather off to World War II, and her tales of endless times
spent alone while he was away.'*

With her military family background in the US, Margaret had
a readymade support network from across the Atlantic, but
she also found support closer to home from the other girlfriends and wives in London:

'*I accompanied Charlie to Brize Norton to see him off and knew
that I had to figure out how to maintain this stability in a foreign
place for the next three months. Within days, I began to receive
invitations from other girlfriends and wives in the Regiment
for which I was very grateful. Unlike the US Army, the British
Regimental system makes for a much stronger family, a unique
element I had not experienced until then. The London group of
girlfriends was particularly empathetic and offered much advice
on how to cope with the added stress of missed calls and grim*

headlines amidst the strains of a city job. Fortunately, Charlie was able to call and email frequently, and if I had not heard from him for several days, it was likely that one of the girls knew where he was and that he was OK. No matter how much easier it is to keep in touch in this age, there were still weeks that would go by without any communication.'

Although the wives and girlfriends obviously endure these separations, we must not forget how other loved ones also have to cope, particularly mothers. They, like many girlfriends, are at a distance from the close-knit community of 'the patch'. Elizabeth Blackledge has known her boyfriend, Charles Maltby, since they were both thirteen years old, although Charlie only passed out as an officer with the Welsh Guards a few months before being deployed to Afghanistan. She formed a close relationship not only with other Army girlfriends but also with Charlie's mother during the tour:

'I was amazed at how the experience brought me closer to his mother. We would phone each other whenever there was word, and just as often when there was no word. She provided me with a connection to him; which I loved. When there was no word from Charlie, his mother and I would continue to ring each other to explain that he was definitely fine. Somehow if someone else said he was having a nice time and still had a full set of working limbs, it was undoubtedly true and our worst fears were diminished. I imagine there can be little anguish greater than waiting for the return of a son from combat.

It was also nice to talk to someone who shared the strange but enormous excitement that came from the news that your boyfriend had received the box of crackers and pâtés that you spent your weekend selecting from four different shops. The news that his Platoon has also tucked in to your offerings was even better. I got to know the ladies at my local post office fairly well and they were brilliant at helping me send the most I possibly could whilst remaining within the weight limit. After sending a package a week, I knew that Charlie would most likely have enough magazines, biltong, and supplies to last him a year, but sending out more made me feel better; it was my only proactive method of helping and offered me something resembling a sense of control.'

Although Elizabeth appreciated the support and phone calls from friends outside the Army, she became

'increasingly amazed at how difficult it was to explain the situation to them … I was certain that in a dust- and IED-free Buckinghamshire, I was not going to be able to prove that I was in any way struggling. Instead, I threw myself into my work, and made sure my weekends were jam-packed to avoid an over-thinking mind. I cannot imagine how hard it must be for all the wives who did not have the luxury of the distraction that comes with a frantic job.'

In relating stories of the well-meant questions from friends as to whether the tour had been hard for Elizabeth, she wrote:

'I often had the niggling suspicion that my truthful tales of insomnia and constant fear would spoil the light mood of quiet drinks parties. In an attempt to shield them from my bad temper, I often had to resort to sarcasm; explaining that it had been nice to be temporarily promoted to chief television remote control operator. I usually added that it had been nice to get rid of him for a while and enjoy the increased space in my apartment.

In truth, the flat had never seemed so empty.'

Living with the constant worry, the endless news bulletins and growing death toll is a stark reminder of the dangers of being a soldier. For those not personally involved, bad news naturally becomes meaningless and it is possible to give it a brief thought and then move on. I feel that bringing war into the comfort of our own homes via TV and radio news gives it a 'soap-opera' image, in which those following the updates are detached from and unable to understand the very real lives and experiences of those who are going through it. Like being on safari from the comfort of a vehicle, knowing that you have a safety barrier and are really just watching the spectacle, the sitting room becomes the vehicle and the television report the spectacle outside it. Being on a foot safari, by contrast, is the equivalent of being an infantryman in real life combat or the wife of a soldier in that situation; it becomes an anxious, adrenaline-charged reality.

I really noticed the impact of that gulf of experience during the Welsh Guards' tour in Afghanistan, which coincided with a time of rising unemployment after the financial crisis. Of course every individual's own worries loom largest in their own minds, but I could not help feeling a big wave of sympathy for one wife, whose husband was out in Afghanistan and had a rather unfortunate reaction from a friend of hers who worked in the banking sector.

'When my husband was on tour a good friend got in touch to invite me to her engagement party in London. When I said I couldn't come, she sounded annoyed and asked why my husband couldn't babysit the children and when I told her that he was still in Afghanistan she said "Oh God – is he still there?" . . . I can't tell you the emotions that ran through me with that one comment – I felt like saying: "Haven't you been watching the news? Don't you realise people are being killed and injured out there every day?" I used to work in investment banking myself before becoming a full-time mother, so I know what she was going through to a certain degree with the crisis, but I don't remember ever being that ignorant to what was going on in the world around me – at least I hope I never was.'

Of course, most people are very aware of the sacrifices being made by serving soldiers and their families, and in fact the media coverage of the casualties in Afghanistan has boosted the much appreciated public support for the nation's Armed Forces. In recent months the military charities have seen a surge in their funds, publicity for the families and the wounded has soared and the country is supporting its troops more than ever. We are hugely grateful for this; a little recognition goes a very long way to boost morale for these servicemen and -women, and their families. But recognition must not be confused with sympathy. Military families are proud of what they do, what their men do, and are not looking for pity, but a little understanding might just give them the strength to carry on.

It is no exaggeration to say that without the support of their families, the Armed Forces wouldn't function as it does. I often feel that without the support of my fellow Army wives and girlfriends, I would not have been able to come through my own darker moments. I do not know of any Army wife who would not extend a helping hand to another when she is in need. Gossip can be irritating, living in a 'goldfish bowl' can be stifling, but on a patch if you need help there is usually someone who knows it before you even admit it to yourself. And when the ultimate price is paid by a soldier of any rank, there are no social differences amongst the bereaved and there is never any hesitation in extending the support of the Army family.

4

Nomadic Children

'There are many things you can do by post; having babies isn't one of them.'

I was newly married when a veteran wife, who had seen many postings and had been through many experiences, spoke these wise words. She seemed like a guru to me at the time and I could not imagine ever clocking up as much mileage in Army life as she had. It did not take me long to realise what she meant though: if you wanted to start a family you just had to make the most of your husband while he was at home, otherwise who knew when he would be around long enough to actually get a family off the ground.

I saw proof of the truth of that veteran wife's words when Richard spent two years at Staff College between 1997 and 1999, where officers do an advanced course in order to be promoted beyond the rank of Major. There were about one hundred and twenty officers on the course, all of a similar age – between thirty and thirty-five. We all seemed to be at the same stage in our lives, all having married within the last few years. The fact that our husbands would not be posted on any operational tours in this time meant that it was an ideal opportunity to start a family. We lived in Shrivenham, Wiltshire for the first year, and Camberley, Surrey for the second year. Oliver was eight months old when Richard began the course; we came back from Oman early for him to start it, and Annabel was born just as it ended. During the course some people managed to have two consecutive babies and during the two years there were eighty babies born; we certainly kept the maternity departments of Swindon and Frimley Park Hospitals in business. The men should have passed the course purely on the grounds that they had to study with newborn babies, young toddlers and sleepless nights, never mind actually passing any exams.

There was always the sound of children playing on the patch, which was made up of a series of very quiet cul-de-sacs. It occurred to me that much of Britain must have been similar to this situation in days gone by, before the roads became busy and when there was more of a community feel to neighbourhoods. There probably still are areas like this today, but whenever I look at old photographs of street scenes, the children playing cricket or football while mothers and grandmothers gossiped at their front doors, they look like images from another life: long forgotten and outdated.

Even the older siblings of the new babies were more or less of preschool age, although some of the overseas officers had older children. These included Arab families who were attending Staff College on an exchange basis, and they would let their children play in the street until it was dark, as they had probably already had an afternoon siesta, so in the summer the children might be playing outside until at least ten o'clock at night. Nobody minded; it was considered a safe place to live, we all looked out for each other and the sight of so many multicultural and international children playing together happily was something to be treasured.

We had been asked to be a point of contact for a Jordanian family with six children during this posting, and so we tried to help them settle in. As Richard could speak Arabic it seemed sensible for us to volunteer for the honour, which meant that the visiting family had someone to come to and a way into meeting the UK officers and their families, and would occasionally be entertained by their hosts and shown some of the local sights. The fact that I did not speak Arabic, other than the pleasantries and the really useful phrase *'Bukra fil mishmish'* ('tomorrow your apricots will ripen') which is rather like saying 'Don't worry, it will all be fine', did not seem to matter. Neither did the small detail that I had responsibility for the wife, who could not speak English. Until, that is, one day when I decided it would be a nice idea to take her and her children out shopping in Camberley.

I squeezed as many children as was legally safe into our car and we all piled out to sample the local, but very large, Marks & Spencer. Now, I do not have a very good sense of direction myself, and always manage to get lost in large department stores, so perhaps it was not the most sensible of choices. I had explained that if we became separated she was to wait at the entrance, so (I thought) all seemed fine. However, obviously my Arabic was not up to scratch because I managed to lose them all within the space of a few minutes and could not see them at the entrance.

I was calm to begin with, but after about half an hour of searching I felt the panic starting to rise; visions of an international incident for which I would be responsible sprang to mind. It was pointless making an announcement over the tannoy since none of the staff could speak Arabic so, along with a string of security guards and a description of the lady and her children, I searched high and low. Eventually I decided to widen the search into the neighbouring Tesco, and there I found her, amongst the vegetables, looking rather pleased to see me, while her children ran happily around the loose potato and mushroom stands. *'Bukra fil mishmish'* seemed an appropriate comment to make at that moment, and she replied with a beaming smile and a huge hug. We returned to the patch for a much needed cardamom coffee for my friend and a cup of tea for me, and let the children return to their favourite pastime of playing in the street.

It still makes me smile to think of all those families taking advantage of the relatively brief period of calm afforded by the time at Staff College to have their babies and let their children enjoy community life. I enjoyed that posting hugely. But of course, not all births are straightforward and well planned. There are many stories of military wives through the ages giving birth in exceptional circumstances and extraordinary locations, and tales of more recent births without the father present, even if the birth is in the UK. Although the Army will do its best to allow a husband home for a birth whenever possible, if only for a few days, leave is not guaranteed, so sometimes a young wife having her first child will be forced to have the baby without her husband by her side. If this is the case, and she lives on the patch, the other wives will invariably rally round and give her as much support as possible.

Victoria Turner has had many overseas postings with her husband Jonathan, including to Cyprus, Germany and Canada, so, without family close by, has had to rely heavily on friends. One of these occasions was when she was pregnant with their second child, Francesca:

'While we were posted to Germany, I was pregnant with my second child who decided she wanted to make an early appearance. Jonathan was away on exercise and I was thirty-one weeks pregnant, with my two-year-old George asleep up stairs when I suffered a placenta bleed in the middle of the night. My neighbour had said "call any time, day or night" if I had any problems. What could I do but pick up the phone and call for help? Moments later, she was taking charge of the situation and organising, with military precision, a plan of attack. She arranged for

her husband to look after George whilst I was taken to the local hospital. I then spent the remainder of my pregnancy in and out of hospital with continual visits and food parcels arriving almost daily – the food in a German hospital comprising mainly of bread and cheese.'

One option for many wives, of course, if the due date coincided with a six-month tour of duty, an exercise or a course, would be to base themselves with extended family. Sue and Martyn Miles' second child Marc was born in Germany at the British Military Hospital, Iserlohn:

'Marc was born at the British Military Hospital in Iserlohn, nearly an hour from Soest in Southern Germany, where my mother and stepfather were living. Martyn and I were actually based in Hohne which was three hours drive away but as he was away in Wales on a course, I decided to stay with my family in Soest for, and immediately after, the birth, then went back to Hohne to wait for Martyn to return. Marc was almost three months old before his father saw him. Something that someone outside of the military would find extremely difficult to understand I would imagine. I often get asked "how do you cope", my reply is usually along the lines of "I may not always like it, but I just get on with it".'

Our first child, Oliver, was born in the Sultanate of Oman and luckily Richard was not away. Rather than us going back to England to have the baby, Richard's parents timed a visit to Oman to coincide with the due date so they could offer a helping hand. However, I was a week overdue when they arrived, and their first week with us was spent twiddling thumbs and waiting for the event.

My pregnancy had been straightforward up to that point but sometimes it was all a bit overwhelming, especially since

I was still missing my mother terribly. I attended the Armed Forces Hospital and with its British midwives and an all-female Indian obstetrics team there was a sense of familiarity that gave me the confidence to give birth there. The only foreigners who were eligible to attend this hospital were military personnel working alongside the Omani military, and their families. The other, non-military, expatriates tended to use the private hospitals in Muscat, mostly paid for by their employers: law firms, oil companies or banks.

Some of the patients in the Armed Forces Hospital were Bedu (Bedouin) wives and children of members of the Omani Armed Forces, entitled to use the hospital just as I was. The true Bedu are still nomadic people, moving their tents and herds of goats, sheep, cattle and camels around the desert depending on where the best grazing is. Many of the women attending the hospital had travelled from the Wahiba Sands, a beautiful area of extensive sand dunes, roughly four hours south of Muscat by road across the Al Hajar mountains. Nowadays most Bedu families own or have access to a jeep or pick-up truck, but it was still a fair trek for an appointment or, indeed, to give birth.

The Bedu in the outlying areas would wear brightly coloured dresses over trousers embroidered at the ankle. Over the dress they would wear a sheer muslin *abaya*, or robe, like fine netting, which revealed the bright colours underneath. However, when away from home the Bedu would often wear opaque *abayas* to hide the dresses, and it is this appearance that we foreigners are more likely to associate with traditional Muslim attire.

They would also cover their heads and shoulders with a muslin cloth, wrapped around in a seemingly complicated way; at least I could never master it until a Bedu showed me how while in her tent in the desert one time. In public, or when they saw a stranger driving towards them in the desert, they would cover their faces with a burqa, which is a stiffened cloth mask, sprayed in gold paint with a ridge down the centre from the forehead to the chin.

On my initial antenatal check I was the only Westerner and had to wait for an hour with about fifty Omani soldiers' wives, all of whom were in opaque *abayas* and burqas and some of whom were Bedu. As a foreigner I was expected to wear a dress or skirt below the knee and to cover my shoulders, but I did not have to cover my head except as a sign of respect when visiting outlying villages. Sitting here in the waiting room, conspicuous in my floral summer dress and a head and shoulders taller than the locals, I waited for my assessment. When the doors opened, all the ladies would jostle through, in an attempt to be the first seen, as there was no appointment system. It reminded me of the rush for a bargain when shop doors are opened on the first day of the sales.

Once through, the first question was: 'What is your tribe?' to which I replied, 'Um ... British', and then 'What is your relationship to your husband?' to which I replied, 'It's very good, thank you.' 'No,' came the response from the rather businesslike obstetrician, 'I mean are you his half-sister or his cousin?' 'Oh, neither,' I stammered. 'We are not related, except of course by marriage.'

My antenatal checks really were a learning curve, and not just for me. I tried to follow the rule – 'when in Rome, do as the Romans', as they say – so when I arrived I would say '*As Salaam alaikum*' ('Peace be upon you') to the entire waiting room, just as the other women did. In reply to my initial, rather self-conscious attempt came a collective stare, followed by the first tentative reply of '*Walaikum as salaam*' ('and peace be upon you'), followed by one or two more until all the ladies in the waiting room had made their replies. In the end I found it quite normal and when I got back to the UK, I was much more aware of the reserved way in which the English often ignore strangers without even smiling in their direction, which felt unfriendly in comparison.

Sometimes my antenatal visits would coincide with one other Westerner, a British Army wife called Joan. She was having her third child and was a great source of comfort, especially as there were few other friends out there who had experienced childbirth. We became friends, and our babies were born within six weeks of each other. We learned to scuba dive together only weeks after they were born and we still laugh at the occasion when Joan gave me the thumbs-up sign underwater, meaning she wanted to go to the surface. Coming up together, she ripped out her mouthpiece and said, with concern, 'You know sharks have an amazing sense of smell, well do you think they can sense when there is milk in the water?'

I looked at her in horror. We both swam and splashed our way for the boat, hauling ourselves over the side and landing very inelegantly in the bottom. When the instructor found out why we had been spooked, he laughed so much we thought he would tip us back into the water again.

I had no idea whether it was the same Omani women returning for antenatal appointments when I went to the hospital, as I could only see their eyes, but some of them seemed to recognise me and smile. They had extremely expressive eyes, maybe as no other facial expressions were visible to give away their feelings, and perhaps this is why the eyes of Arab women are reputed to be so seductive. After this, their children would come to sit next to me in the waiting room as I read my books, and would point to the way I read 'back to front' since Arabic is read from right to left. I started bringing in some children's books, which they loved; they even picked up a few words in

English, mostly relating to 'Baba the Elephant', which was all that I seemed to be able to buy locally.

So, all in all, despite the challenges, my pregnancy had been a happy time and full of moments when I felt that cultural boundaries were breaking down as I shared this fundamental experience with women whose lives were so different from mine. It has to be said, though, that by the time my parents-in-law turned up, I was very ready for Oliver to make his appearance. He, however, had other ideas. We tried to get the baby moving with local Arabic remedies, the hot curry method and Sri Lankan and Philippine therapies from the numerous people from these countries who were working in Oman. Complete strangers were only too happy to offer advice on seeing my very large bump, even when I had not asked for it – frequently in the middle of a supermarket – but nothing worked. Eventually, we decided to make use of the local amenities. We tried 'off-roading' up and down sand dunes in the white, particularly uncomfortable Land Rover we called Fatimah, but it only made me feel queasy and resulted in my bashing my head on the roof when we came over the top of a steeper than usual dune. We tried a trip in a friend's motorboat, but although we went slowly, it was too jarring and only caused my stomach muscles to tie themselves in knots as my body instinctively tried to protect the baby.

So, on Christmas Eve 1996, we decided to go to the park in Muscat to try out the pedalo boats, which sounded far more sedate. The winter over there is much like a hot British summer, so it was bearable to be out in the sun. Having wedged myself into the pedalo, with Richard's father next to me, we set off at a leisurely pace, each turning our own pair of foot pedals. We were out there quite happily for an hour, but then I decided enough was enough, and I think my father-in-law was secretly pleased that I had given up, not wanting to admit defeat before a very pregnant daughter-in-law. Having been assisted out of the boat, which was rather an awkward and ungainly procedure, all seemed fine. We had been looking forward to eating a Christmas Eve supper of finest gammon, brought over by Richard's parents in the absence of decent ham in a Muslim country, and to tasting French champagne which was also hard to come by. However, 'induction by pedalo' was clearly the answer, as halfway through the meal, Oliver decided this was his moment to finally make his appearance. Richard, driving like a true Omani and obviously terrified that I would have the baby in the car, almost flew me to the Armed Forces Hospital in Muscat. I am sure the wheels never actually touched the ground.

And so followed the longest Christmas Eve I have ever known; there was certainly no need to have rushed to the hospital.

During the night I seem to remember Richard sharing a Kentucky Fried Chicken with the nurses, much to my dismay as the smell made me feel decidedly ill. He went for a breather in the corridor and got chatting to an Omani husband who commented that I was taking rather a long time. When Richard replied that it was the first child so he supposed that was normal, the other husband suggested slapping me a little bit, which was sure to work. In the end though, and thankfully with no slapping, Oliver finally arrived at seven o'clock on Christmas morning, the best Christmas present ever.

I had been harbouring an irrational obsession with ensuring that we did not for a moment take our eyes off the baby, as my biggest dread was getting him muddled up with someone else's baby, and bringing up the wrong child for the rest of my life. Consequently, as soon as Oliver was born and was taken off to be weighed, I ordered Richard not to let him out of his sight. After a couple of these paranoid instructions the

Scottish midwife placated me by gently pointing out, 'You have the biggest and bonniest bairn in the hospital, and the only blond one'.

Being a Muslim country, Christmas in Oman is respected although not celebrated, but to the British midwives Oliver was a festive attraction, being the 'Christmas baby', and being blond he was a magnet for the Omani women and their visitors. They also admired his first present (from Father Christmas): a teddy bear, named Qaboos after the Sultan of Oman himself. Then followed goat for Christmas lunch and a box of Matchmakers, before Richard's parents arrived to have a second attempt at feeding me the gammon and the much needed champagne (behind drawn curtains of course, and with a blind eye from the midwives).

Despite these cross-cultural oddities I still considered myself lucky – a friend who gave birth in the military hospital in Salalah, in the south of Oman, had to do so in a room with four other women, the only privacy being a curtain between each.

So, we found that pedalos will get a baby moving. Some people swear by scrubbing the floor (after all, it is one of the recommended methods). It has been known for a wife to move quarters a week after her expected date of delivery and return to the previous quarter the same day to clean it for a 'march out' inspection, only to go into an amazingly quick labour. Perhaps this old wives' tale advice has been passed down by the scores of Army wives who have managed a little last-minute cleaning before squeezing in (or out) a birth between postings.

Annabel Lewis has had her own fair share of unlucky timings. Her husband Mark was on Spearhead Lead Element for Kosovo around the due date of their first child. This meant he was on standby to go out there with just twenty-four hours notice, so it was just not sensible for Annabel to bank on him being around. Instead, in the lead up to the birth she went to live with her parents in Dorset. Luckily, in the end, Mark was not called away but he was commuting every week between London and Dorset. Annabel recalled:

'Mark fortunately made it down from London in time to be present for Harry's birth and it actually all worked out for the best as it meant that my mother was on hand to help us settle into parenthood – it was like having an experienced maternity nurse all to myself.'

Annabel was expecting her second child one month after Mark's deployment to Afghanistan on loan to another Brigade in November 2009, shortly after the rest of the Battalion returned from Afghanistan. She told me that she was disappointed by the lack of support on the patch. Even if most people's experiences of Army life are positive, in the real world sometimes things do not work out perfectly and Army life is certainly not immune to the tensions that affect every one of us, no matter how strong our sense of community. In the event, she relied on family support for the second birth as well as the first:

'The arrival of Lucy loomed in December 2009. We had planned for the birth to happen about a month after his return but Mark's tour dates were altered which meant that Lucy would be due one month into his tour instead. So, back down to my parents – this time two weeks before the due date. I couldn't risk going into labour early on my own with a toddler. I had a planned caesarean this time to enable Mark to plan his leave to coincide with the birth. His journey home took four days though, so he arrived only just in time to take me to hospital. The caesarean was plain sailing, Mark left me the next day

to go back to Afghanistan, and my parents picked me and the
baby up and took us home.

Although the practicalities worked in Annabel's favour – just
– Harry was very thrown by all the upheaval: Mark deploying
four weeks earlier, returning for forty-eight hours before leaving again, then staying with two sets of grandparents, a new
sister to cope with and a mother who could not lift him up for
a cuddle due to her caesarean section.

> '*I couldn't have managed either of the births without our*
> *parents' help but I know many wives are not so fortunate to have*
> *the family support network that I find I have. Both sets were*
> *amazing and went beyond the call of duty for all of us. My parents*
> *looked after me and the babies immediately after both births,*
> *Mark's parents had Harry, our eldest, for as long as I needed and*
> *drove backwards and forwards to the airport on numerous false*
> *alarms, when it turned out that Mark was not actually on the*
> *plane after all.*
>
> *At the time I knew very few people on the patch and not well*
> *enough to rely on – this is a disappointment – I had always known*
> *that it would be difficult when Mark went away and I had always*
> *expected there to be a very supportive community around, but on*
> *this occasion there wasn't.*'

Of course, once babies are born they soon fall into place with
the regular postings and changes of location. 'Have baby, will
travel' is a motto frequently applied to the 'nomadic' children
we nurture. I sometimes wonder whether our son Oliver's very
first experiences, in Oman when we spent time with the Bedu
people, have somehow helped to prepare him for the constant
moving around. I vividly remember our visits to the mountains
where Oliver was endlessly fascinating to the locals because
of his blond hair and blue eyes; the trips to the desert where

we would bump into the same Bedu families in different locations, where he would play with Bedu children on the sand floor of a tent; watching local camel races where five-year-old boys would be strapped to a galloping camel for the reward of a packet of sweets; nights spent camping under vast Arabian skies when we would fall asleep counting shooting stars and galaxies, and the expeditions to watch the giant green turtles lay their hundreds of eggs in the sand at night before returning to the sea; these are all very special experiences which, who knows, may have shaped his character and prepared him for the nomadic lifestyle for which he was predestined.

Moving with preschool-age children is relatively easy from the educational point of view, and packing boxes are always a great source of entertainment. There was one occasion when a removal man taped up a box, picked it up and headed for the stairs with it. He paused to ask me a question while balancing the box over the banisters and at this point we both heard giggling from inside. With horror on our faces, we quickly set the box down and ripped it open. For Annabel, springing out of it like a real live jack-in-the-box' exclaiming 'Ta-dah!' was the highlight of her day, but the poor removal man had to recover outside with a cigarette. I was not exactly amused and the children were banished to play in the garden for the rest of the day. It ended smoothly enough though: as it was Richard's birthday, we saved the last packing box to use as a table, balanced his cake on it and all, including the removal men, gathered round to sing 'Happy Birthday' before heading off to our new destination.

The first thing the children would do as soon as we set off in the car was to request the song 'Funky Town' from *Shrek*, with its lyrics 'Gotta make a move to a town that's right for me', which became our family 'moving house' tune.

Often on a patch there are many children, perhaps more than on an average civilian street. Maybe this is because most serving soldiers are at an age where they have young families, whereas in civilian life there is a greater cross section of ages in the community. Bev Evans told me that she looked back on her posting to the patch in Warminster in Wiltshire with great fondness:

> '*Gareth, the girls and I were on a posting to Warminster in 2005 which was away from the Battalion. During our time there Gareth was also posted unexpectedly to Afghanistan but I have to say that it was a fantastic three years.*
>
> *I felt I really had a taste of life past when children played safely outside in big groups and I knew all the families in the street, even if it was just to say "hello" and "how are you?"*'

Once the children reach school age all the moving becomes much more of a challenge. Moving schools in the UK can have its own set of hurdles, especially if we are not given an address until a couple of weeks before moving to a new camp. Without an address we cannot register a child at a school with the guarantee of a place and if we are not given an address until the summer holidays, we cannot register until the schools open in September. Then follows a mad rush on the first day of term to secure a place, or not, as the case may be. This often means having to settle for a school with an available place, rather than the school of choice. In these situations, buying a new uniform comes low down on the list of priorities.

Many locations abroad have very good primary level schools and in Germany there are service schools; otherwise children must join expatriate schools or simply have to learn the language in a local school. At secondary level there may not be the facilities for teaching the British school curriculum abroad, so attending boarding school in the UK is often the only feasible option.

The decision to put your children into boarding school is

often an agonising one and in every family I have ever known it has prompted endless debate. The alternative, educating the children at a local school, is complicated as it may involve buying a house and the wife and children staying put while the husband spends Monday to Friday at his base; unless, of course, he is lucky enough to be posted nearby. Some parents prefer to send their children to boarding school but they must then live in quarters, moving with each posting. The continuity-of-education allowance provided by the Army covers between fifty and eighty per cent of the fees, depending on the school and your circumstances, and provides stability for children who would otherwise attend a constantly changing string of schools. Whatever the decision, it is a 'Hobson's Choice'; you either do not see your children or do not see your husband. That said, the opportunities at boarding schools are such that many people would give their eye teeth to educate their children at one, so it must of course be seen as a privilege as well; it certainly gives service children the chance, not only for a first-class educa-tion without constant change, but also to make the long lasting friendships that they would otherwise be denied.

We made the difficult decision to send both our children to boarding school, starting at the same time, but only after we had discussed everything with them and were sure it was the right thing to try. Nevertheless, the initial waving goodbye to children as they go away to school is a wrench for every mother; trying to remain cheerful in the car on the way, know-ing that every mile is one further from home, and saying goodbye knowing that the children want to cling on but are trying to put on a brave face in front of new teachers and friends. The memory of nine-year-old Annabel disappear-ing from view, with one of matron's comforting arms around her shoulder while the other arm held a bundle of washing, reminded me of Lucie in Beatrix Potter's *Mrs Tiggy-winkle*. I felt bereft then, but even more so four days later, when I had to say goodbye to Richard for the next nine months as well; two months training and courses followed by seven months deployment to Iraq.

Four weeks before the children started school we had moved from our own house into a quarter in Farnborough, Hampshire. It was our tenth move in thirteen years and suddenly I was alone in a new place with only the dog for company. I missed the children and Richard terribly but just threw myself into full-time work to make the time pass quickly. It was not ideal; I was travelling the fifty miles back to Salisbury once a week to nurse, and had another job as an advisor to a live-in care agency that took me to the south coast, Sussex, Surrey, Hampshire and Wiltshire to assess and visit clients and their carers. Putting a thousand miles on the clock in a week was not unusual if I was collecting the children on a Saturday to bring them home overnight.

After I had dropped them back at school Oliver would smuggle his mobile phone into bed – which should have been handed in for the night – so that he could ring and make sure I had arrived home safely. He would then whisper a muffled 'Night night' before he could get off to sleep peacefully. Looking back now I can see that I was desperately trying to keep busy as a way of avoiding having to face the reality of my situation.

The children and Richard never really felt that they lived in Farnborough, as they were hardly ever there; as soon as the following summer holidays arrived and Richard returned, we were posted again, back to Salisbury. Annabel summed it up that year, saying 'I feel like I've already grown up and left home, and I'm only nine.' By that point, Oliver was on his fifth school and Annabel her fourth, and I tried to console her and myself by reminding her that, had she not started boarding school when she did, she would have added another two schools to her list, totalling six by the time she reached secondary level at the age of eleven.

The pastoral care at school, however, was excellent. Not only did the teachers and house parents take a genuine interest in what was going on at home, so they could understand when the children may have been feeling low, but they were keen to know how I was coping too. During the Remembrance Sunday service at school, the chaplain, headmaster and teachers all made a point of asking after Richard, who was in Iraq. They would email frequently and were never too busy to talk. These small acts of compassion went a long way to helping me through that first year of the children's boarding school life. As a result, they settled well and have never looked back.

Victoria Turner, too, felt the wrench when she said goodbye to her children, who started boarding school together. Francesca (Chessie) was eight, and George ten:

'It is not an easy decision to send your children to boarding school but when my son reached his fourth primary school at the age of ten and he was covering "The Egyptians" for the third time, I knew the moment had come to make a very difficult decision. On the day I dropped both children off at Prep School, once again, I was on my own. I remember driving away, thinking that none of this was the way I had envisaged motherhood. I called a friend, Bee Bedford who I had met whilst our husbands were serving together in Germany, from a lay-by on the A303:

"I just had to stop and talk to someone, Bee. I can hardly drive for the tears, and my shoulders and neck are so tight."

The next day Bee came round with a voucher for a massage; she understood the emotion I was going through and this was her gesture of friendship.

Bee has been the most incredible friend to me and the whole family. I'm currently living three thousand miles away from my children, so they spend some of their weekends with Bee. She and her husband Simon volunteered to be Chessie and George's guardians while we are overseas, and even offered to look after our family dog for two years. She will be doing their laundry, cooking their favourite meals and no doubt washing the mud off dog and children after walking on Salisbury Plain. I should be doing that. I know that my chance will come to reciprocate but these unending acts of friendship and kindness will never be forgotten.'

Karen and Nicky Mott decided to opt for educating their children at a local school. They bought their own home after fifteen years of living in married quarters:

'I found it very hard to make the decision to leave the quarters from the only lifestyle that I had experienced throughout my married life. We wanted to get onto the property ladder and to settle the children so that they only needed to attend one high school. The initial problem we faced was where to settle, as we had fond memories from the eight places we'd been posted in fifteen years.

As a family we had fallen in love with Catterick and surrounding areas within North Yorkshire while Nicky was posted there as the RSM [Regimental Sergeant Major] and decided this was where we wanted to settle down. The children have now grown up as part of the local community and call it home. After his posting to Catterick, though, Nicky has weekly commuted to other postings and I was here alone when he was with the Battalion in Afghanistan. After the close-knit community of camp life I did find it lonely at times without the support of other wives in the same boat.

The one big downside while Nicky remains in the Army is the emotional price we have paid to establish a home for the children, not really understanding the amount of separation involved. We knew all the advantages outweighed the disadvantages to move

*from the patch and put down roots for the children to call home;
still, to this day I dread the moment that Nicky gets on the train
and we live apart for another week.'*

When Sue and Martyn Miles were posted to Northern Ireland
the primary schools took a mixture of Catholic and Protestant
children. Their children were very happy at the local primary;
they learned alongside the local children outside the camp
and played together after school as well. Sue enjoyed her time
working at the primary school for the two years they were in
Ballykelly. She said that religion was rarely discussed and the
only time she would know which teachers were Catholic and
which were Protestant would be on Ash Wednesday:

*'The Catholic children would have Mass as usual, separate to
the assemblies for the Protestant children. On Ash Wednesday
the Catholics would put ash on their foreheads which they were
expected to keep on for the rest of the day. The Catholic teachers
would do the same and only on Ash Wednesday could I tell which
ones were Catholics. Religion was not a big thing at this level.*

*It was when the local children were separated into Catholic and
Protestant schools at secondary level that the troubles began. They
could have been playing together nicely all their lives until this
point, then the hatred and segregation started. All Army children
at secondary level had to go to the Protestant schools, whether they
were Protestant or Catholic, because otherwise they would have
been singled out.*

*When we returned from Northern Ireland the children went to
a local school in Sandhurst, one at primary and one at secondary
school. We have always spoken at length to the children and asked
them how they felt to be moving around so much and having
interruptions to their education – both have always replied that it
didn't bother them and they would always get out of it what they
put into it.*

We spoke about boarding school as an option for them but neither felt that they wanted to go and assured us that they were happy doing what they were, except that they did miss their dad when he was away so much.

We sat the children down and discussed our future when Michelle was in Year 9 and choosing options for her GCSEs and Marc still had a year left at primary school. At this point we had been posted to Central London. Martyn should have only had approximately two years or so left if he achieved the rank of RSM, which he did. The choices were either to move with Martyn to what I saw as "a concrete jungle" or buy our own first property to get on the housing ladder in anticipation of Martyn leaving the Army after twenty-two years.

We as a family made the choice to do the latter. We bought our house in Lincolnshire to be settled close to my family for support whilst Martyn finished his twenty-two years. The children went to the local schools, Michelle going on into further education and university to study sport science. Marc also went into further education and then chose to go to work, but continues to compete in sport for enjoyment. Both are very happy in their chosen lives and do not feel as though their father's life/career in the Army has had any negative effect on their lives. They are very proud of their dad, especially when they visited Buckingham Palace for his investiture where he received the MBE from Prince Charles.'

Martyn did finish his twenty-two years, and then received his commission, becoming an officer in April 2000. (As a Non Commissioned Officer, the natural cut-off is after twenty-two years of service, after which they must leave. An exception to this is if the opportunity arises to become an officer, after which they may stay on until they are fifty-five.) So, after another ten years he left the Army in June 2010, after almost thirty-three years of service and having been on every operational tour with the Battalion since the Falklands Crisis back in 1982. In the last ten years alone he has completed two tours of Bosnia, one of Iraq and finally a tour of Afghanistan. Sue explained:

> 'This was not easy for either of us but we could see the reasons and justifications for the choices we made. It was the right route for us, though people outside of our circle would maybe see it as "strange".'

So how do children cope with Army life? Often, they do not really question it in depth, but the life of an Army child certainly has its own peculiarities.

Michelle and Marc Miles' feelings were that they did miss having their father around for their 'teenage years', Marc especially for not having a male role model around. They do, however, feel that they have certainly never suffered for this; in fact they feel it has had the opposite effect and they are stronger characters for it.

Charlotte Mott was nineteen when she told me a little about her Army childhood.

> *'Moving around the country was normal practice for me until I was nine years of age. During this time, I attended five primary schools, one for a mere two weeks but I wouldn't change this for the world. From a young age I've learnt how to make friends easily and quickly developed good communication skills and confidence. I also learnt how to cope with disruption and change on a regular basis. There was added pressure on my education but it all made me into a hard worker and I always wanted to achieve. The experiences I've had as a child within a military environment have been a challenge, but have certainly had more pros than cons.'*

Charlotte's brother Nathan, twenty-two, also has a story to tell:

I've lived on eight different Army estates and although I remember a lot of excitement, there were challenges as well. It was hard to be constantly making new friends, joining new sports clubs and then leaving them and moving on yet again. Compared to my sister, I didn't find it as easy to settle into so many different schools in such a short period of time. However, looking back, and considering that all the changes to schooling were at an age of eleven or under, this has certainly not affected my education in the longer term. I often revisit estates that I've lived on, and only have fond memories of my childhood which was shared with a group of people who also had similar issues to overcome.'

Michelle and Alun Bowen's daughter Tegan started her schooldays in the reception class of a very small primary school in Wick, South Glamorgan, with our own daughter Annabel, in 2003. On a windswept coast with a sea view from the classroom, it was the perfect beginning to their education. For Annabel it was also her first introduction to the Welsh language; although lessons were in English, they learned the basics of Welsh as well. We moved away from Wales within two years so our children have attended English schools since, but Annabel can still remember how to sing 'Heads, Shoulders, Knees and Toes' in Welsh, and I can very usefully say *'Dim siarad'* ('Be quiet') in Welsh, too, which always makes her stop and think even eight years on. Tegan went on to attend five more schools before starting boarding school at the age of ten. Michelle explains:

'We have not had too many problems with education for Tegan and Harvey. Tegan has had schools in all locations, but thankfully her education did not suffer as we feared it might. Almost the opposite occurred with her having a cosmopolitan outlook and for one so young we felt this was a useful by-product of moving so many times in such a condensed period. This outlook has been

assisted by the fact that her best friend is based in Cardiff and she always has that friendship to draw on as we have moved house and schools.

It has to be said that not all children, in our experience, have managed this inevitable turmoil quite so well.

Boarding school has been a significant step for us all, not least of course for Tegan. Her second term (after the novelty of the first term had worn off) was a bumpy ride but she has shown real maturity and has weathered the storm. She is far more settled now and her education has improved. So we are all happy; so far so good.

Alun deployed to Afghanistan with the Battalion in 2009.It had been a long six months for the family and the kids were excited for his return. It was getting late in the evening when he still had not arrived and Harvey had to go to bed. Tegan happened to be walking past the front door when Alun knocked and she opened the door, mouth agape, exclaiming: "What are you doing here?", as we had tricked the children into thinking that Alun would be home a week later. Harvey, who was fast asleep, was equally surprised when woken by his Daddy.'

Tegan has put some of her own thoughts on life as an Army child on paper for me:

I have been to seven different schools and that is because of my Daddy.

Around May last year [2009] he went to Afghan. I don't like it when my Daddy is there. I remember saying goodbye and I love you when he left home to go to camp and then Afghan the next day I remember getting a few letters off him and they always made me chuckle!!

It was getting nearer to when he was coming home. I was ill the week before he was meant to come home. I remember packing my stuff ready for school one night and there was a knock at the door. I asked if I could answer the door and I was allowed so I did. As

I opened the door I saw this great big giant and straight away I knew it was my Daddy. I was speechless, I almost fainted with joy!

I then gave him the biggest hug EVER!

I don't really like it when he goes away because I get worried and scared but I know he has to. I know he's old enough to look after himself but sometimes he needs my help.

My Daddy is the best, he's my hero!'

Michelle explains how their six-year-old son Harvey copes with Army life:

'Harvey is currently "Army Barmy" and loves everything to do with the military. His teachers asked him if he would give a talk to the reception class a year below him about how he felt with his father in the Army. Harvey was excited but also a bit daunted so Alun offered to go along as a double act. On rehearsing the "lesson" at home and pre-empting the myriad questions that were likely to be asked it was clear that Harvey became tearful on any mention of his Daddy going away and certainly back to Afghanistan. We planned the talk on the fun side of Army life, showing the children different sorts of kit and equipment but the inevitable questions followed. Alun managed to deal with the question of separation by stating the truth ... it is difficult for all families to be separated from their loved ones and the younger someone is the more difficult it can be for them to understand. A ruffle of Harvey's hair and a quick cwtch made it all better.'

[For the non-Welsh amongst us, 'cwtch', pronounced 'cutch' as in 'butch', is a Welsh term for a hug or a cuddle, but it is specifically used to describe the consoling or comforting variety, used to cheer someone up when they need a shoulder to lean on. It is such an expressive word, and not one I could begin to replace with an English alternative. I love it as it is, and it has become part of our own family vocabulary.]

'…*Alun and I have decided to avoid getting too involved in discussing the reasons for all the troubles in Afghanistan as it's hard for a six-year-old to comprehend. We deal with the questions of Army life based upon our own values and we try to explain in such a way as Harvey, in particular, will understand. We find that basing our answers on what we believe is right and wrong works best; as it does for families across the globe. There is not one correct answer but helping our children to understand why Alun has to go away from an Afghan/Bosnian/Iraqi child's perspective and explaining why we need to help these children have a safer and happier life is one way we cope with explaining the inevitable deployments that will follow so long as we are an Army family.*

Harvey has yet to experience the turmoil of leaving friends made in school at an age where it really matters. That will, of course, happen in the not too distant future but with Tegan now settled into boarding school life, Harvey is looking forward to joining her a few years down the line. He is insistent that we won't have any tears off him because he will have his sister there for cwtches and reassurance.'

Asking my own children their opinions on Army life, I am reassured to discover that they seem to mean it when they tell me that all is well. With a lifestyle so at odds with what most people consider normal, there are always moments when the doubts creep in, and after all it is every mother's destiny to worry about her children. Oliver is fourteen and pretty stoical about most aspects of Army life:

'*Living as an Army child is quite challenging at times. But there are memories I will treasure for the rest of my life, for example when my dad was commanding the Trooping of the Colour (the Queen's Birthday Parade).*

I had ten moves and five schools by the time I was eleven, so I was busy. (I did "The Tudors" five times). I wouldn't like to live in the same house for thirteen years but after so many I was pleased to start boarding school where I knew I would keep my friends for longer.

People say to me that moving around the place must be difficult. I say "no, not really" because I have grown up living with it, in different parts of the world, so I adapt quickly to my surroundings. I have learnt to make friends quickly which is a useful skill. Yes it is a hassle to move all our belongings out of the house but I love the change. When you're in your new home there are lots of different adventures that can be found, lurking within the house. When I move the only thing I regret is to leave my friends behind. It is very hard for me to wave them goodbye and to keep in touch with them.

I have friends whose fathers are also in the Army and I know how they feel when their fathers are away; we are in the "same boat" together. The thing I hate about my dad being in the Army is that he has to go to dangerous places like Afghanistan and Iraq and I worry about what he is doing. One job I do like doing for him when he is away though is mowing the lawn. The worst bit is the countdown before he goes away. After that you have to count down the days before he comes home.'

Annabel, at eleven, has also managed to weigh up the pros and cons:

'There are goods and bads about being an Army child. Let's start with bad:

I go to boarding school now and in my first year my daddy was away in Iraq. That was really hard knowing he was in a different country and he wasn't even at home. The other thing about boarding school is that you miss home.

Also there is moving around that is really difficult because once you have settled you have to move again which is annoying.

I have been to lots of schools, but it gets easier to make friends when you have done it so many times.

Then there are the goods:

You can sometimes have the honour of meeting the Royal Family, like I met Prince Charles at Clarence House where he lives which was amazing. I also met the Duchess of Cornwall. I liked seeing the Army horses in the stables after Trooping the Colour.

Also there are lots of fun parties you can go to. Each time we move house I take it in turns with my brother to choose a bedroom first. When it is my turn it is really exciting and I choose the cosiest one. If I can see any horses from the window that's even better.

Daddy asked me "what makes home home?" and I said it is where my family is and my own bed. When I am at school the nice smell of the washing powder on my play clothes reminds me of home too, which makes me feel better.

And that is my view xxx'

The definite disadvantages to being an Army child are when the father is posted away on an operational tour. There is really no 'good' time for the men to leave their children. If they leave newborn babies they miss seeing their development, which changes so quickly at that age; missing those milestones, such as learning to walk and saying the first words, are felt by the absent father rather than the child.

When the children are a little older they cannot understand why Daddy has to go away, or even where he has gone, and cannot be reasoned with. They start to miss their fathers, but do not have a developed concept of time so cannot see an end to it.

I remember one occasion when this was a particular issue for one of the families I got to know. We were living in Aldershot just after Annabel was born, and one wife on the patch was on her own while her husband went to Kosovo. She had told her five-year-old son that Daddy had to go away to work for a long time, rather than to confuse him with explanations of the location. However, this little boy had overheard his mother talking about her husband in Kosovo and made the logical assumption that the barracks in Aldershot, where his father's regiment was based and where he had seen his father go to work before, was Kosovo itself. He passed it every day on his way to school but could not work out why Daddy could not come home to see him when he was working so close by. It was well into the tour when her son asked why Daddy couldn't just pop home to read him a bedtime story before going back to Kosovo, before his mother realised the misunderstanding, and she naturally felt terrible that he had been so confused.

Stacey Merritt-Webb's husband Darren left for Afghanistan when their daughter Milly was six weeks old and their son George six years old. She wrote in her journal while he was away:

> 'Milly is smiling and cooing; it's so lovely to watch, I've recorded it for Darren but it's so not the same . . .
>
> My heart is breaking, Milly is growing so fast and Darren is missing it all, what is the point of all of this?
>
> George is definitely missing Daddy, he is missing someone to play football with or just play fight with, I hope deep down he is coping OK with all of this.
>
> George lost his first tooth today. Daddy should be here to see it, but he is not and me and George are sad, how am I supposed to make George feel better when I feel dead inside?
>
> George's sports day today, really good to watch. He said to me this morning that there will be other people's Daddies there – what can I say to that?
>
> . . . for some reason unknown George just burst into tears, I asked him what was wrong and all he could say was that he was missing Daddy so much, I felt awful as I couldn't say much to make him better – I can't bring Daddy home – we both had a cry.

Darren hasn't been able to write or speak to George for a while now – it obviously affects him worse than we thought.'

Older children may have an understanding of the realities. They cannot fail to see the news bulletins on television and the internet, or listen to radio broadcasts. Knowing that their father is away fighting can lead to worry and tension and often this is an age when children, particularly sons, really need a father figure around.

Richard was deployed to Bosnia for six months during our posting to St Athan. Oliver and Annabel were eight and five years old, and someone casually said to Oliver just after he left, 'Now that Daddy is away you must be the man of the house and look after Mummy and your sister.' For a child who takes the weight of the world on his shoulders anyway this was the worst thing they could have said; he felt the responsibility far too much for one so young and it took a very long time for me to convince him that it was not his job to look after me. During this posting I knew how much they were both missing Richard, although they were too young to express it themselves. I turned to my writing and wrote a few lines, seen through the eyes of an Army child. It was clearly written with my own children in mind, about being alone when Richard was away:

Posted On:

I've done the Romans three times, four styles of maths and badges at swimming galore; had six different schools and memorised names of more people than I can recall. I have good social skills, but not a best friend. I have a broad mind, I'm not shy. My Geography's great and I even speak Welsh but my family's never nearby.

Whenever I've just settled down in one place, when I feel I belong and hang out with new mates, my Dad's posted on

and we up sticks and leave and I'm the freaky new stranger
again. Then there are times when Dad goes 'on tour' – six
months is a lifetime to me. I wish he were here to see all the
matches, come swimming and surf in the sea.

New places, new friends: a challenge, a change. On a limb,
sticking out, all alone, feeling strange at home with my sister,
my Mum and our dog and waiting for Dad to return. But
while he's a soldier it'll always be so, though sometimes you'd
have to agree – that to be normal and stay in one place would
be great, whatever normal may be.

That posting was truly one of the most agonising times for me.
And of course you start to question all your choices. Leading
the 'nomadic' lifestyle can be exciting and rewarding; it can
also be exhausting and inconvenient, and when the men are
on deployment, downright heartbreaking.

But ultimately I return to the experience of my own nomadic
upbringing, when we moved constantly for my father's police
career. I had a wonderful childhood and grew up in numerous
houses that were always full of the love and respect our family
had for each other. In the end that is all I can try to provide for
my own children, as parents do all over the world.

5

Twenty-First Century Army Wife

Although, as a nation, we pride ourselves on the military traditions we have managed to maintain for centuries, the Armed Forces are constantly adapting to the modern world. Not only out on the front line but also at home, the Army increasingly has to take account of the changes that have overtaken women's lives in the last hundred years. These days women are serving on the front line and it is often their husbands and boyfriends who are waiting at home for them. Army wives, who previously might have given up their own jobs when they married or had children, are now keeping their careers going while raising their families, often single-handedly while their partners are away, and all while moving around every two years on postings.

The independence and resilience that come from these constant moves can be fantastically useful skills for modern Army wives to acquire, but, nonetheless, the nomadic life can also be very draining. I have friends who have moved when pregnant, while their husbands were on exercise, so that they could give their older children the chance to start a new school at the beginning of term. Army wives have always had to be capable of turning their hand to whatever domestic tasks need doing, running the family finances and providing both a father's and a mother's parenting to their children when husbands are away. Wives become quite adept at heaving furniture, moving boxes to and from attics, painting the children's bedrooms in bright colours (and then back again to magnolia before moving out again) and putting up shelves. Not to mention the really tricky stuff, like trying to provide boundaries for teenagers when their father is off in a war zone. Of course, family members can be very useful at times like these too, if they are within travelling distance. Once I mentioned to my father that I thought I might benefit from a car maintenance course but he appeared to be quite offended, replying, 'You don't need to do one, that's what fathers are for when husbands are away.' Brothers can also be invaluable; my own brother Simon has stepped in when Richard has been away to mow the lawn for me on occasions (before it became Oliver's prerogative).

On one occasion, my self-sufficiency was stretched to breaking point. By the time Richard went to Iraq in October 2008, just under five weeks after we moved into our quarter in Farnborough, our phone line had still not been installed, nor did we have a mobile signal or a computer connection, though not through lack of trying. Contact with the outside world was becoming increasingly vital to me; I wanted to be able to speak to the children at school the evening Richard left, and was already worrying about not being able to receive a call from him to say he had arrived safely.

Thankfully, by some miracle the day Richard left, workmen arrived to dig up the road outside our quarter in order to repair the faulty line and I went outside with immense relief to offer them cups of tea. One of them started to chat, unaware of how fragile I was feeling. 'Oh, it's terrible how many of the local lads are away fighting at the moment,' he commented innocently. I was suddenly lost for words as the reality of my situation hit home, and did not trust myself to reply without bursting into tears. He looked up and realised that he may have an emotional woman on his hands, not something he had banked on at half past four on a cold, wet

Friday evening. His sympathetic expression had the guaranteed effect of making me lose the thin thread of composure I had been hanging on to, and I could hardly speak: 'Yes, my husband left this morning too – I won't see him until next summer' was all that I could get out, at which point the workman made me the cup of tea, and also wired the modem for our new connection. My in-laws arrived from Suffolk in time to find this kind man lying under the desk so he could get to the back of the computer tower.

Moving around from one set of Army accommodation to the next is one of the defining experiences of being part of the Army family. In some ways it helps to have a few good old-fashioned homemaking skills of the sort that can turn a quarter into a home. Quarters come in all states of repair. Some are notoriously under par, have been 'condemned' by the Army and therefore do not qualify for anything other than vital repair work, despite the fact that families are still placed in them. The compensation for living in a condemned quarter is a reduced rent; you can guarantee that if your quarter has had an upgrade with a new kitchen, a leak-free garage or a 'modern' fireplace your rent will go up accordingly.

There are few things more guaranteed to make me feel as if I am living in the 1950s than the dreaded 'march out' inspections. After they have cleaned their quarter to within an inch of its life, families wait on tenterhooks while every corner is examined for specks of dust, the carpets for dirty marks, the oven for any trace of splattered fat and the garden for any weeds. However, this is done for a good reason; nobody wants to move in to a quarter left dirty and damaged by the previous occupants. Just occasionally, though, quarters are not up to standard on the 'march in' inspection when taking over a quarter. I have a friend who arrived at a quarter with a small baby to find the place infested with fleas, which had 'marched in' of their own accord:

> *'It was terrible. I put the baby down on the carpet when we were "marching in" and when I picked him up he was covered in fleas, and then they all jumped onto me. Luckily there was another quarter available so we had to "de-flea" ourselves in a friend's house and take over the other quarter instead.'*

The AFF (Army Families Federation) is an independent organisation which aims to improve the quality of life for British Army families worldwide and represents families on any aspect that is affected by their lifestyle. Issues surrounding Army housing are the highest of all.

When we were first married there used to be an Estate Warden, now called a Housing Officer, who was allocated to a particular area and would be a point of contact if any repairs or maintenance needed doing. The Estate Warden was a known face on Army patches who was a personal point of contact and requests for repair were dealt with efficiently and effectively. Nowadays, the Housing Officers are often only seen on 'march in' and 'march out' and do not have the same power as their predecessors. Any complaints regarding housing repair or maintenance must now be reported through Defence Estates and its chain of command.

In my own experience, this has caused a significant break-down in communication. Rarely do we see the same work-men twice, if indeed they arrive, and there are so many people involved that few seem to want to take personal responsibility for a job. At the time of writing, a year after a window fell out of its casing when I opened it in our quarter we are still waiting for it to be repaired.

It definitely does get easier to cope with over time and with experience. In fourteen years Richard and I moved house eleven times. After Oman came Shrivenham, then Camberley,

Aldershot, Upavon, St Athan, Salisbury (twice), Farnborough and Salisbury again. Nowadays I get itchy feet after two years in one place, which is the longest we have spent in a quarter. At least moving so often saves me from having to spring clean and we have the chance to get rid of accumulated junk on a frequent basis.

When we lived in Camberley while Richard was at Staff College there were three different types of quarters on the patch, all with different nicknames: the 'railway carriages', long lines of terraced houses; the 'cheese wedges' as they were shaped in a rough triangle; and the 'squash courts' as their roofs sloped down almost to the ground on one side. We were convinced that student architects must have been allowed a free rein to design their own project houses, to be dismantled at the end of their course. In fact, these houses, although now sold off by the Army, are still standing.

We lived in one of the 'cheese wedges' and when we shut our front door the whole house would shake. This was where we were living when our second child, Annabel, was born. It was also where we had a gas leak when, surprise surprise, Richard was away on a course in America for two weeks and Annabel was only a few weeks old.

Oliver was playing in the garden and Annabel was asleep upstairs when I suddenly realised there was a very strong smell of gas. I rushed to the oven, only to find that everything was safely off, then tried to remember where the gas lever was. Oh yes, in the outside shed. Pulling on the lever, though, was difficult and stiff; it just would not budge.

I could feel the panic starting to rise. Do I shout for help to turn it off, do I wake Annabel and get the children out of the house? If I was to apply the same principles as the resuscitation training that had been drilled into me from years of nursing, I knew I should 'make the area safe', but all I wanted to do was to rush upstairs and pick the baby up. After all, was she asleep because she was tired, or because the gas had affected her already?

In the event, the dustbin lorry happened to arrive just at that moment. I called for the men to help me with the lever, which they did (making it look relatively easy) and I ran upstairs, calling out to Oliver to stay in the garden. By now there was a gathering of neighbours, all offering to help; they had followed the smell down the street. We took the children to a friend and called the emergency line. Meanwhile, the dustmen were doing their best to find the source of the smell themselves.

Luckily the gas board and the Army Housing Officer arrived very quickly and the dustmen, duly thanked, went on with their round. However, despite taking all day to attempt to locate the source of the leak, which included ripping up our bathroom floor to inspect the pipes and digging up the road to see whether the problem was underground, they never did find the cause and decided that the area was safe. The smell did die down but I was left on a Friday afternoon with neither a bathroom floor nor a guarantee that it would not happen a second time; cold comfort when I went to bed that night worrying whether we would actually wake up again.

I have grown used to dealing with minor domestic emergencies and it takes a lot to shock me now. For some wives, though, the threat of danger has been real and close enough to require them to be vigilant at all times. The British Army only has a limited presence in Northern Ireland now, but during the height of the Troubles there from the 70s through to the early 90s, living 'behind the wire' close to a combat zone was an extraordinary experience that required Army wives to learn to live with the same stresses of exposure to hostilities as their men. It was a safe environment for families within the confines of the camp, but the wire was there for a reason. Karen Mott's first impressions of Northern Ireland were very memorable:

'My first memory of Northern Ireland was the way I arrived with our children, Nathan who was three at the time, and Charlotte, six months old. We flew on a Hercules with the Army while Nicky drove there, the car full to the roof with the remainder of our personal belongings. When the aircraft landed in Northern Ireland everything was a rush and soldiers were getting off using both exits. I was pulled to an exit by one of the lads and Nathan was taken off a different exit. I didn't know where we were, where Nathan had gone and what to expect when I got off the plane but it soon became clear that this was normal procedure when getting off a military aircraft. One of the lads had seen my hands were full with Charlotte and had naturally got hold of Nathan for me.

It was quite strange to come out of my front door to see the perimeter fence less than one hundred metres to the right. This would be my new life for the next two years. We had friends and family visit us during our time in Northern Ireland and as they arrived at the terminal you could see the anxiety and fear in their faces; no different to mine as I got of the Hercules a couple of months earlier.'

It was not surprising that visitors were nervous; the route from the airport passed a number of known notorious blackspots for IRA activity. Karen tells of an occasion when she was on her way to the airport to fly home for a holiday when the vehicle she was in was caught in traffic due to a local Orange Order parade. The Protestant Orange Order's marches commemorate William of Orange's 1690 Battle of the Boyne victory over Catholic King James II and still are a source of tension between Catholics and Protestants even today. Sometimes the atmosphere surrounding these parades can be intimidating:

'People were coming round to the car windows with buckets rais-ing money for local charities. We just had to pretend that it was all fine and not let on we had English accents.'

However, life for Karen in Northern Ireland soon fell into a routine. Sue Miles also told me that at first they were all very nervous having been given lectures on security. She was issued with a mirror attached to the end of a rod and taught to use it to look for bombs under her car before driving, was told not to drive into Londonderry and if she saw kerbstones with green, orange and white stripes (the colours of the Irish flag) painted on she should go the other way until she saw ones with red, white and blue stripes. After six months or so taking these measures became part of everyday life and the wives learned to shop in safe places such as Coleraine or Limavaddy, rather than in Londonderry.

There was one incident that shook the families on the camp, and was the closest they had come to experiencing violence at first hand. It occurred on Halloween night in 1993. Sue told me about

'an attack in the next village from Ballykelly towards Londonderry called Greysteel. Several people were killed and wounded when terrorists broke into a restaurant, shouting "trick or treat" before they open fired on the clientele. It made us all very nervous for a while as you can imagine.'

In fact, shortly after this, one of the children had a birthday party on camp, during which some of the children innocently decided to burst a few balloons. The wives immediately dived for cover before realising what had happened, assuming that there were gunshots being fired, such was the state of their nerves. Despite this, the Welsh Guards' families considered themselves very lucky. A few years before the Battalion was posted to Ballykelly the IRA had blown up a club next to the camp, the Dropping Well, murdering a number of soldiers and their families.

However, many of the wives posted to Northern Ireland were struck by the good nature of the majority of its people. Apply the Northern Ireland scenario to today's situation in the Middle East surrounding the terrorist threat and it is all too easy to tar the Arab world as a whole with the same radical brush. Perhaps we should be reminded more often that the vast majority of Arabs, and indeed most people the world over, are only concerned with living a law-abiding, decent life and looking after the wellbeing of their families and friends.

Thankfully, most of the time the majority of Army wives do not have to contend with the additional stress of living in a combat zone. But for some women, the Army is their job, not their husband's, and for them and their partners the reversal of traditional roles can have its own intense pressures. The Welsh Guards, being an Infantry Regiment, does not have female personnel as Welsh Guardsmen, but there are a number of jobs that women do. Although officially no women are permitted on the front line, these rules have become increasingly blurred and there have been a number of occasions where women have been in the thick of fighting. Their partners may already be serving, or they may be newcomers to the military life. When both partners are serving, not only do they both experience life on exercise or in direct combat, they also appreciate what each other goes through when left at home. Two such wives are Sarah Hazard and Ina Pollard, both serving in the Army and both with husbands in the Armed Forces. Sarah explained to me her experiences of both serving and of being the one at home:

'I served with the Welsh Guards as their doctor for two and a half fabulous years (including a six month deployment to Bosnia)

and was welcomed into the fold with open arms. A true family regiment, any "outsiders" were offered the opportunity to throw themselves in whole-heartedly and in return were counted as part of the family – a rare gift in most postings.

I am very fortunate as my husband, Lee, is a Naval Officer so he understands the trials and tribulations that forces life may bring. We opted to deploy together rather than go on two separate deployments. For the first three months of my deployment to Bosnia, Lee was assigned on the battlestaff of Commodore Amphibious Task Group who were to deploy to West Africa. Simultaneous deployment had seemed like a great idea at the time, but it was just impossible to communicate from Bosnia to a ship in Sierra Leone! Unfortunately the welfare minutes [the weekly allocated free minutes to phone home] didn't quite cover this one and even if they had, the ship was usually out of range for communications. We were able to email each other on occasion but didn't speak in person for nearly three months, the length of Lee's tour. He was at home to meet me for my R and R and I then returned to Bosnia for another three months while Lee was at home.

When apart, the times you do manage to speak are invaluable and you savour every moment. When you don't know how long it will be until you will next be able to speak to your loved one, there is no time for pettiness or minor squabbles. Telephones do have disadvantages though, as words and lack of them can easily be misinterpreted so one has to be careful if chatting when tired for example. I can think of numerous occasions when people stormed back from the phone angry with spouses for chatting about the wrong thing or asking the wrong questions.

We both write to each other every day when away and the magic of e-blueys [an email that is printed off at the receiving end to resemble an 'airmail' letter, as servicemen and -women do not always have access to email facilities] is a step forward, but a lovely handwritten letter beats all the type in the world.

Lee deployed to Afghanistan when I was twenty weeks pregnant and I became amazingly capable of doing all sorts around the house, such as fixing leaking pipe work to a broken boiler (and that was just his first week away). In this case I didn't just call a plumber; I watched what he did so I could fix emergency stuff next time around. Then, when Lee returned I fell back into the role of the housewife who calls on her husband whenever something goes wrong – quite bizarre.

Being away from home, family and friends is never easy so you have to find a way to cope. Deployments are usually very busy so it's easy to get engrossed in work but when I was in Bosnia with the Welsh Guards my outlets were also the gym and making Christmas cards for everyone back home. I have always enjoyed putting together boxes of goodies for my husband when he is away and I can't stress the importance of receiving them from him when I am the one deployed. One of the best boxes I ever got was a little shoebox of Christmas decorations for my own "space".

Camaraderie on deployments like this is invaluable and friends get you through the hard times. Christmas Day in Bosnia was actually thoroughly enjoyable and it was nearly four o'clock in the afternoon before we had time to even think about ringing home. Very different to what I was expecting as I am a bit of a home girl at times like this.

International relationships were also exploited as the Chilean officers ran a salsa night and the Dutch a language class. I don't quite remember what us Brits had to offer but I also decided to fill my time by teaching GCSE English and A level Biology which was great fun and kept the grey cells working.

On a more serious note, being one of very few women serving with a predominantly male infantry Battalion was difficult. The gossip was relentless; it was difficult to talk to a male colleague without innuendos being made. It was actually quite wearing and started to drag me down. I tended to retreat to the other women and stick together. I certainly felt I put on a hard external shell to combat this and unfortunately brought that home with me. I didn't realise at the time but I came back home quite cold and exceptionally independent. It took a while for me to realise this is what had happened and I am so very lucky to have a kind and patient husband who was experienced enough to spot what was going on even before I did.'

Ina Pollard is also a servicewoman and her husband Mark is a Welsh Guardsman. They deployed on separate tours of Afghanistan shortly after they were married. This was their first taste of married life and although they had both been in the Army for years, instant separation was a whole new experience. Ina met Mark, a Colour Sergeant at the time, when she joined the Battalion in London in 2006. She was the Master Chef for the Battalion and at this point she had already served eighteen years in the Army. Taking into account the time Mark spent training prior to his deployment to Afghanistan they did not really spend any time together for a total of twenty-one months:

'We got married in the Guards Chapel in July 2008. The very next day Mark went on a course for three weeks, then came back and went to Germany for seven weeks to start his Afghan training. Following that I was away on a staff training exercise and we didn't get together until Christmas, after which Mark went straight back into pre-tour training. He had two weeks pre-tour leave but I was on a Brigade Skills competition at the time so we only saw each other in the evenings.

This first eight months of our married life was quite emotional as we hadn't shared the marriage as a "normal" couple. By the time Mark left for Afghanistan it felt like we had already done six months apart. I moved into our first quarter in Aldershot on my own trying to juggle my own job and also going on exercise in preparation for my tour. I was lucky to have found a truly great friend just across the street from me. I didn't know Catrina [Campbell] personally before but I had worked with her husband, Andy, in the Battalion. He was also away in Afghanistan and her daughter Lauren was away at boarding school. If it wasn't for Catrina I wouldn't have been able to get on with my training for Afghan and move in to the house on my own; she made it so much more bearable and we became inseparable.

Catrina cooked for me, listened to me moan and groan, listened to me about my work, loaned me her son for company and let me take her dog Dylan for walks and runs. She let me into her life without a second thought. Catrina kept me motivated with my fitness for Afghan and we would run every day together. She kept me sane when Mark being away got a bit too much to bear.

It wasn't long before Tobie Fasfous was reported as the first Welsh Guardsman killed in action. I knew him, which made it even harder. The Battalion hadn't been out there very long and already they had lost one of their guys.

Time went slowly at first but once I got in to a routine and my work got in to full swing for getting the Brigade Units prepared for deployment it went reasonably steadily. Then the time came for me to go to Afghan for a recce for a week but it's a week I will never forget. Colonel Thorneloe had just been killed and morale was very low within the Welsh Guards.

I flew to Kandahar to meet the person I would be taking over from. I landed the day before Mark's birthday. I then flew down to Bastion to meet the chefs and to see the camp. What I didn't realise was that Mark was in Bastion at the same time as me as he had returned to camp with the RSM for Colonel Thorneloe's repatriation service when I thought he was outside the wire in a FOB [Forward Operating Base].

The next morning, after spending the night in Bastion, I went round to visit the few Welsh Guards who were based in Bastion;

the rest were out on patrols. It was so great to see my old mates but it quickly turned to my tears as Sergeant Dean Williams pulled me to one side to tell me that another Welsh Guardsman, Dane Elson, had been killed who I knew quite well. As I went back to the main kitchen I walked round the corner and actually physically bumped into Mark. I couldn't believe he was in the same place as me. We had twenty minutes together before he had to fly back out to the FOB but we took lots of photos together as a reminder.

I spent a week in Afghan on the recce and I could not believe I actually got to see Mark. I relived our meeting over and over. But my accommodation in Bastion was a stone's throw away from the helicopter landing sight. I lay there each night listening to the ambulances running back and forth throughout the night and the helicopters landing. It sounds silly but I dreaded hearing them land not knowing if it was Mark or someone else I knew on the helicopter. It's the worst feeling I have ever had not having control of what was going on and the worry that if something had happened would I get to know about it. I didn't sleep whilst at Bastion.

I am not sure if I could do a tour in the same place as Mark. Whilst I was deployed to Afghan one of my female chefs working out there was engaged to a Coldstream Guardsman who was also in Afghanistan at the same time. She couldn't cope with the helicopters landing right next to the cookhouse either. I knew how she felt and what she was going through so I got her moved to a FOB out of the way, which was also nowhere near her partner's location.

I went home to Aldershot after the recce and the first thing I did was walk over to Catrina's. I got a great big hug and burst into tears.

Mark came back in the October and we had two weeks together before I had to deploy. It was very strained to say the least. I had got into a routine and Mark was still in Afghan in his mind. I was

raring to go and get my tour over and done with then maybe we
could start our married life together.'

Knowing Catrina as a friend myself, from our first meeting at
Pirbright stables in 2000 and later in St Athan when her son
Oliver and our daughter Annabel were in the same class, it did
not surprise me to hear how supportive she had been to Ina
during this time. She, however, plays this compliment down
and insists that it was Ina who supported her during the time
when her husband Andy was away:

> 'Ina's friendship to me has been so effortless; from day one we just
> seemed to "click". We kept up each other's morale whilst the boys
> were away and Ina became part of our family.
>
> It was great to have adult company and to have someone in the
> same situation going through the same feelings. Life was pretty
> hectic while the boys were away; I was juggling working full-time,
> my ten-year-old son, and my daughter preparing for her GCSEs,
> plus a dog to look after.
>
> Ina often collected Ollie from school and walked Dylan when
> I was working late. It was lovely to see the special relationship
> between the two of them, and listen to their banter. Ollie would
> often go around to see her and her cats and I would end up going
> around after an hour or so to see if he was ever coming home.
>
> Quite often I would get back and Ina would have made tea for
> everyone and mine would be plated up ready for me to reheat. One
> weekend both my children had commitments and I couldn't be in
> two places at the same time. Without being asked Ina offered to
> take Ollie to his rugby festival and she played Mum for the day. I
> am so grateful to her for all her support.'

In fact, it is clear that they supported each other. The camaraderie and understanding between Ina and Catrina has laid
the foundations for another longstanding, if not lifelong,

friendship. Even if they are not living on the same patch for the next operational tour, their bond will not be broken.

Ina and Sarah's experiences of having their own careers in the Armed Forces is increasingly common but it is not the norm. Most Army wives have lives much more similar to Catrina's, in which work is one aspect of a busy nomadic lifestyle that includes children and other family commitments. In many ways, when I talk to my friends, like Catrina, who have young children too, our conversations are probably pretty much the same as those of any other working mothers who are trying to juggle far too many commitments. All women's relationships have to be adaptable and accommodating of change, and the military wife is no different in this respect. The additional stresses arise from the inescapable anxiety of dealing with our partners being on deployment and its effect not just on home life, but also on our ability to maintain our careers, while moving all the time.

Of course, this nomadic lifestyle would have been fairly straightforward in the days when most women stopped working as soon as they got married. Certainly, a working wife was not considered compatible with an Army lifestyle, and in the days when postings were to exotic locations, the job opportunities would have been fairly limited in any case. Nowadays more Army wives have had a career prior to getting married or up until having children, and some manage to continue working full-time when the children are small, though this is the exception.

For all women, although the threads of a career can be picked up when the children are older, some professions are not easily interrupted and many women find themselves at a disadvantage when they return, especially if it is part-time. This general difficulty, coupled with a peripatetic lifestyle, does not bode well for Army wives. Few employers would risk employing an Army wife who may not be able to hold the job for more than two years, and would not be prepared to invest in her if she was likely to leave at short notice. If retraining is required these wives are often not in the area long enough to edge their way up a waiting list either.

No doubt another reason would be given to the prospective wife for not being shortlisted, or not getting through interview, but many Army wives strongly believe that they experience discrimination and are denied jobs, and therefore a career path, because employers overlook their skills or qualifications in favour of someone who appears to be more 'settled'. Despite the unknown risks associated with everyday life common to Army and civilian families alike, such as pregnancy, sickness or a house move, the Army wife is often at a disadvantage.

Consequently, many women, even when highly qualified, find that they must completely change tack in order to accommodate frequent changes of location, and take up different, more flexible vocations such as teaching and teaching assistant roles or telesales jobs working from home. Other jobs, such as freelance beauty therapy, are flexible but it takes time to build up a client base, by which point it is often necessary to move again. Whatever the nature of their work though, Army wives are keen to hold on to an identity of their own, something that shapes their personality, even if they do have to leave the career behind. In this way they can avoid becoming known as 'wife of' their husband's rank, which tends to pigeonhole them and take away their individuality.

Annabel Lewis talked to me about her decision to give up her career when she had her children and her new plans to resume it:

> *I made the decision in the very beginning to give up my work as an IT consultant to relieve the pressure on our family life. As my*

job took me to many locations, in the UK and abroad, we felt that it would not be a healthy family life trying to balance the two careers. It was a hard decision as it removed all my independence, something I had spent the last years of education and early years of my career striving to achieve. Having had the two children, I am now preparing to start a new career as a maths tutor as I am hoping this is something that I can move around with my husband's job.

I find that many more women than I had expected have managed to keep their jobs and succeed at a happy family home and a career. However this reduces their exposure to the companionship and support network of the Army wife community. For those who do decide to stay at home as a full-time mother, the opportunities to get to know other wives and mothers are reduced if they are away working.'

Sue Miles found a job that suited her change in lifestyle:

'Finding work for myself was interesting. Being a "military wife" means you have to be able to turn your hands to almost anything, depending on where you are living and the availability of work. I have a penchant for sewing so when we were posted to Pirbright in Surrey I started work in the Guards Depot tailors' shop as the hours fitted very well around the children, nursery and school.

After a while I found a job working in the village of Pirbright doing admin which was what I originally trained for in the Civil Service. We got posted to RMA Sandhurst and I retained my job in Pirbright to try and get some continuity for the children at preschool and primary school.

. . . Jobs were difficult to find in Northern Ireland, I started off working in the tailor's shop there too, but then got in touch with a training centre in Coleraine which managed to get me employed at the local primary school (which both our children attended) as a general assistant which lasted for the remainder of our stay in Ballykelly.'

Others, such as Michelle Bowen, have managed to use their skills on every posting. She works as a legal secretary and is fortunate that these roles are always in demand wherever the location. As Michelle and Alun have lived in ten quarters in twenty years, she has been lucky:

'I have always wanted to work ... if only to fund my extravagant shopping habit! Living and working within a commutable distance to Central London has been an advantage for the last eleven or so years since starting a family. A lot of the law firms in London have twenty-four-hour secretarial cover and it is therefore possible to work unusual hours to fit around childcare needs. I have worked evenings since having Tegan and Harvey and this effectively means that I have care of the children during the day and Alun has taken over childcare while I am at work. On occasions when Alun is away for a week or two, or when a six-month tour takes place, we have been very fortunate because family (grandparents, nieces, god-daughters) have all helped out and come to stay for varying periods of time to enable me to continue working.'

I am lucky to have a qualification that does travel well. I trained as a nurse before I married although my registration lapsed when I took a break to be at home for the children until Annabel started school. A run of good fortune followed when I was given a place on a 'Return to Practice' course at Salisbury District Hospital in 2005. I knew I would not be able to work shifts while Richard commuted every week to London for two years, during which time he was also on a six-month tour to Bosnia and was away on countless exercises. The children were at the local primary school so I was limited to a job that fitted in with school hours. I began to wonder whether I had made the right choice in going back to nursing when school-hour posts were such a rarity.

Then the next bit of luck; a part-time position became available shortly after I requalified, working school hours as a Staff Nurse on the Respiratory Team. This also led me into a newly appointed post as the hospital's Stop Smoking Advisor, which suited me so well that I was prepared to do the extra commute when we moved to Farnborough. Since going back to nursing I have kept the same job through four house moves; two in Salisbury, out to Farnborough and back to Salisbury again.

Nursing is a great leveller, and I have realised this even more by going back into it having had a taste of life's experiences thrown at me in the meantime. Nursing my own mother before her death, other deaths of family members and friends, being married and having children of my own; all these things enabled me to empathise much more with the lives of my patients when I returned to the job. Nursing makes me appreciate that no matter what our situation, culture or creed, our health and support from our families and friends are what matter the most.

Not only that, but nursing keeps my feet well and truly on the ground; I could be kitted out in best 'bib and tucker' to attend a very formal Army function in the presence of Royalty one day, and then back on the wards seeing patients at their most vulnerable and needy the next. I seem to lead a yo-yo existence between the glitzy 'front cover' of the pomp and ceremony of Army life and its antithesis: the difficulties of separations, anxiety and constant disruption that lie beneath. At times these difficulties do eclipse the grandeur, but then I only need to look around me when I am nursing to realise that there are others out there with far more on their plates and in need of considerably more sympathy than me, which always puts me back in my place. Then I appreciate the many benefits of my lifestyle as well: the friendships, the places and quality family time, which fills my glass to half full again. I feel incredibly grateful that as a twenty-first century Army wife, I can live my own life as well as nurture my relationship with my husband, raise my family and fit in with the needs of the institution that I in some ways swore allegiance to when I married Richard.

6

The Homecoming

The Welsh Guards' homecomings after the gruelling deployment of summer 2009 were even more emotional than usual because of the exceptional stress caused by high casualties and national publicity. I spent a lot of time that summer talking to wives and families, offering my support where I could and trying to be particularly helpful to close friends like Sally. I was at the coffee morning in Aldershot the day the first group of men were expected back to camp. The atmosphere that day was electric. Their wives received texts during the morning saying:

> 'Your Soldier is due to return to ALDERSHOT today at approx 3:00pm. You are welcome at Lille Barracks for their return not before 2pm.'

Each text was read out by the recipient and prompted a cheer followed by tears of relief and hugs from the other wives.

Every homecoming is a huge event though. Whether it is at the end of deployment, or from an exercise, or for R and R, the 'count up' to arrival is a time of excitement, anxiety and high expectations and it can seem to go on forever.

> 22/09/09 'Oh my God, he is coming home soon, can't bloody wait, can't describe the feeling in my belly, just so exciting'...
> 25/09/09 he has called, he is at Bastion waiting for a flight – he is coming home. I'm really nervous about it actually; it's been a while. Will we have to get to know each other all over again?

27/09/09 Tomorrow is the day, we're picking him up from Brize [Norton] *and I can't bloody wait, the feeling in my tummy is so weird, it feels like first date's nerves ... spent the week cleaning the house, getting "things" waxed, cleaning the car etc and there is still so much to do – have to sort out the kids outfits for when we go to pick him up. Oh my God, I haven't done the garden!!!'*

These were Stacey Merritt-Webb's thoughts from her journal while her husband Darren was about to come home for R and R. For the wives, the countdown can seem to last forever, and expectations of the perfect get-together can be high. Luckily for Stacey the leave was perfect:

'What a fantastic R&R, wow, we chilled, we drank, we talked, we had days out – awesome, best 12 days of my life. George loved having Daddy home, he went back to being a 6yr old again. I didn't realise how grown up he had become ... actually quite shocking and sad. Darren seemed fine in body and mind, he seemed a lot more laid back and chilled, we talked about our life and aspirations ...'

Although homecomings are obviously joyous occasions in most ways, they are not without their own particular challenges. It is hard for a wife to take a step back again, so that her husband feels involved, when she has been holding the fort on her own for so long. Richard always says after a tour away that he will come home one day to find that he is not needed. There is little chance of this, however. Car breakdowns, sick children and pets, computer failure, gas leaks and overgrown gardens are an inevitable occurrence, destined to coincide with a separation to make me appreciate how much he is needed. I can cope with these alone to a point, but when they happen I curse the Army for taking him away, feel sorry for myself in a moment of self-indulgence, gather my strength and then deal with the problem.

On an emotional level there is the constant pressure of coping alone, of not being able to halve a problem by sharing it, of not having his shoulder to cry on, or of being able to enjoy the little everyday stories which, after a tour of duty, are forgotten. I often think of single mothers at times like these but at least Army wives know that their husbands are around in spirit, if not always in person. However, once he is home there is normally no problem in reminding him that he is needed to fill both the practical role and the emotional void, although I have learned over the years of homecomings that it is not always a good idea to do so as soon as he walks through the door. I think every Army couple develops its own personal rituals for dealing with being reunited and we are no exception, although luckily we have been very fortunate in not having to deal with issues such as injury and post-traumatic stress disorder. This can make already fraught occasions, with their emotional expectations and sense of wanting to make up for lost time, even more stressful.

Catrina's husband, Andy, also talked about the concerns over whether he would be needed each time he returns from long exercises or operations:

'Going away is something that you get used to, although that doesn't make it any easier to deal with. What I find difficult is the return home. There is an air of expectation and also anxiety over whether things may have changed whilst you've been away; do the family still need you and so on. It's also difficult to fit back in to your normal role, as things can't stop while you're away and things get done differently. There's also the feeling of everybody walking on eggshells around you – everybody wants to know

what you did and what you went through, but don't really want to ask. I got around this by sitting the family down and telling them that they have twenty-four hours to ask ANY questions, and then I didn't really want to go through it all. To be honest, this was okay, but you still have the questions from extended family and friends to deal with at a later date.'

Emotions can often be in turmoil for both partners. Relief that the husband is safe and the desire to make their leave the perfect reunion is often overshadowed by the reality of a rapid readjustment period for both. Sometimes families have been deliberately keeping painful information from their loved ones while they were away. This is usually with only the best intentions, but nonetheless it can cause problems when the men come home and the reality of a situation emerges. When our friends Sue and Martyn Miles came to stay for a weekend to talk about their experiences they told us about a car accident that their daughter Michelle had while Martyn was in Afghanistan. Michelle had asked Sue not to tell her father or her grandparents as she did not want Martyn to worry and Sue decided to respect her decision. It had taken the fire brigade three hours to cut her out from behind the wheel and although she sustained no more than cuts and extensive bruising, she was very shocked by the incident.

Martyn was very angry when he found out about the accident, two days after his return. He felt that his duty as a father had been denied him, but Sue had only kept it from him as there was nothing he could have done, and it was – thankfully – not serious enough for him to come home on compassionate grounds.

In fact, Martyn was still obviously affected by it when telling the story. He said:

'I felt that I wasn't part of the family at that moment. I was detached and wasn't getting involved in decisions within the world I had made for my family.'

No doubt Martyn and Sue will always have to agree to disagree on this one.

The men frequently find it hard to come from a combat situation into the familiar surroundings of their own home, and when on R and R can sometimes feel guilty that they are leaving their comrades out in the field.

At the end of Afghanistan tours servicemen and -women spend a period of one to two days in Cyprus, not intended as a holiday but as a period of readjustment, reflection and winding down before going home. However, when they come home on R and R leave during a tour, there is no time for this readjustment period, so they are often catapulted straight back into a home life which is completely removed from the situations they have recently been in. They could have been in combat with the enemy, dealing with casualties or death in searing desert temperatures one day, and be sitting on their sofa watching a football game with snow falling outside their married quarter forty-eight hours later. This, plus the sudden return to everyday family responsibilities and childcare when the wife takes her opportunity to 'hand over' parental duties for a while, can be quite a shock. Not knowing how to deal with this on both sides may put a damper on a reunion.

While home on R and R, there is always that niggle at the back of the mind that time is precious and soon they will have to do the goodbyes all over again. This can be particularly difficult for children, who can find it hard to readjust. In Stacey and Darren's case, their son George found the second goodbye very difficult:

'12/10/09 Daddy going has definitely hit George worse this time around, I suppose he has done 4 ½ months without seeing

his Daddy, had him for 12 days then he went again. Obviously George doesn't want to revert back to how it was – who would? When Darren went, he went into George's room and said goodbye to him, Darren thought he'd rolled over and gone back to sleep. Me and Darren said our emotional goodbyes. George was stood on the landing sobbing his heart out; he had seen our goodbye. He was so sad, he got into our bed and cried for 35 minutes solid, kids shouldn't cry like that – it's absolutely heartbreaking!

16/10/09 It's been a week now since Darren left, I'm OK, I think George is also, as he knows Daddy is home within the next month. I'm feeling positive; we started to make a welcome home banner at the coffee morning on Tuesday which cheered everybody up. We have permission to hang it outside the gates of Lille Barracks so the boys will see it when they arrive back to camp. All the wives were in such good moods – we could finally see the light at the end of the tunnel.'

The Battalion returned from Afghanistan on several staggered dates. The excitement was beginning to increase among the wives, but many of them would not allow themselves to relax until they were sure the men had arrived in Cyprus. The banner that Stacey described was a large white sheet on which they had painted 'Welcome Home Our Heroes'. It was much photographed and televised at the homecoming of the Battalion.

The 'welcome home' banner greeted the men as they drew in to camp to be reunited with their loved ones. Even though it was dark, the banner was lit by the floodlights on the gates, so was missed by no one. It brought a lump to my throat whenever I drove past it, followed by a surge of pride. As the return dates were staggered, some families were reunited on a crisp October afternoon under a milky autumn sky and others had to wait on a cold, wet night for flights that had been delayed.

Families with young children, who had been allowed to stay up for their fathers' return, were wearing their best clothes and shivering under umbrellas, but did not seem to mind. What was another couple of hours when they had already waited six months? The main thing was that they had landed safely and were on the road home, with no risk of any roadside bombs or ambushes, just the good old British traffic jams and road-works. The atmosphere among the families was a party one.

Stacey described the day both her husband and her friend Laura's husband returned:

> *'On the day they came home, I can't describe the feeling. I took the children to meet Laura and her son Max on camp, and we were all so excited. Even when the coaches kept getting delayed, we walked round to the hangars where we were told to wait and although the weather was shocking, it didn't matter. When the coaches pulled onto camp I remember looking at Laura and saying "we did it".'*

One of the men described the feeling when the coach turned in through the gates:

> *'It was totally overwhelming to see the banner; I never knew how much I had missed home until then, when I could actually let myself believe we were safely back at last and when I knew our families were just around the corner. And I loved the rain; I didn't think I would ever say that, but after months of scorching sun it was fantastic to be in the cold again.'*

Elizabeth Blackledge, waiting for her boyfriend Charlie to return, described the banner herself:

> *'I remember being absolutely ecstatic to see the large welcome home banner outside the fence by the Aldershot guardroom on the televi-sion. This was my first visual indication that some of them were already back, and it finally dawned on me that Charlie really had*

made it back to Bastion and would soon follow the others home. It is truly amazing what a bit of cloth and some paint can do.'

Opposite the gates to the camp is the distinctive Victorian Clocktower House Playgroup where our son Oliver had started at nursery ten years earlier. There was a poignancy in the contrast of occasions the children witnessed from its playground. Not only could they cheer and clap when coach-loads of men pulled into camp on their safe return, welcoming them home with much excitement and waving of flags, but these same children also stood in silence with their teachers as a mark of respect when Rupert Thorneloe's funeral cortège left camp on its way to the service in the Guards Chapel at Wellington Barracks in London.

Seeing the Commanding Officer off the camp after his two-year tour of duty with the Battalion is a ritual for the Welsh Guards. The roads are lined with every man in the Battalion and all the officers have to drag the Commanding Officer out of camp with ropes attached to an open-topped Land Rover while he stands inside the vehicle; yet another quirky tradition. Richard had been escorted off the same barracks nine months earlier when Rupert himself took over as Commanding Officer. Tragically, of course, there was no light-hearted leaving ceremony for Rupert after his short time in command; his vehicle was a hearse passing by the bowed heads of those Guardsmen who were back in camp, wearing black armbands on their combat uniforms.

Each story of the homecoming after a tour is unique and no wife, girlfriend or family member will forget the moment. Elizabeth Blackledge has a close friend, Charlotte, whose boyfriend had been serving with the Fusiliers in Afghanistan at the same time as her boyfriend Charlie. Both girls had become a 'tremendous comfort and support' to each other during this time:

'Charlotte and I would speak every day over emails from our work desks; it was so nice to know that once every day I would receive a line or two that would connect me to Afghanistan and Charlie. For a brief few minutes we would discuss the contents of the next packages we were to send, compare the boys' locations, guess their moods, and continue our countdown of the days before their expected return.'

Elizabeth describes the euphoria she felt when she got the news that Charlotte's boyfriend had arrived home:

'I read her boyfriend Nick was safely back in Bastion on my BlackBerry whilst in a company boardroom and let out rather an embarrassingly high-pitched shriek of excitement. He was to come home within the week. Even though he was not my boyfriend, this was probably the biggest high I experienced whilst they were away. Our job had been to get each other through this first experience of them in combat and I had completed my end of the bargain. I later found out that when Charlotte heard of Charlie reaching Bastion she ran to the ladies loos and did a long victory dance for me. I love the image of her energetically dancing by herself next to the hand dryers. I will be forever grateful for her support and am now aware of how invaluable sharing the experience can be.

Once I knew Charlie was safe the sense of relief was colossal. I started making jokes with his mother about whether it would be possible to make him stay in Bastion for a little longer to work on his sun tan. Another few weeks there would also mean that my flat would remain free from his dirty washing and general untidy habits that were so contrary to those whilst on duty or in the Mess. In fact at his medal's parade, whilst Major Giles Harris was explaining to us that Charlie had really been put in the thick of it and how well he had done, his mother turned to him and said something along the lines of "That's good, but is there any way you could tell me how to get him to tidy his room the next time he comes back home?"'

However, Elizabeth also explains the difficulties in readjusting to 'normal' life, having coped independently for months:

'On the same day Charlie left for Afghanistan, I learnt one of my best friends had found a small tumour in his brain. He had intended to tell me a few days later. However I had already arranged to have him to lunch to cheer me up, and I immediately sensed something was wrong. I could not bring myself to tell Charlie since I knew he would worry about me. The thought of him not concentrating on what he was doing would make me worry more. During my friend's brain surgery I remember explaining that he was resting up for a week because he had flu and was a little down. It was only when Charlie got home that I explained although he was now on the road to recovery, it had been a little worse than man-flu.

It was through things like this that I realised how difficult it was to adjust when Charlie did return. I had become so self-sufficient; it took a while to remember that he was back. Lying to him to reassure him had certainly not come naturally, but somehow it had become my normality. We had led completely different lives, and we now had the task of identifying the fibs which had been lovingly entwined into our narratives. It was also hard to drop the feeling of anxiety. Readjusting was a strange process. I have little doubt that on his next tour we will be more open, but for this first tour it became more about just finding our feet.

Once he had returned, all of our friends wanted to hear all the dangerous details of his trip. While I am naturally incredibly proud of Charlie and his place in the Army, I found this quite tough. I endured endless dinner parties of descriptive tales and political debates surrounding the conflict. For the first time in my life I had started avoiding the news and withdrew from the debates. I was so biased about the conflict – believing in Charlie and believing in the war had had to be synonymous. It was a topic that despite all my efforts to keep my head in the sand, had dominated so many hours of my day for so long. I had prepared myself for his departure, but I had not thought about the endless questions on return. I found that most of my friends who had been through the same thing felt the same way. At this point we had thought about the war enough and were entitled to a couple of weeks of ignorance where we existed in a pleasant, if fictitious, peacetime.'

When Darren arrived back home after the tour, it took a while for him and Stacey to adjust properly:

'I think it is fair to say that we were only back to normal after about three months of the Battalion's return, well as normal as any Army family could be. My husband's homecoming was full of emotions, excitement, and anticipation but also tinged with a bit of worry – as I wasn't sure who I was getting back.

I have many memories of Darren's homecoming; our son's face when he saw him step off the coach, my daughter slowly getting to know her daddy (she was about six weeks old when he deployed and about eight months when he returned), the feeling in my belly when I saw him.

Darren was a little quiet for a while after his return, but I knew not to ask him questions and the main thing was to give him a bit of time, he slowly returned to normal, we ensured we planned loads of family time – we had a lot to make up.'

The clichéd scene of the women welcoming home their husbands is perhaps the image that most people have of a homecoming, but there are of course a number of men who wait with these women, to welcome their wives and girlfriends back if they were the ones deployed.

For Ina Pollard, whose six-month tour to Afghanistan followed on from her husband's tour there with the Battalion, adjusting back to married life was especially hard as she and Mark had not had the chance to experience married life in the first place. She described her homecoming and the adjustment period afterwards:

'It was dark, cold and a typical April evening. There were around twenty people on our coach from Brize Norton. I had slept most of the way, it helped the journey go more quickly and hold off the excitement. I didn't even know if Mark was coming to meet me at camp as I said I would ring him when I got there.

The camp was dark when we pulled up, but underneath the armoury shelter there was a small group of people. I couldn't make them out but there were two very MAD people jumping up and down waving Union Jacks. I remember thinking to myself "how embarrassing do they look?" but as the coach pulled up these two people were screaming and cheering and everyone on the coach was looking and pointing. Then one of the guys said: "Here Ina, isn't that Mark?" and, yes, to my horror it was Mark but not only that, Catrina was with him. I couldn't believe it. I had a massive big smile on my face, I totally forget how mad they looked, jumped off the coach and they both ran over and engulfed me in their arms with big hugs. I was so chuffed to see them it was all a bit surreal. Not twenty-four hours ago I was in Afghanistan, the next I was wrapped in Mark and Catrina's arms. We all jumped in the car, all trying to talk at the same time. Mark dropped Catrina off at her house then a couple of yards up the road pulled in to our drive. He had painted a massive pink bed sheet and tied it to the garage door, it said, "Welcome Home Ina". I think he thought he would get in trouble as he said, "I found it in the cupboard, I'm sure we don't use it any more."

It took me two months to adjust to being home and even more so sharing the same house with Mark. It wasn't easy as we had effectively been living single lives for a year and had got into our own little worlds. I had to learn to be more tolerant and patient with Mark and remember he had been on his own in the house for a long time so he was set in his little ways. I know he didn't like being at home on his own and he put all his effort in to work so as to keep himself busy whilst I was away.

I couldn't even share a bed when I got home as I was so used to having my own space. Mark was like a kangaroo in the bed, always fidgeting. The hardest part was getting used to having someone around you all the time and having to look after them; he would not pick his clothes up or do the washing-up to my stand-ard. On tour you look after yourself. I found I needed my space and just little things annoyed me. I felt on edge and frustrated but I couldn't put my finger on one thing. We needed to find each other again.

I did speak to one of the guys who were on tour with me and he had the same feelings so at least we knew it was normal. I felt very frustrated that I wasn't busy doing something as on opera-tions you are always busy or you were missing out on something. After about three weeks that feeling went away.

We haven't discussed what we experienced on tour as I think we had a silent understanding of what we have been witness to. To both know people personally who have died is a comfort in a way as we both know how painful it feels.'

Lee Hazard, a serving Naval Officer, told me about his wife Sarah's homecoming from Bosnia with the Welsh Guards in 2007:

'The Battalion arrived home in London towards the end of March 2007 and I waited with wives and girlfriends to welcome the returning troops home. I felt slightly uncomfortable being one of the few men waiting in a crowd of loving women looking proudly at their brave soldiers but equally sharing their pride. I spoke to the wife of a senior officer who was asked "how do you cope with the separation?" to which she answered "you cope". I challenged this because I believe it is not so much a matter of

coping but existing as I certainly failed to cope, finding it harder to say goodbye and watch them leave on operations than be deployed myself. I did not cope and partly existed, hoping never to have to say goodbye again.'

Ina's husband, Mark Pollard, gave me his perspective on her homecoming after a total of a year apart:

'The days were getting fewer. What could I do to make it special for her return? I made a big pink banner that covered the whole garage with "Welcome Home Ina". (She was never pleased that I used her best bed sheet). She stepped off the coach very embarrassed that I and her best friend Catrina were holding a big Union flag between us trying to make enough noise for the crowd that was not there. I had an emotional time during my wife's deployment. It was not over. We now had to find each other again.'

The after-effects of separation can be long lasting and many couples struggle for a while. There can be other effects of being in combat that only make themselves known gradually, after a homecoming, such as post-traumatic stress. The Army is very aware that returning soldiers and their families have a lot of issues to deal with and there is an official response to this need, which I had a taste of when, just before the Battalion came home from Afghanistan, I attended a briefing for the wives in Aldershot given by the Welfare Officers and the Army Welfare Service (AWS). The AWS has staff trained in bereavement counselling and is responsible for the 'HIVES', which are support services with centres in most of the large military units. These are staffed mainly by spouses and partners of serving personnel and produce information packs for families covering topics from the local services available in a new location to information on other support agencies.

The purpose of this meeting was to explain about trauma risk management, which is the recognition and treatment of mental health issues within the Army and the reduction of the stigma that can be associated with them. Preparing wives for the possibility that their husbands will have to go through such normal stress reactions to extraordinary circumstances is vital in ensuring that the homecoming and readjustment period is not jeopardised. Coping with a husband who has been away on an exercise, firing blank rounds and simulating scenarios is a very different matter to coping with his reactions when he has participated in live firefights and been the target of roadside bombs for six months.

Although some people may not have had any physical injuries, there may still be a possibility of psychological trauma, which can take months or even years to manifest itself. Making the families aware of this is vital in order to prepare them for this eventuality. Wives may then approach the Welfare Office, the AWS or the Army Families Federation if necessary for advice and support, all of which will be dealt with in confidence.

I was impressed by the Army's approach and by the amount of help available to wives and families, but of course, as with other areas of Army life, the first line of support is usually immediate family and the Regimental family. Friendships like Ina's and Catrina's allow family members to let off steam, and it is the love and support between partners that helps them to pull through the bad times and enjoy the homecomings that they have been longing for.

7

The Wounded

There is another, very different, sort of homecoming, which has been given more publicity since British troops have been deployed to Afghanistan, and that is the return home of the wounded. Their arrival is rarely glamorous, with no recuperation in Cyprus and no happy crowds to meet them; rather the anxious and shocked families, who may not know the extent of their loved ones' injuries until they are back in the UK.

Writing about the wounded deserves a book in itself, but I wanted to look at the situation from the families' perspectives, so I set out to explore the way they cope with a wounded loved one. Although these men fortunately did not pay the ultimate price, as did their fellow Guardsmen and Officers who were killed in action, many have sustained life-changing injuries and face a future of uncertainty about their careers. They joined the Army as fit young men in their prime; if they are lucky they will be offered a job with the Battalion on camp, but may never be able to fight on the front line again. For those not fit to be fully deployable this compromise can be hard to accept; they want to remain loyal to their Battalion but being surrounded by their contemporaries, who are fit to deploy again, can be very frustrating. The Battalion is always keen to offer these men jobs where they can, but it is in the knowledge that they may not be happy with what could be seen as second best. Injured men need to have other options for the long term.

The men, whether or not they are also physically wounded, may also suffer from post-traumatic stress, with symptoms like flashbacks, panic attacks and nightmares. Symptoms such as these in the weeks after the men return home do not necessarily mean that there will be any long-term issues, but if they continue for more than a few weeks they can develop into Post-traumatic stress disorder (PTSD). Thankfully this condition no longer has the stigma it once had, during and after the First World War when it was known as 'Shell shock' and was rarely discussed. These days it is regarded more appropriately – as a wound to the mind which, like any injury, will heal better the sooner it is treated.

I decided to visit two of the wounded Guardsmen with members of their families to talk about their experiences. Richard has never, thank God, suffered an injury but of course I know many families whose lives have been affected. My nursing means that I am also familiar with the reality of working with people with injuries and trauma. I felt nervous about asking the two young Guardsmen to open up about something so painful and personal, but I felt strongly that there was a need for their stories to be told, and so I stepped into the pub in South Wales where we had arranged to meet feeling determined to get the job done.

When I walked into the Black Lion in Llandaff, just outside Cardiff, a group of older men just inside the bar nodded and we exchanged hellos, then I asked at the bar whether Tim Hillard was around. Tim is the father of Geraint, one of the Guardsmen I had arranged to meet, and he works in the Black Lion. He told me that the group of men I had just passed were ex-Welsh Guardsmen. There were a few of them living locally, all of them still wholeheartedly supporting their old Regiment, and each one had given Tim the support he needed when they heard that Geraint had been injured. It was that sort of place;

a place with a thriving community spirit between friends who had grown up and lived together for many years.

This setting, a warm spring Sunday lunchtime, with the daffodils just emerging and locals gathering after a Welsh rugby international at Cardiff's Millennium Stadium, could not have been further removed from the scene nine months earlier where Lance Corporal Geraint Hillard and Drummer Dale Leach had sustained their injuries. Although life appears to go on as usual in their home towns, their own lives have changed significantly since then.

Geraint and his girlfriend Jo were the first to arrive, arm in arm. As we sat together, Geraint's right leg was propped on the seat beside me, externally fixed in a metal frame with pins running from one side of the leg to the other. For me, being a nurse, this did not seem particularly strange, but it did occur to me that this kind of sight might make difficult viewing for other people.

After I originally asked Geraint if he would contribute to the book he replied, saying:

'I'd like you to know that when I received your letter it brought a tear to my eye and got me quite upset to know that people do care and it got me thinking of the boys that we lost ... It touched me to hear that someone has decided to write a book on the important role that the families play in our lives being part of the close-knit family of the Welsh Guards ...'

I also noticed Dale the moment he walked into the pub. He was hard to miss, swinging between crutches with one good leg and one stump. They were all pleased to see each other and made me feel very welcome too.

I was profoundly moved by what Geraint and Dale told me; they spoke at length about their injuries and the impact they have had on their lives.

Geraint and Dale had been part of a team travelling in a Jackal – an open-topped vehicle mounted with weapons and some mine protection on the hull – about nine miles from Bastion, clearing roads for supply vehicles in summer desert temperatures of 40°C plus, when an IED detonated directly underneath them. In the carnage of flying debris and metal they were all blown clear of the vehicle. Dale and Geraint both suffered serious blast injuries, Dale lying unconscious after losing his left leg. They were airlifted to hospital in Bastion, leaving behind a firefight between the Taliban and those soldiers still on the scene.

Geraint and Jo Mason were boyfriend and girlfriend while at school and although they drifted apart when Geraint initially moved back to the UK, they got back together again a few weeks after his injury, as Jo explained:

> '*Before Geraint went to Afghan I added him on Facebook and then we started to email each other. We chatted for a while then decided to meet up in Cardiff for a coffee and a catch-up. We kind of rekindled a closeness that we had when we were going out together whilst in school in Germany (both our parents were in the Army).*'

Geraint introduced Jo to some friends before he deployed and it was through them that Jo heard about his injury. They emailed her to say that Geraint had been involved in a 'minor incident' and could she phone his uncle who had been trying to get hold of her.

> '*As soon as I had the email I was on the phone trying to get information of Geraint and what had happened and if he was OK. That's when I found out the truth that Geraint was in a bad way and my heart sank and all sorts of things went through my mind. We had had our ups and downs whilst he was in Afghan but from then on my*

phone was stuck to my hand in case any news of him came through. When I got to the hospital Geraint was in intensive care. I took sick leave to stay by his side until he was onto a ward. From there I went up every weekend and after a few weeks Geraint was allowed out over night. We had time to ourselves and we both got talking and became really close. We could talk about anything and every- thing and we never got bored. We went shopping and did loads of things together which rekindled the feelings that once were there. Eventually we decided that we were more than just friends, admit- ted to each other how we felt and decided to give it another go.'

Jo remarked on Geraint's selflessness:

'Geraint always said before he went on operations that he would rather be blown up than someone with families or girlfriends, and he was.'

However, getting into a relationship on his return has obvi- ously benefited Geraint's recovery enormously; he told me that Jo gave him something to look forward to when he was recovering. The support she has received from the Battalion has been considerable and although she was not an official next of kin, she was acknowledged as a partner once she became close to Geraint.

Geraint knows he will never be fit enough to fight on another FOB (Forward Operating Base), and will probably not be able to remain at the main base in Bastion for the next operational tour to Afghanistan in 2012. His spleen, part of his liver and his pancreas were all seriously damaged in the blast, leaving him with a severely reduced immune system. As a result, he has been medically downgraded. Although he has been given a job in the Battalion's stores, he regards this as a position for the 'sick and the lame' and would rather be in recruitment, talking to potential Guardsmen about the reality of combat.

To be surrounded by men who are as fit as Geraint used to be is hard for him, but it does at least give him the motivation to perform his duties to his best ability.

Geraint's father, Tim, served in the Falklands Conflict in 1982 with the Royal Marines. During the conflict there was no communication between the Battalion and the families until and unless their own loved ones were injured, and even then details could take days to reach them. Although communication has improved since then, the full extent of a serious injury may still not be known until the wounded are flown back to the UK and can be assessed at Selly Oak Hospital in Birmingham. During Geraint's tour to Afghanistan, Tim received text messages nearly every day to say that there had been an incident but that Geraint had not been involved – until, of course, Geraint *was* the one injured.

Tim told me about the moment he heard the news of Geraint's injury:

> *'I saw a person in uniform walking down the drive and thought it must be Geraint, but then realised it was a Casualty Visiting Officer. When he told me the news I couldn't take it all in and I was shaking like a leaf, then panicked when he couldn't tell me the full extent of his injuries.'*

Since then he has had amazing support from the Welfare Office: 'Anything I have needed they have provided it.' One of them even offered to help me behind the bar but he admitted that 'there wouldn't be much drink left if he did'.

Geraint's mother, Debbie Mackenzie, spent the first three weeks after the incident at Geraint's side in Selly Oak in Birmingham, where the strength and support she gave him were invaluable. She was not at the Black Lion but when I spoke to her later she explained to me that even though she was not close to Geraint before the injury, she became so during his convalescence and their relationship is now very strong. Debbie has been an Army wife for twenty-seven years; she divorced when Geraint was eight and remarried another serving soldier. Her outlook on life is very pragmatic; her description of the way the wives coped with living on an Army base in Germany was that:

> *'We were all in the same boat. We either got on with it or went back home to be with our families.'*

Her experience of just 'getting on with it' stood her in good stead for the times ahead. She also said of Jo that

> *'even if they had not got together when Geraint came home, Jo would have been there for him as a friend. She is just that sort of girl; one of life's really good people.'*

Debbie is now actively involved with SSAFA Forces Help (Soldiers, Sailors, Airmen and Families Association) and is keen to work to help relocate the wounded into areas within the Army where they would be most useful.

Having been airlifted to Bastion from the scene of the incident, Dale was then flown to the Queen Elizabeth (QE) Hospital in Birmingham where the severely injured are taken into Intensive Care. He remembers nothing of his three and a half weeks there; his first memory is of his transfer to Selly Oak Hospital two miles away, where he found himself on the same ward as Geraint. Dale was in Selly Oak for a further eight weeks, after which he spent five weeks at Headley Court, the Defence Medical Rehabilitation Centre in Surrey, and continued for several months to convalesce there on weekly visits. He was still receiving regular treatment there around the time of our meeting.

Dale's fiancé, Alex, was newly pregnant when he deployed to Afghanistan and stood by him throughout his recovery. She had to cope with morning sickness and the emotional rollercoaster that always goes with pregnancy as well as supporting Dale. Their son Mathew was born the following January and was in the Black Lion with us when I met the men and their families.

Dale, holding Mathew, was happy to let his mother Sue and his stepfather Mark Mellars do most of the talking for him.

I asked Dale what reaction he received from people when he had to use a wheelchair, before he had his prosthetic leg fitted, and he replied that he had not realised how difficult things could be in a wheelchair and that he had 'lots of stares but never any verbal grief'. Joking about his first outing in it, he described how he 'got mugged by a rail of clothes' when he steered the wheelchair into a shop and piled into a clothes rack, having to fight his way out of a tangle of jackets.

Sue described the moment she was informed of his injury in person while she was at work:

> *'You think it's not happening, that it's not real ... they couldn't tell us any details so I had visions of going to hospital, seeing him sitting up smiling.'*

The reality was very different: he was critically ill and it was two weeks before he was taken off sedation and a ventilator. Mark described the wounds Dale had sustained, including blast injuries to his lungs, a fractured skull and bleeding on the brain, three spinal fractures, a shattered heel and a fractured eye socket. He lost the hearing in one ear and his speech has been affected ever since.

Mark kept a detailed journal from the day of the incident to Dale's discharge from the QE Hospital, and was kind enough to lend it to me along with Dale's visitors' diary. The diary, which contains personal messages from friends, family, ward staff and visitors during the first three and a half weeks of his recovery, will serve as a record for him of those lost days of his life. One of the first entries on arrival at Selly Oak was from Alex:

'14/06/09 830am. Hello Baby, I got a phone call Friday morning saying you've been in an accident. We all came to see you straight away. I haven't left your side (only when the nurse told me to). I'm talking away to you Babe. Be strong and hang in there. Me, Ellie and Baby need you to pull through this. You're meant to be my husband in Dec you Ninny! Please keep strong for me my angel. I love you so much my baby. All my love for ever and always, Al xxx'

Dale's mother Sue's first entry is equally poignant:

'Hi Honey, it's Mum. You look lots better today, but you have to have an operation to make your tummy better. Dad, Mark, Mel and Alex are all here with you and having lots of chats and kisses with you. You have to stay strong through all this and we are by your side all the way and with what else may come in the future. We will have you back home before you know it my angel. We all love you so very much and can't wait for you to open your eyes. You just enjoy your big sleep for now.

Love you more than life and would swap places with you if I could. Love you, Mum xxxx'

Both diaries are a true testament to the devotion of Dale's family and friends, including the men who visited him while they were home on leave from Afghanistan. They all rallied round and supported each other during these fragile few weeks and their genuine feelings and love for Dale are clearly there in all their comments in the visitors' diary. Mark's entry in his journal on the day of Dale's injury reads:

'How do you tell a room full of people who love him about the severe injury Dale has sustained? I felt sick. I knew the distress I was about to cause will stay with them forever.

> *Lots of tears and reassuring hugs ... what a family, everyone pulling together in a time of togetherness. I love them all ...'*

Day five was a very black day for the family; Dale's vital signs deteriorated, his pupils dilated, his intracranial pressure had risen and he had to have a brain scan. Mark described the course of events:

> *'I couldn't take it all in. All I understood was that there is a stem in the brain and if this was not functioning Dale would be brain dead and the only thing keeping him alive would be his ventilator. It was like being hit by a bus. I saw the colour literally drain out of Sue's face. Everyone was shocked as this really brought home the extent of Dale's injuries. They had told us to expect bad days but this was the worst day of my life ... everything was going through my mind, even the worst case scenario. How would I deal with that? How would we all deal with it? Please don't let it come to that ...*
>
> *... It has now been a week since we first had the news about Dale's injury; the longest week of my life. I never knew sitting next to a bed not knowing what was going to happen could be so tiring both physically and mentally but most of all emotionally. I think we all at some stage went through every emotion possible, and I am sure there is more to come. All I want is the doctor to say he is going to be alright, I could then relax a little instead of living on a razor's edge day by day.'*

Luckily, Dale's condition improved, and continued to do so over the next ten days. When the sedation was reduced and Dale started recovering consciousness, Alex's relief was plainly recorded in the visitors' diary:

> *'24/06/09. Hello Hansome!! I can't believe how much you were moving today! When you looked at me and you said 'I love you' I just wanted to jump on you and smooch you but I'd probably get banned from your bedside!*

I saw your pretty eyes today; I've missed them so much. It upsets me to see you like this but Babe I'm the luckiest and the proudest fiancée in the world. You know how much I love you and vice versa! I can't wait to talk to you properly. I've got stories bubbling out of my ears! Better go Sweetness ... all my love, forever and always, Al xxx'

The visitors' diary also includes a handwritten entry from Prince Charles when he visited Selly Oak Hospital, expressing regret at Dale's injury and pride at his 'courage and fortitude'. He also wrote that he hoped to thank Dale in person when he was fully recovered. This he did, at the Medals Ceremony in Aldershot the following December.

Looking back on the support that Dale received from family, friends and the Battalion during this testing time, Mark commented:

'Dale has a very supportive family who will encourage him throughout his recovery process, and also his Army family who have been so supportive especially throughout the two weeks I have spent in Birmingham and who I have had the privilege to meet. These boys never cease to amaze me. You don't realise what they go through and the public don't know the half. All you hear on the news is of a fatality but for everyone losing their life they don't mention the horrific injuries that are suffered by the lucky survivors and until you are in our position you don't appreciate the hell, suffering and anguish that families and friends go through.'

I found meeting Geraint and Dale and their families incredibly moving. It was obvious that a large part of the men's recovery had been due to the constant support from friends, family, Army family and the wider community. The value of that last element of the support network became even clearer on the next stage of my journey. I drove on to the Rhondda Valley in Mid Glamorgan. Nestling among the hills, the town of Treherbert is in the heart of ex-coalmining country, and driving down the terraced rows of old miners' cottages and past the Constitution Club it was not hard to imagine how close-knit such a community must have been until the mines were closed in the 1970s. When the siren sounded the end of a shift, the miners would have walked back from the collieries together to their homes, perhaps calling at the Con Club for a drink first. These clubs, really the local equivalent of the English pub, remain very much a part of life in these areas and have changed so little that some still have men-only bars. The British Legion clubs are of a similar ilk and remain staunchly traditional, a very male domain. It did not take me long to realise that the traditional community spirit in a place like this also remains as strong as ever. I went to see Lance Corporal Gareth Davies' father Stephen, his stepmother Helen and his girlfriend Kayliegh Williams at the house shared by Kayliegh and Gareth.

Gareth was involved in a contact (firefight) with the Taliban and sustained a severe gunshot wound to his left arm, leaving a scar fourteen inches long. His day sack was also left with four bullets embedded in it. Telling me about the impact of visiting Gareth in Selly Oak Hospital, his father Stephen said:

'To see the amount of injured in Selly Oak was unbelievable; seeing the boys lying there with no one beside them was really sad.'

When I visited Kayliegh, Gareth had regained sixty per cent use of his arm but had two metal plates inserted which were affected by the extremes of temperature due to expansion and contraction and caused considerable pain. He returned to work but found it hard to stay positive at times. Gareth also suffered from post-traumatic stress and experienced panic attacks and flashbacks to the incident. The attacks prevented him from going out with the boys as he did not want his friends to see him experiencing them, but as Gareth himself acknowledged, part of the recovery process will be to share his concerns and learn that others have similar troubles.

In the Valleys around Treherbert, I found that the locals had all taken a very active role in supporting the troops in Afghanistan. They had raised money for Forces' charities and had been sending out shoeboxes full of treats for the men. Kayliegh says:

> 'I think it's a Valleys thing. Church, chapel and schools all do the boxes and they all come together to support the troops. They all want to be involved and genuinely care; the people are just so close they are like one big family. The news that Gareth had been injured spread like wild fire and people were coming down the street crying when they found out he was wounded.'

The tradition of joining the Welsh Guards is a longstanding one in this area. Kayliegh discovered that the husband of a lady who used to babysit for her was a Welsh Guardsman; his name is Gavin Evans and he helped to get Gareth into the helicopter after his incident.

On Gareth's return the whole street was decorated with bunting and 'Welcome Home' banners, and one hundred and fifty locals all joined in a street party. It was a double celebration, as another local soldier with the Royal Welsh Regiment had also been injured in Afghanistan and was returning home at the same time.

Although exhausted and much in need of rest that night, Gareth went straight to Treherbert's local pub, The New Inn, to be reunited with his friends. It was here where Kayliegh was singing, which she had been doing lately on Friday, Saturday and

Sunday nights to earn money while studying television and radio journalism at Cardiff University. They got talking and arranged to meet again the following week: the rest, as they say, is history.

Since Gareth's homecoming Kayliegh has become his rock and, as Helen said, she is 'the best thing that has happened to Gareth'. His father Stephen commented that 'Gareth has spoken and opened up a lot more since you met.' Kayliegh brushed off the praise, saying only:

'I know it's a lot to take on but I support him dearly and help him how I can.

When I first met Gareth he would drink excessive amounts of alcohol to hide his panic attacks and it made him forget things. Then he was diagnosed with PTSD almost a year after his injury. I helped him understand that drinking wasn't the way and he only drinks on weekends now. The PTSD has stopped Gareth doing duties with guns and he's not allowed to do any guard duties. He can't be deployed either and has been medically downgraded. When he has a panic attack he gets very agitated and starts breaking out in a sweat. Nobody can tell him not to worry; he describes it as like having a heart attack.

Gareth's panic attacks do affect his day-to-day life and even our relationship. If there are too many people in our home he can't deal with that. He walks out of shops if they get too packed. He can't come singing with me. We can't go out for meals together; just the thought of getting ready to go brings one on; just before walking out through the door he would have one and then we wouldn't be able to go. Since treatment this has slowed down but he still gets them.

Sometimes when he feels an attack coming on he just goes to bed and stays there 'til the next day as it would take all his energy out of him. I always try to be very patient and supportive and he has a supportive family but it is horrible seeing someone going through this.

> *Gareth wants to go back to Afghanistan on the next tour in 2012; I wouldn't like it but at the end of the day I'm here to support him and that's all I can do. Sometimes I go upstairs to have a cry but then tell myself to pull myself together and get on with it. I've got to support what he chooses and what he does. It's his job and I knew what I was getting into at the start of the relationship.'*

Kayliegh's stepfather was in the Army and she used to visit him with her mother during the holidays wherever he was posted, so has an insight into the Army setup. Consequently she says she would not mind living on a camp, but Gareth himself would rather return home at weekends than live with the Battalion permanently. She does feel that there may be more support in a place like Treherbert where families are so close-knit. On camp, she says, 'the wives haven't got their Mams to talk to; here everyone comes together'.

Kayliegh would like to have talked to more wives and girlfriends to get a better sense that what Gareth is going through is normal. In some ways she missed out; because she didn't know Gareth before he deployed, she didn't attend the briefing session before the Battalion returned, which was designed to help prepare partners and families for the impact and implications of their loved ones returning from combat.

Gareth told me about the Medals Parade that took place in Aldershot for the Battalion shortly after its return. Gareth was amongst those able to march, so did not have the opportunity to speak to Prince Charles who had made a point of talking to all the injured who were unable to march, although he included as many of the rest of the Battalion as he could. When Prince Charles realised after the event that he had not spoken to Gareth, he wrote a personal letter of apology. The letter, now framed, expressed regret at not having spoken to

Gareth on the day and described his accompanying present as a 'small bottle of medicine which I hope will help you through the coming months'. This 'medicine' was a bottle of whisky in a presentation box from Highgrove; another example of Prince Charles' pride in the Battalion and the personal touch he so often displays to the men.

Another of the injured men was Lance Corporal Jamie Evans, who was the driver of a Jackal vehicle hit by an IED. I spoke to him on a different occasion and he told me his story. He had been injured in the same incident that tragically killed Major Sean Birchall. Jamie was in a routine patrol from Lashkar Gah, the capital of Helmand Province, to visit North and South Checkpoints: joint Afghan Army/British checkpoints which they were resupplying with stores and equipment. Jamie told me what happened:

'We were on a routine patrol from Lashkar Gah down to Checkpoint North. Our task was to resupply the Mercian Regiment and the ANA [Afghan National Army] *who were patrolling up there. The Grenadier Guards Company that would take over from us was on their recce and we were showing them around.*

At Checkpoint North we stopped, stripped our gear off and chatted with friends there. I had prepared a bacon and egg sandwich for the resident stray dog, nicknamed Shit Lips by Company Sergeant Major Campbell. He was a scruffy beaten up flea bag of a dog who was found tied up with wire in a corner of the compound. The boys cut him free and he returned every day after that for rations and he would lie all day in the shade of the Mastiffs [heavily armed patrol vehicles]. *After two weeks he trusted us enough to let me stroke him.*

Andy Campbell (Catrina's husband) described his decision to keep the dog:

'Shit Lips was a mass of sores and matted fur, over a bag of bones.
He was in a bad way when we first took over Checkpoint North,
having been subjected to a pretty hard time by the Afghan police
who were in the compound before us. I thought it better to put him
out of his misery and was going to take him around the side of
the compound and shoot him. Deciding to give the condemned his
rightful last meal before execution, I gave him a pouch of corned
beef hash. The way he wolfed it down and seemed to almost
instantly perk up, made me change his sentence from execution
by firing squad to death by overfeeding by thirty British soldiers!!
His rather crude name came from his habit of leaving half his food
around his mouth – obviously not sure whether he would be fed
again and keeping half for later.'

The irony of the compassion displayed by the men to a stray
dog, when surrounded by so much hostility in the form of
hidden IEDs and the possibility of ambush and firefights, was
to become clear within minutes. Jamie continues the account:

'After maybe half an hour Major Birchall emerged from the ops
room and said we need to run down to Checkpoint South and
that he would ride with me in the Jackal.

  Roughly a quarter of the way to Checkpoint South there
was a crater in the middle of the track where two days ago an
ANA patrol had been hit. As we passed this hole I said to Major
Birchall: "this is where the ANA must have got hit the other day."
He leaned over the side of the Jackal and said: "That's a bloody
big one."

  We carried on for maybe twenty metres. The next thing I
remember is waking up thinking I was under water. My helmet
was holding me under and I couldn't breathe. I removed my
helmet and tried to stand up but was very dazed and confused.
My immediate thoughts were that I couldn't remember being
anywhere near water and how the hell did I get in there.

I was dragged out and evacuated to Camp Bastion where I was told some time later that Major Birchall had not survived. I was still confused and it was not until I saw the news that it really hit me.'

Jamie sustained blast injuries; shrapnel in his left arm, buttocks and fingers and an open compound fracture to his left femur. His girlfriend Donna Billington, who is a teacher, wrote an account of her experiences following the injury:

'I was trying to keep busy as the weekends and weeks were dragging as I awaited Jamie's return. I ploughed myself into my school work, and saw friends and family on the weekends to make time go as fast as possible. I was scared to listen to the radio as more and more Welsh Guards seemed to be getting injured as the weeks went on. My best friend in work had her husband out in Afghan and we used to talk and keep each other going and count the days until their leave. The time he was away was painful. I would wait for 'blueys' [British Forces airmail letters, which fold in on themselves and are blue] to land on my doorstep. One which landed was only half written and the last line said "and then we were patrolling in the river and the Taliban were behind us …" He had continued in a second bluey that I did not receive until 3 days later, and this filled me with utter dread wondering what had happened during the patrol.*

I have loads of friends and a fabulous family but I felt utterly alone. On loads of occasions I just wanted to talk to Jamie, and then when he did finally call I would forget everything I wanted to say and remember when he went, and it was too late. I had to wait another week to speak to him again.

On this Friday I had driven to my parents' for the weekend and I received a call from Jamie's dad. It was an answerphone message, which said: "Jamie's phoned, something has happened. It's nothing to worry about but phone me back, it's nothing to worry about!" From the way John repeatedly said "it's nothing to worry about" I knew immediately to be worried. I phoned him back and sat in my parents' living room. He said it couldn't be too bad because Jamie was allowed to phone himself. He was only allowed one call and phoned his dad as I had repeatedly missed calls in the previous week. No one was at my parents' yet, and I sat there in shock from what I was hearing.

My mum came home and I told her what had happened. We were meant to go to my sister's school fayre and I just went on autopilot. I wore sunglasses and cried all the way around the stalls as it hit me. I got home and it just sunk in. I stayed at my parents, then drove to Birmingham and was met by two men. I had to be sat down and was told about Jamie's accident and what to expect. I was in total shock. It still hadn't really hit me. Until the next day when I saw Jamie.

I went up on the ward in Selly Oak and saw all the young injured soldiers around. I felt very naive that I had no idea this number of men were being injured and sent back with cages on their legs, in wheelchairs and faces scarred with shrapnel. I didn't know where to look. Jamie was in a side ward. We went in to see him. He looked strange, vacant. He had bandages on all his wounds; he was really tanned but really dirty. His hair was full of dirt and grit. Still at this point I tried to keep it together. His mum and I chatted about nothing and we didn't really talk about the accident; it was really surreal.

We were not allowed to stay long. After the nurses explained what had happened and Jamie's injuries were explained we sorted out our accommodation. As I was not Jamie's wife and only his girlfriend I was told I was allowed a space only until a wife or a family came as I was not next of kin. This was really hurtful to me as I didn't love Jamie any less just because we weren't married.

As the bandages came off and the surgery began it became clear that the injuries were worse than they previously looked.

We went to the flat that we had been allocated and sat and talked over his accident. His mum and I just cried in the kitchen and his dad went for a walk. This pattern continued for the next two weeks where Birmingham became our second home. Our discussions were only about Jamie: What mood would he be in? What would he eat? Would he talk? We went back to the flat in between visiting hours and sat and talked and cried and waited for the next visiting hours.

Jamie began to change. As time went on and he was not recovering as quickly as he wanted he became aggressive and depressed. On one occasion I went to visit and Jamie had asked for Snack a Jacks so I took them up and he threw them out of the window, saying: "Why are you bringing me this shit? It won't make me any better!" He wouldn't wash or get changed and stopped eating. He lost three stone while in hospital and contracted C. difficile where he was isolated on a ward and we had to wear gloves and an apron when visiting him. This was the lowest point of the whole time. Seeing Jamie at ten stone sweating and on two crutches trying to get to the toilet was unbearable. His mum and I washed him at his bedside with wet wipes, changed his bed as he nipped to the loos as he never wanted any fuss and if we said: "You have been sweating, let's get a nurse to change your bed sheets" he would say "No I don't want any fuss".

We were constantly walking on eggshells awaiting an outburst. Eventually as he got more depressed and ate less the doctors took us to one side and said if he didn't eat they would force feed him and put him on more drips, so he began to try food again. We would take him to the canteen in a wheelchair and he would ask to go back upstairs, we would take him to the local pub and he wouldn't speak and would ask to go back to the ward. He asked for steak which we would cook and take to him, then he would refuse to eat it. He became unrecognisable. I remember having a conversation with him where I shouted and said: "You should be *thankful you're alive not sat here moping and looking out of the window." He replied: "Do you know there are 105 bricks in that wall? I counted them." The mental health people would come and talk to him but he would say what they wanted to hear and didn't want anyone else prying.*

One funny memory Jamie and I often laugh at is when he had a second accident at the hospital.

Wheelchairs were few and far between on the ward but on one occasion I managed to get a wheelchair but little did I know it was for transporting people INSIDE the hospital. I took Jamie outside in this and he was swearing that it was really bumpy. We then realised and saw a wheelchair parked up on the grass. We swapped him over which was a mission in itself only to realise that this one had been discarded as it was broken! We carried on and Jamie said he was hungry and wanted to go for some chips down the road. I was so happy he actually wanted food so I left Jamie on the top of a hill while I went to a bank to get money out. The brakes were broken and Jamie went flying down the hill and fell out of the wheelchair. I was at the hole in the wall and some ladies shouted at me, saying that he had just fallen out of his chair! A lady with a broken arm went past and tried to pick Jamie up. He was so angry and said; "I'm not hungry any more, just get me back upstairs before you do any more damage."

We laugh about this now and say we were like Lou and Andy from Little Britain *in his wheelchair but at the time it wasn't funny.*

I got to know his parents really well. They were so supportive and we got through it together. I had only met them three times before Jamie's accident but lived with them for a month and we bonded so much. We were moved from our flat to the 'Big Brother House' as we called it. It was called Norton House where we had our own room but a shared kitchen dining room and garden. Everyone there was ill or looking after somebody in the hospital. I didn't like it there much. Everyone was friendly but I didn't want to sit and talk and share how I felt and talk about Jamie with strangers. I just wanted to be on my own.

After a few days I was asked to leave as a family needed my room and as I wasn't a wife and was only a girlfriend I had to find somewhere else to stay in Birmingham. I found a B&B down the road and phoned the Army Welfare Officer who was excellent and took a lot of the pressure off me. He met me straight away and organised that I could stay there and they would pay for a few nights. This was really stressful, thinking about Jamie then having to move and organise this was something I just couldn't cope with at the time.

I found a local gym and went training most mornings to be alone, saw Jamie and his parents throughout the day and went back to my room for peace and alone time in the evenings. I had to return to work to send my school reports out to parents so I left the B&B and the next thing I heard Jamie was coming home. I was so happy.

This was nowhere near the end of his journey. This was the beginning.

Following the injury Jamie was diagnosed with Post-traumatic stress disorder. Although PTSD does receive more recognition now than in the past, the cry for help often still has to come from the person affected before treatment can be offered. Even if relatives raise their concerns with the Army the person concerned might not want to admit to a problem or seek help. In that case it is not only the sufferer but also the families who miss out on vital support and guidance. In Jamie's case, his symptoms were spotted because he was in hospital already, but nonetheless it has been one of the most challenging aspects of his recovery. He and Donna are still constantly learning about how to deal with it. Donna is frustrated that so little is known about the treatment of PTSD and that more cannot be done to speed up Jamie's recovery, that there is little information on what sort of behaviour to expect from him, how to behave around him to ease the situation, or insight into how she can help him in his recovery. Despite the increasing availability of resources on the subject and reading as much as she can about it, Donna, still feels isolated.

Captain Tom Spencer Smith was also one of the injured in Afghanistan and told me about the incident. He was a Platoon Commander on a foot patrol when his interpreter stepped on an IED less than four feet behind him:

'*I had seen Ahmed* [the interpreter] *in the corner of my eye milliseconds before and was turning to tell him to stay directly behind me and spread out. Suddenly there was an explosion that threw me forward with a force I had never before experienced, like being hit by the 1st XV scrum in one blow. I blanked out momentarily before I hit the wall to my right; my senses were on fire and immediately I was thinking "where was the crackle of enemy fire following the explosion". That didn't last long as it was replaced by the dull throb and ringing in my ears and the feeling that my neck and head had been sandblasted and then dunked in a hot bath. The heat from the blast was extraordinarily painful. I think I knew something was wrong with my neck and my shoulder as I couldn't really move but I jumped back onto the cleared area so we could sort out what had happened.*

... the medic treated Ahmed as best he could although he was by our assessment already dead ... the pain in my head and ear started to appear but was not so bad that it needed morphine. When I got on the MERT [Medical Emergency Response Team] *Chinook they cut my top off and tried to give me an IV drip, there was no chance that the chap with a ruddy great needle was going to stick it in my arm as we were bouncing around in*

the back of the chopper. When we got into the hospital at Bastion I could see the black "slug" of metal in my shoulder and seeing the blood down my back and the entry point the pain suddenly swept over me. Within fifteen minutes I was in surgery.

Soon after waking up, feeling somewhat bruised and battered, the Danish surgeon came to see me and explained my injuries. Although at the time I didn't take it on board I realise how close I had come to losing an arm or being killed outright. Now when I look back and read his report he talks about a millimetre here or a millimetre there making the difference, I understand now why he wanted a photo of us together and why he referred to me as the luckiest man he had operated on in six months. Despite having minor shoulder injuries, and a ruptured eardrum it was odd spending six weeks in hospital at Selly Oak. I was acutely aware of other people there who had not lost limbs per se but had large chunks of muscle torn from their bodies as they stood next to people who had trodden on an IED. It made me realise that I had got away very lightly indeed with not a scratch on my lower limbs'.

Tom's wife Pari described the moment she heard about his injury:

'I was used to Tom calling me at random hours of the night and day – whenever he managed to get to the phone. He mostly called at unsociable hours so that his men, most of whom had small children, could call their families before bedtime. It was a Saturday morning. I was not surprised when the phone rang at around 7.30 a.m. – I knew it would be Tom. He asked me how I was and if I was awake. I told him I was – just about … mainly because he had woken me! He went on to describe the events that had taken place in the early hours of that morning.

"Darling, there was an IED explosion last night." I was used to this kind of comment as it happened often and most notably Tom's Commanding Officer Lt Col Rupert Thorneloe had recently been

killed by one. My immediate reaction was to make sure none of his men had been hurt and to check that no one had been killed, it didn't occur to me that he could have been injured. Injury and death always happen to other people and it's easy to think it won't happen to our loved ones. It was only then that he started to tell me that his interpreter had strayed from the cleared path on patrol and stood on the IED causing it to explode. He explained that Ahmed was killed instantly. Without giving me a chance to put two and two together and come up with an answer Tom immediately gave me my "debrief":

"I was hit by shrapnel, but I'm fine, all my limbs are intact, I only have shrapnel wounds, I'm OK, I'll be home on Monday."

At that stage blind panic set in – I kept thinking that he could have died. I kept asking him if he was really OK – Tom has a habit of toning injuries down and I was worried I'd be faced with a husband with rather more severe injuries than he was letting on.

"Stop worrying, I'm fine, I'll see you on Monday – Welfare will call you and let you know when I'm flying back."

When the phone goes dead who do you call? I had forgotten to ask if he'd called his parents, I didn't relish the prospect of having to tell them their son had been blown up by an IED. When I finally pulled myself together and stopped shaking I called them around 8 a.m. They gingerly asked if Tom had called me recently and I immediately asked if he had called them. Luckily he'd already called his parents and told them. It didn't really seem real till I spoke to the Welsh Guards Welfare Office on Sunday and even then it was only really real when I walked up to S4 [the ward in Selly Oak] and there he was – injured – but still in his combats and still covered in Afghanistan dust. Relief that he was OK washed over me, but, much to the disbelief of friends and family, I wasn't relieved that he was back. I'd much rather have had him serve for the full tour and return safe and sound.'

Pari, like the families of all the wounded admitted to Selly Oak, was looked after extremely well. She praised the support she received from the Welfare team, in particular Captain Darren Pridmore and Colour Sergeant Jiffy Myers, who organised for her to stay in B&Bs and hotels for as long as she needed and covered bills for petrol to the hospital:

'It reduced the extra worry of having a loved one stuck in hospital with home and immediate family over a hundred miles away.'

She also spoke of the support she received from family and friends:

'They have been immensely supportive of Tom and me. Calling to check up on him and me and lending an ear whenever I needed to talk. What helped boost Tom's morale most during his six-week stay in hospital was seeing his friends who made the effort to travel to Selly Oak to visit him. It was tiring to be inundated with concerned friends and family every weekend, but very comforting at the same time.

When Tom was in hospital one of his friends, who came from an Army background herself, brought me a bottle of nice bubble bath. She told me to go and have a long relaxing soak. It was a small gift but a wonderful gesture from someone who understood what it is to be part of the Army family – and how stressful things can get.

Most family and friends did not realise the extent of injury or the number of patients and the sights they would witness on entering S4 Ward of Selly Oak. I had to warn them to expect the worst. Many of them commented on how brave our boys were and how they never expected to see so many young men injured with such severe injuries. They asked why the public weren't made aware that Selly Oak military wing was bursting at the seams with injured soldiers when they only saw the fatalities in the papers and on the television. I think people are still very much in the dark about the number of severe injuries sustained by our brave men.'

All those I spoke to while gathering material about the wounded commented on the lack of media coverage of the sheer extent of the injuries that were being sustained. Perhaps there were so many being killed that the fatalities had to take priority in the news, and there is no denying that the lives of those bereaved will be devastated and changed for ever, but the wounded and their families felt that the public was not made aware of the constant suffering endured by these men and women and the impact their injuries would have on their futures.

One of my friends, Joan, who was pregnant in Oman at the same time as me, is a physiotherapist working at an Army Medical Centre. Our paths crossed four years after leaving Oman, in the playground when taking our children to their first day at school in Wiltshire. Her daughter, Catherine, and my son Oliver were to be in the same class. We have both been posted on several times since then, but after fourteen years we are still in touch and our friendship is firmly sealed.

Not only is Joan an Army wife, but in her work she also sees at first hand the injuries sustained by the servicemen and -women returning from Afghanistan. It can be hard to distance herself when caring for the injured, when it could so easily be her own husband in the same situation:

'Of course you hear all the stories in the media, but when your own husband is out there or you live with the wives whose husbands are away, it is different. Constantly fretting about their safety let alone juggling all at home, obsessively watching the news and hearing that now familiar phrase: "The family has been informed" and counting our blessings when the Welfare Officer has not knocked on our own door.

When our first double amputee wheeled himself into our physio department, it was a very sobering moment. He was quite relaxed, which helped hugely, but we were all tense around him, in the nicest possible way. All of us were really chummy without trying to be patronising.

He joked away, swearing like the trooper that he was, as if he had nothing to be worried about any more. In a way, that made it easier for us to break the ice. Within minutes there were loud whoops of laughter between him and his physio coming from their cubicle. The laughter was so loud I spun round from where I was, while on my knees assessing another soldier's foot problem, peeped under the curtain and saw what looked like something out of a skittle game – the body of a man, only from the hips up, bobbing around and relearning how to balance without the counterweight of his legs, while his physio threw balls at him, expecting him to reach out and catch, which he did. What a sad, happy, sorry, hopeful sight to see.

Slowly, over the next few months, there would be a single below-knee amputee, another two double mid thigh amputees, countless other less life-changing injuries and the day came when I finally had my own amputee patient on my list – I dreaded it.

The experience was so emotional, not because this twenty-year-old soldier was in any way negative or miserable, but because Afghanistan had come to me, to my hands and I had to deal with it. Afghanistan became so REAL. He had lost both his legs while on operations out there, stepping on an IED four months earlier. The first thing I said to him after reading through his medical documents was: "Well, how do you feel it has gone so far?" Why did I say that? His response was not expected: "Brilliant" he chirped!

He was articulate and helpful. My previous experience had been mostly with sports injuries but never any amputees and he showed me what to do with his prosthetic legs when I attached them at an awkward angle, reassuring me that it was easily done. I just felt I was making things worse. But he had a good repertoire of banter as soldiers always do. Again, this helped when it came to handling his mangled stumps that looked like cuts of raw meat you'd buy from a butcher to cook for a large roast meal. They were not nicely shaped but truly deformed with dents of shrapnel wounds still obvious in the red flesh and skin grafts that were left. Professional training kicked in so I touched them, and let my hands rest on them so he did not feel that they were awful to look at. At the end of the appointment, I felt totally drained by the emotion of it all. He could have been my husband, any of my husband's friends and he was so young. The other physio came up and spoke to me earnestly about how to cope with the horror of it all. The moment passed when we heard him joking with our receptionist who told him to go and put his feet up if he was tired!

That day changed my life. I just had to do something. I had never really done anything out of my comfort zone for charity before, so I signed up to raise money for Help for Heroes, cycling seventy miles in a day. I didn't tell my patient. Every time my training programme caused irritation or pain, I just thought of him struggling to get on/off our physio plinth from his wheelchair, and just got on with what I had to do.

Visiting Headley Court was like stepping onto a film set of bionic people. There were dozens and dozens of soldiers coming along the corridors with all sorts of contraptions around them: metal framework around legs, bodies and necks encased in plaster of Paris, amputees on trainee legs coming up to my shoulder height and men with facial injuries. I tried not to stare.

I watched a rehabilitation class which had two teams of four, one of whom was a therapist. They were playing volleyball. They all had above-knee amputations and were sitting on the floor balancing on their bodies, laughing away and throwing themselves everywhere to catch a ball. There was not one sorry, pitiful look on *their faces. My patient then arrived, wheeling himself in at high speed, having missed the start of the match as he was having his prosthetic legs re-fitted and to my horror, he threw himself off his wheelchair and onto his hands, landing with the "blunt" end of his stumps on the floor. He then swiftly dragged himself forwards using his knuckles to join in with the game. He always says he loves it at Headley Court, having fag breaks outdoors with all the other injured soldiers, joking about and comparing notes/injuries to make light of their disabilities.*

It is normal for those who have been wounded in this way to experience similar stages as those going through the grieving process including denial, anger and depression before, finally, acceptance. He went through his depressive phase after that and put on a great deal of weight, so his prosthetics had to be refitted. He moved back home to live with his mother but then turned himself around and is back to being the cheerful chap he must have been before his injury.

Soldiers' camaraderie is amazing in all sorts of conditions. They see each other succeed and walk normally, so their competitive spirit comes through and they seem determined to match a "perfect gait" or outdo each other on the adventure side, some even aiming to climb Kilimanjaro or to train for the Paralympics.

We are getting used to the sight of a soldier coming just about high enough up to the level of the desk, instead of towering above it. Whenever there is a soldier in a wheelchair, all the other soldiers in the department are obviously moved and disturbed, and make excuses that they are "wasting your time" because theirs is a minor injury in comparison. They seem to feel guilty that they survived a tour away without a significant injury.

I think of my husband, Michael, who did not tell me that his camp was being mortared while he was on tour. He was actually on the phone to my eldest son during the weekly allocated phone call when sirens blared out short notice of a rocket attack. My son heard some of the bangs going on and asked what that was, so Michael replied that it was fireworks. He had thrown himself under his desk and carried on talking so as not to alarm us. He always teases me that when it was my turn to speak, all I could do was complain about the car breaking down (always does when he goes away) while he cowered away to keep safe. I so often think of that moment, and how it could be so different, and he could have lost his legs.

How would I and the kids cope if he had lost his legs? How would Michael cope? Michael has, thankfully, only ever had one injury that stopped him playing his sport for six months, and like most soldiers who are generally quite fit and active, the inactivity made him so unhappy. As a physio, I see it happen so often and now see these young men with no legs and the thought of that uphill struggle all their lives. I think of their families. How do they manage? I can only console myself by taking inspiration from the sheer determination that these people show and from the support that their families so readily give them.'

I was lucky enough to be able to speak to Simon Weston, an ex-Welsh Guardsman and very well-known Falklands veteran who sustained extensive injuries while deployed on operations during the conflict in 1982. I phoned him on his mobile at an inconvenient time – he was driving from Cardiff to Liverpool to give a lecture – but he was only too happy to help. I explained that I wanted to give the stories of these newly injured men, and others like them, some balance. Simon's story of the way he turned his life around after he was wounded may just give them some hope while they begin their very long road to recovery and a new life.

Simon was originally from Nelson, in the Welsh Valleys, and joined the Welsh Guards at the age of sixteen, deploying to the Falklands four years later. While on RFA *Sir Galahad* in

Bluff Cove with other members of the Battalion, the ship was bombed by Argentinian fighter jets. It was carrying ammunition and thousands of gallons of diesel and petrol, which magnified the fireball that swept through the ship. Twenty-two out of his platoon of thirty men were killed and the Welsh Guards lost forty-eight men in the incident, with ninety-seven injured. Simon survived with forty-six per cent burns.

Simon told me that when his mother was informed of his injuries, the only thing she could focus on and the thing that kept her sane was the sound of the next-door neighbour's lawnmower. To this day, the sound takes her straight back to that day. He reflected with wry humour on the desperate situation he was in:

'*I was kept down there to die, 8,500 miles away. I had septicaemia and wound infections and had lost ten stone in weight. I went from being an eighteen-stone rugby prop, down to eight stone. It was three and a half weeks before I was taken to Montevideo in Uruguay, then flown home. This was not without its dramas either: while on takeoff, the RAF plane lost its engine. It fell out on the runway. But you have to laugh, don't you? If you can't take a joke you shouldn't have joined.*

I was not offered a job in the Army again, and it would have been a mistake to hang onto the past even if one had come my way. I left the Battalion while I still had respect for the Army and while they had respect for me. All of us in the Army have to get used to being a civvy [civilian] *at some point.*'

Simon went through years of reconstructive surgery, including over seventy operations. His recovery was tough and he suffered psychological trauma and setbacks, but gradually he began to pick up.

His convalescence saw him getting involved with an increasing number of ventures. He became patron to several charities which support people with disfigurements and founded his own youth charity, Weston Spirit. He was awarded the OBE in 1992. He has been a commentator for news programmes, has written autobiographies and children's novels and is a motivational speaker for businesses, as well as being in demand as an inspiring and humorous after dinner speaker. He married Lucy in 1990 and they have three children. Simon's determination is a fine example of how a positive attitude can achieve success.

The moment I first spoke to Simon I realised how very modest he was, so I was not surprised at his response when he read the list of his achievements written in draft for the book:

'Fiona, could you also add that I was voted number 75 in the top one hundred Scousers, coming in one behind a dead horse, Red Rum?'

I replied that I thought it was very respectable to come in just behind such a famous racehorse.

We talked about the future for the wounded today. There are many more opportunities available to them than in the past, as prosthetics improve and medicine continues to advance. Simon also pointed out that

> *'the severely wounded are surviving in Afghanistan now whereas a few years ago they would not have stood a chance. The medical services are in solid situ and casevac* [casualty evacuation] *is so quick now. We also have top surgeons out there with a massive amount of experience.'*

As an ex-Welsh Guardsman who has come through so much, and has shown such determination and courage, Simon is an inspiration. He still keeps in touch with old friends from the Battalion, whom I have included in this book; Martyn Miles or 'Milo' as he calls him, and the Mott brothers. I hope his story and example will inspire not only other Welsh Guardsmen but also countless other wounded servicemen and -women to carry on and accept their change in fortune, and even to use their situation to their own advantage. As Simon said:

'With the amount of determination these men and women have and the opportunities open to them, we will have one hell of a Paralympic team next time round, that's for sure. They are all the right age and right mentality.'

8

The Knock on the Door

The reality of being deployed is that men return wounded, and worse. For the Welsh Guards, the summer of 2009 was a brutal reminder of this reality. It had been a terrible few weeks during Operation Panchai Palang ('Panthers Claw') when the Army as a whole suffered a large number of casualties. The nightmare that the Army families live with on a daily basis was played out over and over again and they felt they were living on a knife-edge.

When the events of that awful summer began to unfold, I wanted to lend my support in some way. I visited a few of the Welsh Guards wives' coffee mornings in Aldershot, just before the Battalion was due to return home. I knew some of the girls already, and used to bring my own children to the same coffee morning when we were posted to Aldershot ten years previously.

Richard had served his term as Commanding Officer only four months before the Welsh Guards were due to deploy to Afghanistan, handing over to Rupert Thorneloe, who would have been in command for the following two years had he not been killed. Richard had very recently returned from Iraq, where he had been short-toured from nine to seven months when British troops withdrew from the region. It was highly unusual, if not unprecedented, for a tour to be cut short and we considered ourselves very lucky. He was out of harm's way, but visiting the wives whose husbands were still in Afghanistan I was very aware that I had a comfort zone and they did not.

Walking up the familiar path to the coffee morning, I felt slightly nervous that perhaps my presence would be tolerated rather than welcomed. Maybe I should not be there at all; my own husband was not amongst theirs and I had the luxury of being able to stand back from a highly emotional situation. Rupert had been killed two months previously; maybe the girls would think I was usurping Sally's role amongst the wives. She was living in Aldershot and sometimes still went along to see them. I had told her I was going and asked her if she wanted to come too, but she was busy that morning, although I had said I would visit her afterwards. For me to walk in without her when my husband was no longer with the Battalion might have seemed presumptuous. Of course, as soon as I arrived, Marlo Bettinson's welcoming face greeted me with 'Hi Fiona, how lovely to see you here,' and then the old familiar faces appeared: Leanne Peters, Beth Pullen and Stacey Merritt-Webb.

My silly worries need never have been; walking back into such a group of genuine, down-to-earth women reminded me that the Welsh Guards truly is a family. Even if you move away, you are always welcomed back into the fold on your return, regardless of your husband's rank, or even if he has left the Regiment. Richard was not in Afghanistan, but this did not alienate me; why should it? None of us choose our circumstances or where our husbands are posted. From then on I knew I would be accepted, and I scolded myself to have entertained the idea that these friends would even mind.

It was obvious that the atmosphere this time round, with the men away in Afghanistan, was very different from the last time I had visited. The air was charged with anxiety and emotion. I could see that the girls were all putting on brave faces when I asked them how they were coping; but the worry and stress was clearly etched around their tired eyes. Every knock on the door caused pain and drained their reserves of energy. Despite this, they were happy to talk, to release some of the burden of stress. Their oblivious toddlers and babies still demanded their attention, and there would still be the endless routine of motherhood when they went home. Perhaps this routine was a blessing, in that it would keep them occupied and make the time pass more quickly, but the weekly coffee morning offered a chance to recharge, to realise that they were all in it together, to laugh together, and to cry.

The fear of answering the phone or the front door was very common amongst the wives, girlfriends and mothers. No innocent caller could have imagined the heart-stopping moment they might have caused. Marlo told me her coping strategy. 'Please don't ring the bell; just tap on the window, then I'll know not to panic,' she urged her friends after one nerve-racking morning which made her feel physically sick. There had been a knock on the door of Marlo's Army quarter at 7 a.m.; she stood in the hall, frozen to the spot, not daring to answer. When she could finally bring herself to open it, she saw the postman and trembled with relief. He was so concerned when he saw her looking pale and terrified that he swore he would always tap on the window from then on, for her and all the other wives on the patch whose husbands were away.

Elizabeth Blackledge, whose boyfriend, 2nd Lieutenant Charles Maltby, was serving with the Battalion in Afghanistan, told me about the arrangements that she and her fellow wives and girlfriends had made in the event of her receiving bad news. Actually, though well intentioned, they antagonised a mind already poised to hear the worst:

'We had already discussed who would come and tell me of any bad news and we settled on a long list of contenders so that I would not

be overly paranoid whenever I heard from one poor soul who was innocently calling for a catch-up, and so that one of them would hopefully be able to get to me quickly. Ironically my tired mind often became anxious when anyone on this list rang; envisaging that they were calling to check I was at home or at work before they came to the house and delivered some news. I was also aware that his mother would hear of any serious news first and it was unlikely to be passed on to me over the phone. This meant there was bound to be a further delay while a messenger travelled to me, and I often thought this could account for Charlie's lack of contact. In these now embarrassing paranoid phases I was very grateful for the consistency of his mother's phone calls, since they were an indication that no bad news had arrived.

Obviously a mother or a wife has priority to learn of news of her son or husband, and I would never refute that. However it was slightly unnerving that any news concerning Charlie was to come from someone else because we are not married. I was so used to hearing every bit of his news from him each day. If Charlie were to be injured I would not hear it from him, which left me feeling slightly isolated. If he were to die, I would not receive a last letter from him unless someone discovered it on his person and delivered it to his mother so she could pass it on to me. In either case, I felt slightly unconnected and helpless, and although perhaps unjustified, this did increase my apprehension.'

Despite all the planning, there was an incident which shook Elizabeth badly; a simple misunderstanding but one she would not wish to experience again:

'The biggest low I personally experienced was late one Saturday night when we had had no word from Charlie for well over a week, and he had said he would call. I am always amazed at how these intelligent, practical men still make promises to call within the next few days when realistically they have no idea whether

they will be able to do so. Even though I knew how changeable the situation must have been, Charlie is not one to go back on his word and it was the first time I'd heard nothing for such a long time. I began to worry. I had stayed at home that weekend to try to shift a small bout of flu, and had gone to bed early to avoid staring at my phone for another hour. At 2 a.m. I was woken by a loud, authoritative knock at the door. As I walked I spent a bizarre few seconds consciously wishing that my boyfriend was injured, since at that hour, and feeling as ill as I did, I was fairly certain I was about to hear the worst. When I answered the door I found a young gentleman who had mistaken my flat for one on the floor above me where there was apparently a party. I won't repeat what I said to him. I remember thinking the next day that I should go and apologise. Unfortunately, amid my angry rant I never actually discovered where the party was.'

Soldiers' mothers often feel isolated when their sons are away. They are sometimes listed as the next of kin, but usually not if their son is married. I recall an occasion when we lived in St Athan; I received a phone call from Mary Spry, mother of one of the Captains, Alexander (Ali) Spry. I had only met her once but she had remembered that I was a nurse and she had received news that Ali had been taken ill while on exercise in South Africa. Although he had received medical attention, had returned home and was being treated, she just wanted to offload her anxieties with someone connected to the Battalion, and with some medical knowledge. I tried to source some information, as the problem was not my speciality, but despite the fact that my medical advice was not much use she was eternally grateful for the contact and the chance to talk it through. After Ali deployed with the Battalion to Afghanistan, Mary explained to me how she avoided the agony of waiting for the 'knock on the door': the only way for her and her husband to cope was to get away from the house. Mary made sure she could be contacted, and then the couple got away from not only the house but also the country for good measure:

'We made an extraordinary journey for two and a half months touring Europe with no agenda, just going where and when it suited us. We had no media information, no television and no newspapers and no one rushing up to us and saying: "How are you coping?" The only contact we had was by our mobile telephone. We both found that it was an immense relief to read the text messages from the Welsh Guards, horrified that there had been a casualty, but to know that it was not Alexander who was involved. At the same time we were always overcome by a feeling of guilt that it was somebody else's son or brother, husband or boyfriend and huge sadness for the families involved. Our being away in a completely different environment helped us to cope, but the fear was with us every day and when the mobile telephone beeped to alert us to a message our hearts were in our mouths.

On our return we attended the funerals of the brave men, including that of Lt Colonel Rupert Thorneloe at which Alexander was an usher. He was on his R and R and seeing him there in his uniform made us both think "There but for the grace of God." The funerals were harrowing and agony for the poor families but there were beautiful tributes to the men who were lost.

The next most difficult thing was when Alexander, after a whirlwind R and R filled with anxiety and sadness and emotion, also lots of laughs and happiness, had to return to what he knew. By that time we knew what he was going back to for the remaining time of his deployment. That was very hard because now we were home and saw daily on the television and in the newspapers the horror of the war and the number of casualties the Welsh Guards were receiving. All the people we knew and saw, although well meaning and concerned for us, asked us if we were all right and how we were managing, saying that it must be so worrying for us. So I kept myself out of the way and busy doing mundane jobs. I think the last ten weeks of his tour were the longest and most worrying and it seemed it would never end.'

One of the topics that came up over and over again when I was talking to the families of the Welsh Guardsmen who were deployed was communication, and its importance to the loved ones at home. The speed of communication has of course improved significantly over the last few years. It is possible with modern technology to receive news almost as it happens, and live television coverage leaves nothing to the imagination. Despite this, stringent measures are taken to ensure that the next of kin is the first to be informed of a fatality or a serious injury, and that the wounded or killed are not named publicly until this has taken place. Communications from Afghanistan back to the UK through mobile phone and internet routes shut down immediately (a process known as 'Op Minimise') until the news has been officially broken to the families. At the same time, back home, the next of kin of all the Welsh Guards who have not been involved in the incident receive a text message notifying them that the families of those concerned have been informed. Some of the messages received were these:

'We are sad to report that there has been a fatal incident in Afghanistan involving a member of 1WG. NEXT OF KIN HAVE BEEN INFORMED. Details will be published shortly.'

'There has been a non-fatal but serious incident in Afghanistan involving Welsh Guardsmen. All NOKs have been notified.'

'There has been a serious incident in Afghanistan on ... NO MEMBERS OF THE WELSH GUARDS BATTLEGROUP WERE INVOLVED. DO NOT REPLY TO THIS MESSAGE.'

All the people I spoke to said they hugely appreciated the Army's systems for releasing accurate information as fast as possible. Compare this sort of information to that available during the Falklands Conflict in 1982. Media coverage for the duration of the ten-and-a-half-week-long crisis was very different to today's reports from news teams in Afghanistan. It was even unlike the previous conflicts in Vietnam and the Middle East; these were at least recorded in photographs by the international press, whereas in the Falklands only two professional photographers and two television crews accompanied the Task Force to the South Atlantic. Communication between the men and their families was also less frequent, not only because of the relatively limited technology available at the time but also because of the strict regulations around sending 'familygrams' from the ships before they reached the Falkland Islands. A government regulation specified that the sender had to declare that he had not received mail for a specific length of time before he was allowed to send one, otherwise the cost of sending would not be approved.

The Welsh Guards were among the three thousand three hundred men who were transported to the South Atlantic aboard the *QEII* on 12 May, making up only half of the Task Force as a whole. Each one of the men was allowed a minimum number of phone calls home, but once they were on the islands they were not permitted to make contact with home at all. The spread of rumours, both on the ground and at home, was rife and it took ten days for a telegram to reach the rear headquarters in the UK, from where the families could be informed of the men's welfare. Of course, by the time the news was received, the conflict had moved on, so it was 'old' news anyway. For Sue Miles, at home and expecting their first child, she had no option but to try to get on with everyday life as best she could:

'I discovered that I was pregnant with our first child (Michelle) whilst Martyn was in Brecon [Mid-Wales] *on a course in March*

1982 which came to an abrupt end when he was sent back to the Battalion to deploy to the Falklands in the April.

Rumour had it that the Welsh Guards would NOT actually be sent to the Falklands, I suppose it lulled me, together with a lot of other wives, into a false sense of security. Of course it turned out not to be true, and when Martyn told me that he would be going, I can remember having that feeling of dread and anxiety.

Martyn would not let me travel to see the QEII off. He thought (quite rightly) that I would have been too distressed. As it was I had been to see the doctor as my blood pressure had become raised, obviously due to my anxiety. He signed me off from work for a couple of weeks to get some bed rest, but that just meant extra time to worry. I was terribly scared but knew that there was little that I could do but get on with it.

Once I went back to work full-time I managed to keep busy. I was an avid watcher of the news as I imagine all wives were (and still are today). On 8th June 1982 news of the attack on the Sir Galahad was on the 6 o'clock evening news. I was at home watching this alone, not sure what to do. I can't remember what time I received the "knock at the door", but I do remember feeling quite sick immediately; it all seemed surreal, like a dream, as though it wasn't happening to me.

The Families Officer [now called the Welfare Officer] was there together with at least two other people. He told me that Martyn had been injured. They could not at that time tell me exactly what his injuries were, but they did tell me that he had not been burned. Over the next couple of weeks I ran on auto-pilot. When I was driving I would get to places and not recollect anything much about the journey, I would just be surprised to have arrived at my destination. Sounds pretty dangerous I know, but, it happened.

It took what seemed like ages for more detailed information to get to me. Communication was appalling; I felt very isolated and *felt I was not being told everything – I realise now though that this was a case of when there was something to tell me I was told. Obviously, since the Falklands Conflict, communications have made a vast improvement, thank goodness.'*

Over the following ten days or so, Sue was told that Martyn might have lost his leg, but none of the reports were confirmed. He was held on the hospital ship *Uganda* for two weeks before sailing home with the returning troops at the end of the conflict. By the time Martyn came home Sue had found out that four of his ankle bones had collapsed while he was trapped under a bulkhead fire door in the explosion. As her stepfather was ex-Welsh Guards himself, he managed to get confirmation of Martyn's injuries by contacting the MOD in London. If he had not done this, Sue could have been waiting much longer:

'I was obviously one of the lucky ones; my husband returned, but at the time it was one of the most traumatic experiences of my life, a situation which I hoped I would never have to face again, but that was not to be the case. Martyn still carried out his duties and deployed on every operational tour with the Battalion until he left the Army after thirty-three years. On every one of these, I never knew what was going to happen to him.'

In Sally Thorneloe's case the knock on the door came at 9 p.m., an equally suspicious time as 2 a.m. or 7 a.m., and she knew what it meant as soon as she saw the Army uniforms through the glass in the front door. For Sally it was a moment that will haunt her for ever. The grim job of the Casualty Notification Officer was to inform her that her husband, Rupert, had been killed by a roadside bomb while serving as Commanding Officer of the Welsh Guards in Helmand. Lieutenant Colonel Rupert Thorneloe was the most senior officer to be killed in action since Lieutenant Colonel 'H' Jones, the Commanding

Officer of 2 Para in the Falklands Conflict, twenty-seven years previously. Rupert had been visiting his men on the ground when the bomb exploded, killing him and his driver, Trooper Joshua Hammond. At that moment, Sally's world was torn apart.

Sally came to visit me the following day to escape the relentless ringing of the home phone. There was an agonising paradox in trying to comfort her on a hot July day, the garden in full flower and the birds in full song while her world was plunged into a cold, dark void filled with desolation and despair.

'Rupert was a big bear of a man; he was so gentle and made me feel so safe, and I only came up to here on him,' recalled Sally, pointing to his chest on the photo taken just before he deployed to Afghanistan. He was described at his funeral as 'quite simply the best of his generation' and was passionate about the Army and its role in Afghanistan. His love of history and politics made being a soldier the perfect vocation for him as he could combine the two interests; his bookshelves were bursting with military and historical titles. But to Sally, he was simply her best friend, a loyal and devoted husband and a wonderful father.

Rupert had a great love of the outdoors and was both a keen sailor and accomplished polo player. Sally told me that they used to spend their weekends and holidays gently sailing along the south coast and down to the Scilly Isles and Channel Islands in their boat, *Valentina*:

'They are some of my favourite memories, planning our trips around tides and timetables, laughing and chatting as we left the boat's mooring on the Hamble, heading downriver to the open sea. The boat has now been given to the Household Division Yacht Club where it will be used by all the members in years to come.'

As a friend of Sally's this is the most difficult part of the book for me to write. I do not want to betray the trust she has in me, having confided to me her darkest moments. So we worked on it together; it is the result of spontaneous conversations on dog walks, over glasses of wine, during a pub lunch or over cups of tea around the kitchen table – anywhere that did not seem like an interview room.

Sally's daughters, Hannah and Sophie, were her raison d'être through the horror of the weeks following Rupert's death. The realisation of her enormous responsibility as a widow and a single mother was overwhelming; especially as Sally knew that she and the girls would now never have the perfect family unit that had always been so important to her.

On the surface, Hannah and Sophie continued to live for the moment, as do any children of their age. Nevertheless, Hannah, at four, seemed to have grasped that Daddy had gone to heaven and would sing prayer songs to him with Sally every night after bedtime stories. This was an appropriate time for her to remember him as Rupert always used to phone Hannah from work every night at 7 p.m., no matter how busy he was, to find out how her day had gone. It really mattered to him; he was devoted to his family and he always looked forward to that special time of day.

Hannah talked openly to her class in 'show and tell' about how brave her Daddy was, displaying her painting of him painted from the photo that was used in the press after his death, of Rupert in his yellow mackintosh, kneeling down with Hannah, Sophie on his back. The emotion, of course, ran much deeper. She became drawn to male family and friends, craving the affection that she would never again receive from her own father. Her sensitivity to Sally's feelings after Rupert's death, though, was amazingly mature; she has led Sally by the hand to a chair and, making sure she was sitting down, has reassured her that 'it's OK Mummy, everything will be all right.' She has had to grow up fast.

Sophie, at two, appeared to be oblivious and would run to photos of Rupert calling 'Daddy, Daddy.' It was hard to explain to her that he will never come home, when she had been used to him walking through the door after a spell away, as he always did, eventually. The most telling thing of all was Sophie's own painting, done the day after Rupert's death. She would usually make a beeline for fluorescent colours, but on this occasion she drew a green central circle surrounded by a red circle with a yellow line underneath.

'Maybe it's me reading into it too much,' commented Sally, 'but I am convinced it is supposed to be Rupert in the centre wearing combats, surrounded by a ring of fire [the bomb blast] and the yellow is the sand of the desert.'

Perhaps, at two years old, children have a much clearer head than we think; maybe it was Sophie's way of communicating that she understood.

One of the vital factors in Sally's life in the first few months after Rupert's death was the support she received through the Welsh Guards Welfare Office. When there is a fatality the next of kin is allocated a Casualty Visiting Officer, in Sally's case Major Nigel Overton, Coldstream Guards, or 'Ovy' as he likes to be called. Sally told me many times that he was immensely kind and his practical help was invaluable to her. His role was to provide her with support and guidance, from when she was reeling at the initial shock through to the adjustment of their lives without Rupert and their preparations for a new life ahead. His duties ranged from corralling financial information, and dealing with the media interest, the scores of emails, texts and phone calls, to accompanying Sally to some of the many events she has been invited to as a result of Rupert's death. He also helped to assemble Hannah and Sophie's new trampoline. Sally and the girls bounced on it every morning those first few weeks; they would jump as high as they could to see how close they could get to Daddy in heaven.

Sally appreciates how valuable the support from the Battalion has been: 'The Welfare Office and Ovy have picked me up when I needed help, and put me down when I needed space; I have literally been carried along in the tidal wave and they have been professional and sensitive enough to get it exactly right,' she said.

Ovy also had to honour his regular Regimental duties; the role of Casualty Visiting Officer was in addition to his daily role as a Major in the Coldstream Guards. When the Coldstreams took over from the Welsh Guards in Afghanistan, Ovy went on a tour of duty with his own Battalion. At the end of the tour, one of his first calls was to Sally and the girls to catch up with their news. Sally considers herself 'incredibly lucky; Ovy was exactly the right person for the job of Visiting Officer: he could sympathise with my situation having his own wife and family, and the dedication he showed was above and beyond the call of duty.'

Family and friends, of course, have been amazing to Sally as well, although she misses her mother terribly since her death five years previously. Sally is a very well-loved person; one of the Guardsmen's wives told me that she did not know who Sally's husband was for weeks when she was getting to know her at the Welsh Guards' coffee mornings early on in the tour. When she found out and asked why Sally never told her that her husband was the Commanding Officer, Sally replied that 'it isn't important who my husband is; I am here to make friends as myself, not as Rupert's wife.'

Sally is not alone in this attitude. The Welsh Guards officers' wives seem to have an unwritten code: they do not wear their own husband's rank and they are on equal terms with all other wives, whatever the husband's standing or background. Lifelong friendships are formed within this unique lifestyle; the separations, postings, house moves, even the glamour of supporting the men in their public duties, all these shared experiences strengthen bonds and create empathy when the worst happens. This is where the beauty of a small regiment comes into its own; it becomes an 'extended family', doing what blood relatives would do in times of crisis. Of course, Sally has received countless letters, about seven hundred, from well-wishers around the world, presents for the girls, and offers of help. She is hugely grateful for them all, but in reality, the day-to-day support has to come from hers and Rupert's close-knit family and the Regimental family itself.

The losses to this Regimental family have been significant. Six other men also lost their lives that summer of 2009. Lance Sergeant Tobie Fasfous was twenty-nine and the first Welsh Guardsman to be killed in Afghanistan. He was a specialist mortarman with the Mortar Platoon and was killed by an IED while on a foot patrol with soldiers from the Afghan National Army in Helmand Province. Tobie was born in Chesterfield, England but grew up in the United Arab Emirates, where he lived until he moved back to the UK after leaving college, and settled in South Wales. His mother Anne talked to me about her perceptions of the conflict in Afghanistan and about Tobie as a soldier:

> *'This conflict seems all the more real to me as, living in Dubai, we are geographically much closer than those in the UK. The Middle East Region in general is not such an alien environment to us and Tobie would have been familiar with both the ground conditions and the heat out there; it would not have phased him, even in the summer temperatures. He could speak Arabic, and whilst*

not the national language of Afghanistan, as Muslims it would be familiar to them and he would have enjoyed exchanging pleasantries with locals whilst out on patrol. He kept quiet about his Arabic in his early Army years as he didn't want to be singled out, just preferring to be "one of the boys", but people noticed he could speak it when the Battalion went to Iraq in 2004, and communicating with the locals became an unofficial role for him. It was also very handy to be able to listen in on the interpreters to make sure they were translating correctly!

Tobie originally wanted to join the Navy and work with helicopters but they had strict rules about being a UK resident for two years before joining and at the time he did not qualify. Instead, after returning to the UK with a Higher National Diploma in electronics and communications engineering he had several jobs before joining the Welsh Guards in late 2000. He became highly respected as a Senior Non Commissioned Officer [SNCO]. Before Tobie went to Afghanistan he had asked for a transfer to the Army Air Corps, so he could learn to fly helicopters at last, something that sadly never happened, but he never regretted his decision to join the Army for a minute, it was very much him, and he spent an action-packed and very happy eight and a half years with the Welsh Guards.'

Richard has told me the story of when he promoted Tobie while on exercise in Germany, just before he handed over command of the Battalion to Rupert Thorneloe. In order to be promoted to Lance Sergeant, Tobie had to pass the SNCO mortar course, which he had recently completed. Richard had received the results of this while they were on exercise and went with the Regimental Sergeant Major (RSM) to find Tobie, who was live-firing on the range. In order to get a better view, Richard and the RSM climbed the two-hundred-foot-high observation tower adjacent to the mortar line. Once the firing had finished Richard decided it would be a good idea to combine promoting Tobie with giving him the news of having passed his course. He was called to the top of the tower to receive the news:

> *'I took great delight in promoting Tobie in the field in front of his section. He only just fell short of being the top student and had proved he was more than good enough for promotion on the course. Crucially, he was an excellent mortarman who went the extra mile to look after his men. They all really respected him for that.'*

Anne described to me how she coped immediately after Tobie's death:

> *'When I was told the news it was like someone flipped a switch and I went into autopilot, going through the motions but not really knowing what I was doing or why. I had to be told of Tobie's death over the phone as it was already evening in Dubai and my emergency contact number was registered to the office address, so nobody knew where my house was to make a personal visit. Brian, the senior Royal Naval Officer attached to the British Embassy in Dubai was tasked with being my Visiting Officer and when he came round to the house the following morning I remember answering the door and greeting him with the words, "Oh, I expected to see someone in uniform." I have no idea why those words came out of my mouth. Poor Brian had never had to do this before and had changed three times that morning as he couldn't decide what would be best: uniform, a suit or a shirt and tie. I don't doubt I spoke hours worth of nonsense in those first few weeks, especially while Brian accompanied me on flights to and from the UK for Tobie's repatriation and funeral; he was "a captive audience" at 38,000 feet.*
>
> *My memory of those very early days after we heard the news is very patchy. Perhaps this was a natural defence mechanism so*

I didn't take too much in at once, but some memories started to be drip fed back as time passed. It was weeks before I recognised myself in the mirror; I would see my reflection whilst doing my hair or my makeup but just didn't register who I was. A friend told me later that when she saw me the first time "there was nothing there, just an empty look" on my face.

Tobie's loss so early in the tour was a huge shock not only to us but to the Regiment too. It has been incredibly painful and extremely hard going at times, but there is no going back so we have had to try moving forward as best we can. Brian has become a good friend since those early days. For me, Dubai, my home here with my younger son Alex, my work and work colleagues, my network of close friends, and Brian have become my comfort zone. I'm well away from all the media hype in the UK, and whilst I remained mindful of the rest of the Welsh Guards out in Afghanistan after Tobie's death, and felt the pain of subsequent losses, to a great extent we've at least been allowed the privacy to grieve in peace.'

Lieutenant Mark Evison was fatally shot in Helmand during an ambush. He was flown back from Camp Bastion to the UK, ventilated and unresponsive and the agonising decision was made to turn off life support three days later, while his family said their last goodbyes. He was twenty-six years old.

I met Mark's mother Margaret during the autumn after he died and she spoke to me about the wonderful relationship she had had with him and of their 'bond of understanding'. She is clearly a supporter of the youth of today, which is refreshing when we hear so much criticism. She described Mark's friends as 'energetic, caring, giving and idealistic'.

She told me about the moment when she received news of Mark's injury on a beautiful, calm May Saturday morning. She was about to collect a paper from the local shop when she saw a man talking to a neighbour. He was looking for her house and Margaret's heart sank as he introduced himself as a Major in the Army. 'I could feel the panic starting to rise in my throat. He explained that Mark had been shot, very seriously injured. He said there were three categories of injury; very very serious (mortal), very serious, and serious.'

Margaret spent the weekend waiting for more news; all she had been told was that Mark was stable and on life support. Then on the Sunday, she realised that as he was still in Camp Bastion, he must be fighting for his life:

> *'That was almost exactly the time his body gave up and his pupils finally dilated in Camp Bastion Hospital, and they gave up hope also. I did not know that until much later'.*

On the Sunday afternoon Mark was flown back to the UK. Margaret drove to Birmingham with her daughter Elizabeth to wait for him, and hope.

Mark did arrive at the Queen Elizabeth Hospital in Birmingham, still on a ventilator. She spent the next two days just talking, whispering and holding him, willing him to wake up again. There was a hospital diary by his bedside which had been filled in by the medical staff at Bastion, with good wishes for Mark's family and praise of his bravery. There were also messages sent through from his friends out on the patrol bases and Deiniol Morgan, the Welsh Guards' Padre. The dedication of the Bastion medical team was astounding; as Mark used up the hospital blood supply, the medical staff donated theirs as well. In their dedication and compassion they went the extra mile to try to save him. Rupert Thorneloe, only days before he was killed, offered to come to Bastion with some men to give more blood.

On the Tuesday Margaret and Mark's father, David, waited for the agonising procedure of brainstem tests to be carried out. It was the news they had all feared. Margaret and her family said their final farewells in private before the ventilator was switched off.

While we were having lunch and talking in the sunshine on the South Bank in London, Margaret told me about her job as a psychologist just a short walk away from us and how ironic it was that she often deals with bereaved families.

With so much life around us that afternoon; the tourists, the business of city life and the street artists on the Embankment, framed by the Houses of Parliament across the river, it was hard to imagine the combat scene in a desert country so different from our own.

Mark's soldiers described his unusual understanding of them, his smile and fun under all circumstances, and his professionalism. He was a very charismatic, generous person with a love of the outdoors and of adventure, and his thoughtful, gentle side, showed through in his love of music and art. The last entry in Mark's journal from Afghanistan read: 'if life was easy then it would be easily boring.' It epitomised his inexhaustible enthusiasm for life. One of the Guardsmen, Jon Caswell, said:

'Lt Evison was loved by everyone; he was a friend of every Guardsman. We always used to say he had a face "sculpted by angels" and he was an inspirational man; one of the best blokes you could ever meet.'

Mark shared his love of writing and poetry with Margaret; her feelings, written at a time of great anguish shortly after Mark's death are best portrayed through her own 'Meditation on the Death of a Soldier':

'They say I have lost my son. Where did I lose him? Perhaps he has turned away from me, left me. Is he somewhere, that warm

radiance, that understanding smile, that young love flowing without guile, that cocked head and lithe body, that gentle loving nagging. If I have lost him, can I find him? They say death is just another room, just around the corner. Should I go too, to find him, to be with him as I always have? But then I would leave behind other loves, who would suffer as I have.

Perhaps as they say he has gone to another world. Can I believe this, and if he is there, will he be happy looking down and not being part of all the fun, as he has always been? Perhaps for his sake it is better that he is now nothing. But I can't manage the impossibility of never seeing him again, this longing for the presence at the front door, the smile around the corner, and that warm young love.

I am told that he died selflessly, helping the soldiers he cared about to safety, ignoring his own pain and injury. Such is the stuff of what they call heroism. It is cold comfort, when his gentle smile is so close. I cannot say goodbye.'

For each life lost there are scores of family and friends who grieve, whose own lives will change for ever. Lance Corporal Dane Elson was killed by an IED while in Afghanistan with the Welsh Guards in 2009, aged twenty-two. From the age of six, Dane had lived with his father Stuart and his step-mother Alison when they moved from Wales to Stroud in Gloucestershire. Dane's sister, Rowenna, continued to live with their mother, Debby.

Stuart, a police officer in Bridgend, recounts Dane's childhood:

'Dane was a robust young man and loved sport, was always out playing on his bicycle or playing football in the local park, but if there was trouble he would find it. Few parents can have spent so much time in the headmaster's office; I had my very own chair, which was well used.'

Although Dane was mischievous and fun-loving, he never got into any serious trouble and was always there for his family when it mattered, showing great love and compassion.

Stuart recalled one occasion, when the family horse, Holly, had had to be put to sleep not long after Dane joined the Army. Holly had been 'one of the family' throughout Dane's childhood:

> *'Dane lay on the grass, along Holly's neck, all the while stroking her face as his tears fell on her. It was a very emotional sight, and an incredibly sad situation, but his words brought a smile to all our faces – "Oh, Holly, you made so much shit for me to shovel, but I loved you – so much!" Typical of Dane to be realistic about things. Afterwards, Alison drove Dane back into the village and as he got out of the car she said to him, "Thank you for being there, Dane." Dane replied, "I'll always be there for you, Ali." Dane had been so naughty growing up but he knew what was right and when he needed to be there for his family.'*

Stuart explained that Dane had three sisters; Rowenna, his natural sister, as well as Jessica and Rebecca, his stepsisters, with whom he grew up:

> *'Sadly we don't see much of Rowenna, but I see comments left by her on Dane's Facebook page and knowing her, I can see her hurt etched into her words.*
>
> *Jessica, the eldest, is immensely strong. The way she tells stories about Dane to her two young daughters is so moving. Jess takes the two girls to where Dane lies, and they will leave him presents and cards.*
>
> *Dane was very close to Rebecca. As they grew up she was the one he would relate to, and she was so very protective of him. She laughs at the fond memories of him, but she also cries so many tears. Sometimes Bec will send her mum worrying text messages.*

It's clear that she has been talking to Dane, sometimes through the night. At the moment she seems unable to throw off her sadness.

Stuart also recalled Dane's ability as a sportsman:

'*Dane was a keen sportsman and played for Stroud RFC from the age of seven. He loved his rugby. One of the things I am most proud of, and most grateful for, was that I was able to play rugby with Dane at senior level. Firstly at Cainscross, our local rugby club in Stroud, and then for South Wales Police just before Dane joined the Army. Just after he went to Afghanistan, Dane telephoned me and told me that he had obtained permission from his Company Commander to come on tour with the police in May 2010. The tour was to the Cayman Islands. Of course, Dane never made it.*

We played two games on tour and after playing the second game I remember sitting alone in the stand, exhausted. Overlooking the Caribbean Sea, in such a beautiful part of the world, all I could do was cry for my son, who should have been there.'

Dane's mother, Debby Morris, tells of her pride for him, describing him as

'*a loveable rogue, always in some kind of trouble as a child, but nothing nasty, only mischievous. He always had a cheeky grin on his face. Everybody loved Dane and wanted to be in his company. He was very much a Mammy's boy and we were both very proud of that, (all his mates used to tease him about it but he just laughed at them), he was man enough not to be embarrassed by it. He was very close to his big sister, Rowenna, and stepdad, Terry.*

The support we've received from the Army has been incredible. The funeral was arranged with precision and went off perfectly. Everyone who attended said they had never seen anything like it and I said it was fit for a king, which he deserved. There were about 650 people there. There was so much dignity and respect. I was so very proud of our Hero.

But to me the thing that keeps me going the most is his Welsh Guards comrades. Even those that were coming home on R and R would take the time to come and visit, no matter where they lived, to see us. We had phone calls, even on his birthday the lads phoned from Afghan and they took it in turns to speak to me. Since their return to the UK the lads have kept in touch. We have his "bruvs" (as they call each other) calling to see us and I think it is as important for them as it is for us. It's like we have gained a huge new family.

His civilian friends have also kept in touch and come to see us [in Bridgend] *regularly. Whenever we go to the grave there are always signs that one of them has been there. You cannot see the grave for things that people are putting down. They go regularly to have a can of Strongbow and a cigarette with him.*

In every room in my house there are Dane's clothes scattered, CDs, books, and photos on almost every wall which I smile at and talk to every day. In his display cabinet are his cap, belt, flag, medals, you name it and it is so proudly displayed. I wear his sweatshirts and T-shirts in the house as does his sister, his stepdad wears his tops, we just want to feel closer to him. And the poor dog just misses him so much she is still pining, he loved her to bits.

I am so, so proud of him and miss him so very, very much, Mammy's Smiler.'

Private John Brackpool was attached to the Welsh Guards from the Princess of Wales' Royal Regiment, Territorial Army, when he was fatally shot in Afghanistan. It was two days before his twenty-eighth birthday. After his death, while the Welsh Guards were still on operations, his mother Carol found that her way of coping was to imagine that he was still on duty in Afghanistan, because if that were the case she would not be seeing him anyway. During this time she felt that: 'I had come out of my own body; that it was not really happening' and it was not until the Battalion returned that the reality really hit; when the others were back home and he was not:

'I had many messages from the lads Johnny was with and they all said he fitted in well but that was my Johnny; he always made friends very quickly and I think he always felt the Army were his second family. I can't describe how much losing my son has affected me, it's broken my heart and I have a void in my life that I can never fill. I have not only lost a son but a very good friend.'

John's father Alan said:

'Joining the Army at the age of seventeen was the best thing John ever did. It gave him direction in life and we were so proud of him.'

On passing out, John signed on for three years as a Regular soldier and then became a Regular Reservist, which meant he had a civilian job but could volunteer at any time to serve. His civilian job as a security guard, though, did not give him the excitement he needed. Alan explained that:

'He was known as "Bracks" by the lads in the Guards; he was just happy to be one of them; he didn't want to climb up through the ranks. He could have fitted into a Platoon of Eskimos in the desert he was that easy going. And the girls loved him too; Lord knows how many he promised to marry.'

In a tribute book that his Platoon put together after he was killed, the men remarked that 'John gave his life protecting his comrades', and remembered him for his 'good sense of humour and compassion'. They commented that he was 'always happy and upbeat, never moaning', 'had a laugh, usually at his own expense' and that he was 'always willing to help out with anything and anyone'.

Major Giles Harris was his Company Commander and said of John after his death:

'That an Englishman could be so quickly and genuinely brought into the fold of a Welsh Platoon was a testament to his character and good nature.'

In Afghanistan, John fell through the roof of a derelict house while on patrol and his Platoon had to knock a wall down to get him out. When Alan heard this story at John's funeral, he thought to himself that it could not have been anyone other than his John. When he was about twelve, John was playing amongst some derelict buildings in his home town of Crawley and fell through a roof, and had to be rescued by the fire brigade.

Alan talked of the 'fanfare' when John was repatriated, the ensuing funeral and all the organising that follows a death in the family:

'After it was all over I just expected him to walk back through the door again. I still expect him to now. It's so surreal. I had lost my best friend to cancer in the January of 2009, then my brother-in-law died while John was in Afghanistan. We were going to break the news to John when he came home but of course he never knew. It was a terrible few months.

After all that happened though, I can still say that John has done his duty, he served his Queen and country, and I am so proud of him.'

As a Company Commander in charge of around one hundred men, Major Sean Birchall was involved in leading his Company into Basharan, near Lashkar Gar, with the aim of establishing a firm presence in the village and driving the insurgents away. The operation had been a huge success and they were quickly accepted by the village elders. The headmaster of the local school had been beheaded by the Taliban in front of the terrified schoolchildren and the remaining teachers had been too afraid to teach, so the school had fallen into disrepair. As a result of Sean's work and commitment to his project the teachers were encouraged to come forward and within a few weeks the stabilisation plans were in full swing. However, at this point the Company and the Battalion as a whole were dealt a tragic blow when Sean was killed by a roadside bomb while on a routine patrol in a Jackal. Lance Corporal Jamie Evans was the driver of the Jackal and was wounded in the incident. He said of Sean:

'Sean Birchall was a fit, driven, professional soldier. I had not worked with him long but he would be one hundred and ten per cent behind any ideas we had and was always ready to listen.'

WO2 Andrew Campbell (Catrina's husband) was in the vehicle behind Sean's when he was killed and said of him:

'He was a great man to work for as he firmly believed in Mission Command – tell somebody what to do, but leave the how to do it up to them. The men in the Company trusted his judgement completely, knowing that he would never get them to do something he wasn't willing to do himself. He would regularly accompany patrols onto the ground acting as a Rifleman, rather than a Commander, just to give the soldiers a bit of downtime.

When the Company first deployed, he was a bit of an unknown entity to the majority of the men, and it took them a while to get used to his very dry sense of humour, especially his fellow officers. A few of them came up to me to question me on him, as they didn't know how to take him!

Personally I couldn't have asked for a better Commander, he let me get on with my job, trusting my judgement. He was the consummate professional, and expected others to strive to attain the same levels as him, although he was understanding of those who didn't achieve this.'

Major Alex Corbet Burcher took over from Sean as Company Commander and said:

'I think Sean would be proud of the guys' achievements. It's what he would have expected us to have done. It makes us all feel better that some good has come from his sacrifice – something tangible for us and his family to see.'

Perhaps one day Sean's wife Jo and their son Charlie, who was sixteen months old at the time his father was killed, will be able to visit the school and see the good that came out of his death, but for the moment they have to face a future without him and must attempt to rebuild their lives.

Christopher King was a Coldstream Guardsman, attached to the Welsh Guards in Afghanistan, when he was killed by an undetected IED. In a move typical of his character, he volunteered to be the lead man in a foot patrol, clearing IEDs to make a route secure for military vehicles to pass through. He was twenty years old.

I arranged to meet his grandmother, Judy Mugliston at her home in Devon, a few miles from Christopher's village and the small churchyard where his gravestone can be seen from his family home. When Christopher was five and his brother six, they moved as a family from the Wirral in Merseyside to start a new life together in Devon. However, after two years their parents' marriage sadly broke up and Christopher's father David found himself bringing the boys up as a lone parent. This proved very difficult when he had to work full time as well, so when the boys were ten and twelve David's mother Judy joined him to help 'for a little while'. She ended up staying for ten years, even when David remarried. She became so much a part of the immediate family that she only moved to her own place just after Christopher had deployed to Afghanistan.

Christopher's father had suggested that I speak to Judy, as the one who was most involved in the boys' upbringing while he and his second wife Shelagh worked full-time as teachers. I knew I was going to meet someone very special: David had requested that the Elizabeth Cross, which is awarded to the serviceman or -woman's next of kin after their death and therefore, by default, to David himself, was awarded to Judy instead. David said his mother had

'*shown a degree of love and caring for my sons that could not have been equalled. In every important sense, she was their mum and they viewed her as such. Without her influence and dedication Christopher would not have had such a full and happy life and would not have matured into the man we all became so proud of.*'

David's request was granted and it was one of the proudest days of Judy's life. The Elizabeth Cross was presented at the National Memorial Arboretum, the UK's Centre of Remembrance, in Staffordshire by the Duke of Edinburgh. The presentation was part of a service of dedication for a new Guards' Memorial at the Arboretum.

Judy welcomed me warmly into her home and I shared a sofa with her retired greyhound, who gazed at me as Judy told the King family's story:

'*I hope I did well as a grandma. I realise I had a really special time as a grandparent. I was the lucky one, hard work though that may have been. I had the advantage of having teenagers before with my own four children, and I am glad I had a chance to do it all again. When you pitch into a situation, you just roll your sleeves up and get on with it. When Michael was married just*

after Christopher joined the Army I was put on the top table at the
reception and Mike mentioned me in his speech. He said "Chris
and I wouldn't be the fellas we are today without Nan." I realised
then how lucky I was to have them.'

Judy talked about Christopher as a child, saying he was a

'come day, go day, young chap. He would rather build a den or
a go-kart, and keep worms in a matchbox than get on with his
homework. He was always outdoors fishing, or camping in the
garden. He joined the Army Cadets for two years where his shooting skills were noticed. He then left school at sixteen to become an
assistant gamekeeper for two years. Ray Mears' programmes on
TV greatly influenced him.

   He found the Army training hard as he wasn't a natural athlete
but he stuck it out and was totally committed to it. When he passed
out as a Coldstream Guardsman it was a defining moment for
Christopher; he was proud of his uniform and what it stood for, his
Regiment and the history behind it. He was applauded, admired
and liked and above all he was proud of making us proud of him.'

In 2009 Christopher volunteered, along with a few other
Coldstream Guardsmen, to make up numbers for the Welsh
Guards in Afghanistan, even though his own Regiment would
anyway be following on from them after a few months.

'He soon settled in and became well liked amongst the
Welsh Guards,' said Judy; 'he had the ability to crack a joke
with a deadpan face; it was the Scouser sense of humour in
him. He was known for it wherever he went.'

He was reputed for his improvisational skills: making tables
and chairs and finding wild game to add to the rations. He had
passed the Sharpshooters' course prior to deployment and
was recommended to advance to the Snipers' course upon his
return. Of course, this never happened.

Judy told me that the support she has had, both from the Coldstream and the Welsh Guards, since Christopher's death has been overwhelming. She said she feels as though she has been 'wrapped up in a big blanket', from the moment Christopher's body was brought into RAF Lyneham, to organising the military funeral and beyond. The funeral was a very big event for Christopher's village, which was closed to through traffic on the day. A holly tree was chopped down to make a space for his grave, which is, fittingly, next to the war memorial.

Christopher's brother Michael spoke to me about his memories of Christopher. He was very philosophical about his brother's death. He strongly believes that, though cut short, his life was lived to the full, and that it was quality, not quantity, that mattered:

'On the back of his Army training notes, Christopher had written: "live each day as if the last". It was almost as though he knew he was going to die, but he wasn't afraid of this and he was always able to put a positive spin on a negative situation.

Before Christopher joined the Army he was a rebellious teenager. He died a very able and responsible man.'

Michael tells of the love of rock climbing and the outdoors that Christopher shared with him, and with his father David and uncle Jim. One of his first memories of climbing was when David and his uncle took him and Christopher up Tryfan in Snowdonia (where Richard had proposed to me a few years earlier). Christopher was about ten years old at the time and while on the summit they saw a Brocken Spectre. Also known as a Brocken Bow or Mountain Spectre, this is a magnified shadow of someone standing on a mountain. It appears when the sun shines from behind the climber who is looking down from a ridge or peak into mist, fog or clouds. The 'ghost' or spectre can appear to move because of the movement of the cloud layer and its 'head' is often surrounded by a glowing halo like a ring of rainbow-coloured light, called a 'glory'.

This was the only time that Christopher had seen a Brocken Spectre, although he had climbed many mountains. David had seen one again while climbing in Spain just before Christopher deployed to Afghanistan, and after Christopher was killed David returned with Michael and Jim to the same peak in Spain to climb in Christopher's memory. As they were all acknowledging his life and spending a few moments of silence remembering him, another Brocken Spectre appeared on the clouds below. As Michael reflected:

> '*It was a moment that will stay with me for ever; it was as if Christopher had appeared amongst us, where he would have been had he been alive. It was so significant for us on that day; something special we will never forget.*'

Perhaps Christopher's family understood why he wanted to join the Army because they shared his love of climbing and the outdoors. There are similarities between the climber's mentality and that of the soldier. They both have a strong bond with the friends who share their risky, sometimes life-threatening, situations and the camaraderie that comes from this may be lifelong. They also thrive on living 'in the moment', when they have to focus one hundred per cent on the task in hand, switching off to all distractions until the job is complete. Michael, though not a soldier himself, certainly understands this, and rather than asking himself why Christopher joined up, he has nothing but pride and praise for his brother and what he did for his friends and his country.

The shock wave that spread on hearing the news of each death during those dreadful six months showed in the eyes of all the families at each of the funerals. It was as though every wife, girlfriend and parent was waiting in a queue to receive their ration of bad news, not knowing when they would reach the front and hoping that they could slip to the back.

In her journal after hearing of Rupert's death, Stacey Merritt-Webb wrote:

'Another death, when will this end? When I receive the text to say that the families have been informed of a death I feel relief as I know it's not Darren but someone somewhere has just lost a husband/daddy/brother. I feel so bad for them …

Could not sleep at all, don't know what's come over me last night, just sat in bed rocking, hugging Darren's t-shirt and smelling it, crying uncontrollably – I've got it into my head he is not coming back.

… saw Sally today, I didn't know what to say, I tried to act as normal as I could, I'm now reliving the conversation hoping I didn't come across as too chirpy but I didn't want it to be depressing, for her sake as much as mine. It was a lovely conversation considering, we talked about the kids and the other wives, I obviously asked after her and if she is OK – maybe I could have asked more, oh I don't know. I feel so sad for her, but so relieved it's not Darren – how awful is that!'

These mixed feelings are typical of all those families who suffered that summer but whose loved ones didn't, thankfully, pay the ultimate price. They continue to endure the anguish of supporting their husbands, sons, brothers and fathers, in the knowledge that the Battalion is due to return to Afghanistan in 2012. For the bereaved, of course, the worst has already happened. Writing about the lives of these wonderful men and their grieving families was heartbreaking; so often I would strain to see through my tears and would have to leave the computer and clear my head. Living in the country has luckily meant that I was able to take our dog for a walk on occasions like these, hoping I would not meet anybody en route while I wandered along in a blur, my mind numb but at the same time spinning with life's injustice and tragedy. I would remind myself that my sadness has been nothing compared to that of the bereaved, who have been on a rollercoaster of emotions since the day they received the knock on their door and the devastating news that would change their lives.

At times like these I would also reread the poem 'If Only', which I wrote after returning from Oman, not long after my mother died. It helped me to come to terms with her death, to see the situation in black and white, rather than in so many shades of grey. Sometimes there are too many 'what ifs' and 'if onlys'. We are in danger of constantly looking back rather than forward, as if we could undo what is done by sheer willpower.

One thing I learned from living in an Arab country was an appreciation of their often fatalistic attitude. To our minds in the West, geared to problem solving, this fatalism could perhaps be confused with apathy or an acceptance of a situation when it seemed that something could in fact be done to change it. I became convinced, though, that this approach helps them to cope with death, which, after all, is still very much a part of their everyday lives.

In Oman as recently as the 1980s, infant mortality was still very high in some of the outlying villages and large families were produced in the hope that at least some would survive. Although it has improved, the commonplace deaths from curable diseases or malnutrition are still very much in living memory for many Omanis. Although every death is mourned by those left behind, the Arabs believe fundamentally in 'Allah's will', just as many Christians believe in God's will, and that will is final, whatever the reasons why. This fatalistic approach seemed to me to provide them with the crutch they needed to carry on, and I admired their way of coping. Their outlook on life, and death, helped me to accept my own mother's death and prompted me to write the poem. For me, rereading it after the deaths in the Battalion was, once again, strangely cathartic.

'If Only'

'If only' is irrelevant
When things weren't meant to be.
'If only' surely racks the soul
Consumed by misery.

If only we could change the past;
One more day, one more chance.
If only we could start afresh.
If only, not so lonely.

When our hand runs out we leave the stage,
We draw the final curtain.
Though mortal hearts stay in a game
Predestined but uncertain.

And when life's circle comes around
It leaves a rich bequest;
A spirit to live in each of us,
The courage to try our best.

These fragile hearts must then be strong
To curb 'if only's' chance.
Let cherished warmth and love live on
And so our lives enhance.

'If only' is irrelevant;
Some things were meant to be.
Eternal life, peace at last.
If only we could see.

9

What the Men Say

Even after times of great crisis like the summer of 2009, life has to go on. The death of colleagues and friends obviously has a devastating effect on the men of the Battalion as well as the families, and everyone has had to learn how to pull forward. I wanted to write this book to take a look at the Army from the families' points of view, to tell the story of those left behind, but those stories would not be complete without some comments from their husbands and boyfriends. What do the men say about their lives, how do their lifestyles work together with their relationships, and how do they see their future? I talked to recent recruits as well as the men whose wives and girlfriends are already represented in the book, some of whom have served twenty-two years.

What I discovered was a huge appreciation of the support from home, which the men were only too happy to express. Coming from a traditionally British 'stiff upper lip', no-nonsense establishment like the Army, I found this a refreshing and welcome revelation. Many men spoke very movingly about their relationships with their partners and how their perspectives have changed after having been on operational deployments. They talked openly of love and commitment and the importance of good communication. They told me how they cope with the homecomings. I was particularly interested to hear from two men whose partners are also serving, about how they cope with a double Army lifestyle.

When I visited four young Welsh Guardsmen at Lille Barracks in Aldershot, I asked them to compare their hopes and aspirations on joining the Army, to their thoughts once they had experienced an operational tour. How and why had their perspectives changed following their time in real combat in Afghanistan in 2009? Over cups of tea and coffee they were happy to talk to me about how they have been affected and their plans for the future.

The ages of the men I talked to ranged from twenty to twenty-three and the youngest, Guardsman (Gdsm) Daryl Hughes, was only seventeen when he joined the Army and eighteen when he went to Afghanistan:

'Ever since I was a kid I always wanted to be in the Army. I wanted to travel the world, meet new friends, further my education and get my driving licence. I was fresh out of school when I joined, so I struggled at Catterick [the training depot in Yorkshire for all Guardsmen]. *It was so far away from home in South Wales.*

My family was very upset about me going to Afghan but they sort of understood that I wanted to go and do my part. My farewell was like having my own funeral party before I'd even died and not many people expected to see me back. It was hard for them because I'd never really been away from them before.

When I went to Afghan a lot of us never thought we'd get it as bad as we did, ever. It was one of the worst things I've ever done. I had to grow up so quickly. I was the youngest in my Company. The boys were like fathers and brothers; you wouldn't believe you could have friends like that. Then you would start to lose friends and the panic would set in. We lost our Commanding Officer and then I lost my best friend, Chris King. I cried a lot when people were dying.

In my first contact [firefight] *I thought I was going to die; I didn't know what to expect. You would hear the bullets whistling* past and I started praying to God to get me out of it alive. I was praying for my life, and I'm not a religious person.

But we had to cheer ourselves up when we could. We made a "swimming pool" in a section of river and played rugby in the evenings. We even had our own "Squaddies got Talent" competition. After going without mail for seven weeks we had to raise morale somehow.

When I went home for R and R I couldn't relax. I wished I'd stayed in Afghan. I watched the news all the time in case anything had happened to our boys. When we came home at the end of the tour I went to sit on the beach for two hours before returning to my family; I was scared to see them.'

Gdsm Chris Davies is twenty years old and joined the Army at seventeen. When in North Wales he lives with his aunt, uncle and three cousins:

'I joined the Army for a varied, exciting life with a physical aspect and to get all my driving licences and medical training qualifications. The tour to Afghan put a totally different perspective on how I see life and the things I take for granted on a daily basis.'

Chris was in Lashkar Gah with Major Sean Birchall's Company, working on the school project. He was clearing the roads of IEDs when Sean was killed, and gave Jamie Evans first aid after the incident. He spoke of the local Afghan people:

'It was terrifying at first, being surrounded by so many locals. You didn't trust any of them to begin with. We gave the children footballs and boiled sweets and they were like scavengers, all fighting over them.'

Gdsm Jon Caswell, from Coventry, is twenty-three. When I asked him why at the age of twenty he decided to join the Army, he said he wanted to follow in his granddad's footsteps:

'*Before you join you hear exaggerated stories about how excit-ing it is. There were people who inspired me, but you have to take the stories with a pinch of salt. What you don't hear are the stories about the lads who cry in their pit* [bed] *for days after shooting someone. We tell the new recruits coming in now how bad it was. They sit there, wide eyed, soaking it up, and they still want to go.*

My family was very proud overall but some of them thought I was a bit daft. The tour was very emotional and trying. We were in the main Battlegroup so we had it real bad. When I came home for R and R I was in Birmingham in my desert combats. Everyone stared and as I was on my own without a rifle or helmet; I felt very threatened.'

Jon was in the same platoon as Guardsman Luke Langley. Turning to Luke, Jon said:

'*Luke was my right-hand man. We shared a bed space and went on every patrol together. We dragged each other through a lot of stuff; the emotional side of things was shocking. I wasn't out there to be a hero; I was out there to get home safe. We were fighting for the man next to us; simple as that. We were brothers in arms, a massive family, and made bonds that will never be broken.*'

Luke, twenty-one, comes from Anglesey in North Wales. He joined the Army at seventeen as there was very little work for young men locally, plus he wanted some money, a career and to fight for his country. He plans to stay in the Army and will be deployed to Afghanistan with the Battalion in 2012:

'*In some ways I want to get out of the Army but it would be hard to find a job, so I'm staying. My mother and brothers found it very difficult to cope while I was away but they know I'll just get on with it; I'll know how to conduct myself when I've done it before. First time round you don't know if you're going to freeze up, cry or go nuts and spray bullets everywhere but I will be better prepared next time and my senses will be honed.'*

Daryl, too, has decided to stay in:

'I won't be leaving; I'll go back out and crack on. I'll still have the thoughts that others have been before and survived again, but others die on their first time, but I'll be better prepared.

I wouldn't mind doing some ceremonial duties either; I haven't done any yet. I want to have done Afghan and Trooping the Colour, for the honour of standing outside Buckingham Palace; there's no need to be a Guardsman if you don't do the Guards' duties.'

Chris will be leaving, however. His family and girlfriend live three hundred and fifty miles away and he has had enough of being a 'part-time boyfriend':

'Every weekend I share the journey to North Wales. It's not worth it. There were three of us from the same town who went to Afghan. We all grew up together. Our families don't want us to do it again; they were very proud of us but scared at the same time. One of the main reasons for getting out is the families; it is very hard for them and it is hard on my girlfriend. Everything I wanted to do in the Army I've done now. I don't need to do it again.'

Jon is considering leaving for family reasons. He is married with two children and he said that missing the birth of his second child while he was in Afghanistan was a 'kick in the teeth':

'There are lots of parameters. If it was financially worth it, or if I could stay in Camp Bastion for twelve months and not go out to FOBs I'd definitely stay in. I was short-toured from Afghan with PTSD after four and a half months; I had a panic attack while on sentry and was casevaced to Bastion. I didn't care about anyone

and had treatment for five months. I am cautious about having to go through that a second time. I may go back to Coventry and drive a van; happy days.'

It was a life-changing experience for these Guardsmen to experience real combat at such a young age, but by no means unprecedented. My great-grandfather was in his early twenties when he joined the Royal Horse Artillery, and went straight off to fight in the First World War as a shoeing smith. He saw action on the Western Front at Passchendaele from 1915 to 1918. While lying in a communication trench playing cards with a gun team of soldiers in a 'quiet moment', they ran out of cigarettes. My great-grandfather volunteered to crawl to the next group of men about fifty yards away to borrow cigarettes off them, but as he did so a mortar attack struck. Both gun teams were completely wiped out, leaving him, alive, in between the two. The experience affected him for the rest of his life but my family never heard him talk about it until one Christmas when he was eighty years old. There had just been a war film on the television and when it was over we decided to have a game of cards. He did not want to join in, and when we turned on the lights, we saw that he was in silent floods of tears. The story came out for the first time: 'and that's why I have never played cards since,' he said. 'Until you have to shoot your own horses and see your mates blown up you wouldn't understand.' He had felt forever guilty that he did not die with his friends that day, but it had simply never been discussed, which seems unbelievable in today's much more open society.

I was pleased that the Guardsmen I met in Aldershot did feel that they could discuss their experiences. No matter what decisions they make about the future, at least they have the ability, and the opportunity, to vent their feelings. These Guardsmen had been fighting in Afghanistan alongside Falklands veterans who had been sent out there, twenty seven years earlier, when they were a similar age. Many Falklands veterans never talked about their experiences at all, although others have spoken out for the purpose of this book. Many left the Army after the conflict; others stayed on; but they all dealt with it in their own private ways.

Richard, unlike the young Guardsmen, did not have exposure to an operational tour immediately after joining the Army. Opportunities are very much in the hands of fate and the political climate for those in the Army, and it is impossible to engineer one's career to always be in the right place at the right time. Richard joined the Army at the age of nineteen because he wanted adventure, travel, a challenge, the chance for leadership and to see some active service. The Army offered him all this and for the next nine years he had only himself to please. With few personal responsibilities and a disposable income, life as a single soldier could be lived for the moment. When a serious relationship, marriage and responsibility for a family came into the equation though, his outlook and considerations inevitably had to change. His experiences, though, have still been varied and challenging:

'For most of us an operational tour is something to be looked forward to, to be able to put into practice the job that we have trained to do. That does not mean that we are all bloodthirsty individuals who are looking for a fight but it does mean that we have trained in a certain way and, if there is a job that the government wants us to do then we are the people who are trained to do it. Not going on an operational tour is a bit like training to be a plumber and then never seeing a pipe.

It is at this juncture that a married man, or someone in a long-term partnership, becomes very torn between the professional who wants to get on with the job and the family man who wants to stay *at home and look after his wife/partner and children, rather than leave them to fend for themselves. We don't want to miss birthdays, anniversaries and children growing up, perhaps even the birth of a child, their first steps and other significant events.*

There are a number of emotions that we go through on a deployment but uppermost is the feeling of guilt at leaving the family at home. Will my wife and family know how to deal with all the jobs that I normally do, be that admin or repair jobs? Battling with banks and insurance companies is always a nightmare if the husband is the first named in a joint account or first named on the policy. Through endless battles such as these Fiona and I have learnt to cope the hard way, and there is always a new challenge every time I go away.

Our wives cope fantastically with all the stresses and strains of us being away. Fiona was likened to a single parent by one teacher; there are similarities of course but this comparison does not take into account the additional pressure of someone they love being in harm's way and the risk of death or serious injury.

I often feel that the wives go through far more than we do when we are away. We tend to know when we are in danger and equally we know when the risks are less and so can relax to a degree. The same cannot be said for our wives who do not know when we really are in the firing line and when we may not be.

The phone calls home are often the best, and the worst times. How much admin can one get into a phone call, on top of the sensitive conversations about dying grandparents and dying pets. Phone calls are also times to talk of love, mundane matters, chat to the children and just catch up with life at home. The timing of calls is out of our control; either there is an emergency at our end, or we catch the family at a bad time. I vividly remember one phone call when Fiona and I were chatting and catching up when there was a huge explosion just outside my camp in downtown Basra [in Iraq]. I don't think Fiona heard the explosion but in as nonchalant a way as I could I had to sign off rapidly and head off to do my job all without trying to cause alarm at home. There are plenty of such examples which are often made far worse when the wife has heard the explosion or shooting at the other end of the phone call. It is often not possible to phone back to let home know that all is well for days; the family have to live with the doubt when we just get on with the job.

There are some interesting and difficult decisions to make when we go away on an operational tour. Obviously none of us want to die when we are away but we do want to make sure that our families are catered for in the best way possible should the worst happen. Some husbands chose to write a letter to their wife and children to be opened in the event of death. I chose not to do so because I don't want Fiona and the children to cling to a single piece of paper to represent a lifetime together; I feel that the best memories are in one's head and that they are not best represented by a couple of sides of paper.

On return from operations there is often the worry that we have become surplus to requirement, no longer needed to do repairs, do the gardening or sort the car out. How will the family have changed, how will we have changed given what we may have been through?

So with all these concerns why do we join the Army in the first place? Most of us join as young men looking for adventure, excitement, challenge and responsibility at a young age. We also know that when we join we hand in a blank cheque for our lives; we obviously hope that it is never cashed in but we know that it is there and we have signed it. We know that there is no such thing as a risk-free war, a casualty-free war or a fatality-free war. We are not victims; we have joined to do a job and we are trained very well for it. When we get married or enter into a long-term partnership we have to make a joint decision on that blank cheque. Does our wife really understand what it means? Do we know what it *means for the family? We write the cheque but it is the family in the end who pays the bill.*

To stay in the Army as a couple requires a very special sort of wife. The decision to stay has to be a joint decision. Fiona has been amazingly supportive and has been through so much over the years. I don't think I always realise how hard it is for her and the children. It takes a very special sort of person to support the family and our strange way of life; to live with the unknown, never knowing where we will be living in twelve months time, to get on with a normal life in the face of an abnormal job, turning a quarter into a home, to give a stable home to the children in a nomadic existence. Amongst all this turmoil Fiona has been my rock throughout.

Fiona has been there whenever I have needed her; to share those private thoughts and worries away from the gaze of others; to lend a listening ear and to give common sense advice and ideas. She is there when it matters, not just for me and Oliver and Annabel but also for the wives, mothers and girlfriends of others in the Battalion. We are all in it together and in the face of adversity very close bonds are formed.

Winston Churchill said we make a living by what we get, but we make a life by what we give. While we, the soldiers, make a life by serving Queen and country it is our wives, supporting us as they do, who make our lives by giving so much to us.'

Tom Spencer-Smith suffered an injury on his second deployment to Afghanistan. He and I discussed the expectations that he and Pari had had at the start of their relationship. Now married, and after two operational tours to Afghanistan, have these expectations changed?:

'Before we were a couple I asked Pari's opinion about going to Sandhurst. She was sceptical and didn't really think it was for me. After we started dating and subsequently got engaged, Pari knew the caveats that came with the job. However her support

changes over time and as my career goes in cycles I am sure it waxes and wanes with the pressures we face. I know for example that she really enjoyed the time we spent in London and thought the ceremonial aspect of what we do is a lot of fun, and when my first Afghanistan tour came up in 2007 I felt that she supported me one hundred per cent. I have no doubt she was apprehensive but I do not think the publicity machine for Afghanistan had quite reached the level it is today, so the decision to support me in what I was doing was probably an easier one.

After I got injured I knew that I still wanted to remain in this job. The sacrifices we make as a family are hard, but equally they can be rewarding. Looking at friends of my parents who were in the Army and have ended up achieving all they set out to do and are on the cusp of retirement, I think that those sacrifices are worthwhile and we have to make them together.

In the build-up to the Welsh Guards' next operational tour in 2012 I imagine there will be a lot of apprehension about going back out. The last tour has shown that it doesn't matter who you are, there is potential for something to go wrong. I believe that this experience has made Pari and me more aware of each other's strengths and weaknesses though, and I am now much more aware of what Pari goes through while I am away.

There's no doubt that if we continue to go back to Afghanistan then you enter into a numbers game. At Headley Court there were four soldiers I knew who had also served in Afghanistan in 2007. Every one of us had been injured on our second tour, and the chances of getting injured or killed can only get greater the more times you return.

In full knowledge of this and in maybe a rather blasé way I assume Pari will support me as I continue in my career, but ultimately this is the career I have chosen and for the meantime Pari does support me. Until that changes then we continue to manage the strain by supporting each other.'

In recent years the British Army has been deployed more often, and for longer lengths of tour, so this has become much more of a limiting factor in many relationships. Martyn Miles looks back on twenty-nine years of marriage and the way expectations of Army life have changed over time. Luckily, his marriage was strong enough to cope with the changes:

> *'When Sue and I were first married in the 80s the British Army was not really involved in any conflicts as we are today, other than in Northern Ireland. Apart from the two-year accompanied postings to Northern Ireland, the shorter unaccompanied tours were four months, not six. These only came up every two and a half years so I didn't really think about the separation side of things. We went on other tours to places such as Kenya, Canada and Belize, to name but a few, but these were exercises, not conflicts. Then I went to the Falklands and after that things started to get serious in the Balkans.*
>
> *A soldier entering the Army today knows that he will be on tours of duty more often so will at least be more prepared for separations. Until you experience Army life together you don't really know how it will be, but luckily Sue is a strong character and we have built up a relationship based on love.'*

A solid foundation based on love; it keeps cropping up in the conversations I've had. Alun Bowen reinforces this view:

> *'Married life in the Army is based upon so many factors but if you boil it down to basics it becomes crystal clear, I believe. Do you want to be together? If one answers in the affirmative, which we always have from the day we started out all those years ago, then you make an unwritten and probably unstated pledge that being together is <u>the</u> most important factor. We don't labour the thought, it is just there, all the time, like a comfort blanket as we looked towards the future and nothing has changed to this day in that respect.*

Honesty, loyalty and without any question whatsoever the ability for me to compromise, is absolute. If Michelle says we are going on holiday I simply agree and ask to whom I write the cheque. If she says the house needs a clean I throw on my pinafore. If the grass needs cutting I simply say how short? I do, however, draw the line at shopping, which in my small world serves no purpose whatsoever unless it is going to result in a good meal. The ability to compromise here is also supremely important so I do shop, once a year at Christmas!

Army life so far has allowed us to remain as a solid unit which has been largely based upon Michelle's ability to work almost independently, rarely having to rely on me with the exception of the obvious childcare balances. This, I am sure, has been a major factor on our ability to laugh our way through twenty plus years together. We often say we would have served less "time" for murder. We are completely in love of course but do not wear our love on our sleeves or make a big deal of it. What you see with us is what you get, old cliché but so true. We simply enjoy each other's company as soulmates and to have had the kids later on has allowed us to "bed in and dig a good trench with sound foundations".'

The importance of effective communication, in particular receiving letters, is also mentioned frequently. Letters are often more gratefully received than emails or phone calls, and if the system allows, the printed-out emails known as e-blueys are also popular, no doubt at least partly because the recipient can take them away and keep them on his or her person. Andrew Speed told me his thoughts on leaving Alannah when he was deployed to Afghanistan in 2009, and the joy in receiving news:

'I deployed on operations to Afghanistan comfortable in the knowledge that I had a girlfriend who would support me through all the challenges ahead. Alannah has always been one to raise

matters of the heart whereas I am the average Army Officer that spends his life avoiding such conversations. We found ourselves in Oxford on a weekend away. Alannah had gone into one of her silent moments (this is obvious as she normally talks as if she has a word limit that she needs to hit each day). Over a rather dodgy Chinese dish we discussed how our relationship was going to proceed as I was going away for six months. I think in my rather ham-fisted way I explained that I was very serious about "us" and that we should certainly stay together as there was, in my mind, a great future ahead on my return. I think this satisfied her as she started talking again.

In my mind the "goodbye" worked very well. Tears normally disarm men and I am no different. So a short wait for a train and then a quick goodbye with no tears was perfect. I know Alannah was worried about me but I appreciated her fortitude as it showed to me that she was going to be strong throughout my time away.

During the easy times of the tour, support from home mani-fested itself in parcels and letters. The simple memories of home can bring great pleasure when stuck in forty degrees. Alannah would send pictures via the e-bluey system. So around my desk I had pictures of summer lunches; my dog Scrumpy chasing balls; my parents home in the sun; and ones of Alannah taken in that awkward way where you hold the camera at arm's length. She would send me things that made me laugh (a tennis ball that Scrumpy had chewed to bits). She would send food parcels full of my favourite things. And of course, many letters ranging from the frivolous to the serious. The serious ones came in the wake of casualties; they came when I was not selected for promotion. I remember being very nearly moved to tears as one arrived while I was waiting for the repatriation of Lieutenant Colonel Rupert Thorneloe. It was full of support and despite the vagaries of the postal system, perfectly timed just when support was needed.

The bond that kept all the girls together in the UK had a far-reaching effect in Afghanistan. We would distract ourselves from the rigours of the day by discussing what the girls had been up to. A particularly nice touch was a photo from three of the girls having dinner together. Each one was holding a napkin that said "We" "Miss" "You". This kept us amused for days.

Operational tours are, in many ways, harder for the girls than the boys. We have a very clear focus and, to a certain degree, we are masters of our own destiny. We can relax in the knowledge that the girls are safe at home. They, on the other hand, have tenuous communications to men who could be in danger. They cannot call when they feel upset or concerned. They just have to wait hoping that the call will get through and that the man on the other end is not too distracted to have a normal conversation. That waiting must be hellish.

Personally, I think the whole tour made my relationship with Alannah much stronger. Her support and love made a difficult tour less difficult. Life throws up all sorts of challenges and being away on an operational tour probably rates up there with the most difficult. So any couple that comes out of the other side still smiling, laughing and together is going to have a bright future.'

I found it fascinating to talk to men whose partners are also in the Forces about their experience of family life. Perhaps, having had both experiences, they are even more aware of the demands that Army life has on a relationship. Lee Hazard, a serving Naval Officer, talked very honestly about how he dealt with being the one at home when his wife Sarah deployed to Bosnia:

'When you hear in passing that someone's partner is deployed on operations, the natural assumption is that the husband is doing his duty whilst the devoted wife remains at home. I have experienced both sides of the coin, being both the one deployed and the one at home.

I first met Sarah when she was doing her new entry officer training as a Medical Officer in the Royal Army Medical Corps. We were married two years later and were incredibly lucky to be in the same country for just over a year before Sarah was posted to the Welsh Guards. Then, in the summer of 2006, she embarked on her first operational tour to Bosnia with a predominantly male regiment.

Thomas Haynes Bayly wrote that "absence makes the heart grow fonder" but I could never appreciate the pain that a "fonder heart" could cause with absence. It is not all gloom though and the art of handwritten letters brings the excitement of reading the innermost thoughts of your partner. Receiving mail really is one of the greatest morale boosts.

Sarah was deployed to Bosnia at the same time as I was deployed to West Africa. Email and telephone calls were exceedingly difficult. We rarely spoke in three months, and only got sporadic mail drops.

The loneliness of deployment could only be surpassed by the loneliness of the homecoming whilst having a wife away. While you're on operations you at least share the hollowness with your colleagues, but at home an empty house makes it so hard to stay strong. The paranoia about missing a phone call prevented me from distracting myself with a busy social life so all of my energy was pushed into work. Many non-military friends thought that if one of us was away, we were both away, so in any case my invitations got sparser.

I am sure women are better at coping with the fluctuation of emotions that love brings. As a man and a serving officer I felt more nervous about my wife's homecoming on mid-tour leave than I have on any operational event I can think of. Despite the hours of trying to choreograph the perfect first meeting after so many months apart, it's almost impossible to live up to the expectations of a Hollywood love scene. I was also very conscious of this being Sarah's first deployment and the emotional changes that occur on tour.

I was unprepared for the change in our relationship that had occurred since Sarah had deployed. This in part was due to the independence and barriers that had to be adopted in her environment. No matter what anyone says, you can never fully shake doubts from your mind. The two weeks were tense, as we both tip-toed around our innermost thoughts, each not wanting to say what they felt in case the response was negative. As the leave period came to an end and the sadness of further separation loomed, both our tempers flared. It is only when you care so much for someone that you fear their loss and as I said goodbye to Sarah I hoped that the relationship would survive until the end of tour. It is only now that we both appreciate that our relationship has strengthened as we have grown closer and have a far deeper understanding of each other.

That final three months was the hardest of my life. I retreated further into myself, spending Christmas alone and not wanting to be the spare part at others' family festivities. Much was resolved in the last three months, our letters to each other even more meaningful as we made promises and shared dreams and our commitment to each other strengthened.

Thomas Haynes Bayly may have been right, but I never wish to test the theory again.'

Mark Pollard, too, found the separation from his wife, Ina, very hard. Perhaps the fundamental male instinct to be the protector was the limiting factor for him and Lee. Being at home while their wives were away and in dangerous situations was a role reversal that many men would find unbearable, especially when they know the dangers themselves. One could argue that these men were safer in the knowledge that their wives were fully trained to deal with combat situations, and that there was no fear of the unknown for them back at home as they were familiar with these same situations themselves. In reality though, this did not actually make it any easier. Mark describes his experience of the separation from Ina during the first year of their marriage; both he and Ina were desperate to make a start to their married life but knew that it must be put on hold for another six months before Ina returned from her tour:

'*As I was getting ready to go home from deployment I watched everyone packing their bags with big smiles on their faces for in a couple of days they would be with their wives and family. My wife, however, was getting focused and ready to deploy herself.*

The short time we had together in between my return and her departure was like a whirlwind of emotions: pleased to see each other but in the next breath saddened to see each other go again. It felt like my world had been given and taken away within the space of two weeks.

The time came to say goodbye; I drove Ina to the airport and it was a very painful and emotional time bearing in mind I had experienced first-hand what my wife was about to experience.

I have never felt such overwhelming emotions take over. After she'd left I could not drive so I parked in a lay-by for half an hour and wept like a four-year-old boy. I then sat there staring into space until I felt I could drive back to an empty house.

I wanted to keep my six months as busy as possible; I have a large family as well as a large family of Welsh Guards friends so I planned on visiting them to keep myself occupied. At home, I gave myself a routine of work, gym, food, TV, sleep – pity the food was mainly Pot Noodle or beans on toast. I had two cats to keep me company, not a substitute but a small token.

But I could not help but watch the news all the time. I was still at work for the first two weeks of Ina's deployment so she could ring me daily on the military line; a small bonus for the time we are apart. I emailed her daily, wrote twice a week and sent parcels weekly. I knew what she would be missing so I sent what I would have liked myself.

After two weeks I was on my own, without the military line. My post-operational tour leave was to last for four weeks. As planned I visited everyone I knew; I spent a weekend in Yorkshire with my best friend and as it was Remembrance Sunday we attended a service in uniform.

I spent a lot of time with my eldest brother who is a house-husband, a weekend with another good friend. I finally found that my friends were true friends who insisted I could stay without asking. They knew I was going through an emotional roller coaster of missing Ina.

Nothing prepares you for a year away from your wife. It saddened me when I was watching boring reality shows such as Big Brother *and* I'm a Celebrity ... Get Me Out of Here! *hearing them say they are missing their wife or family after a week. Try doing it for a year.*

After a slow month passed it was not getting any easier but thankfully not any worse. Another month later Ina was due home on her R and R so I had time to plan the best Christmas she has ever had; we both deserved it.

I planned a hotel in the country so we could find each other once again. I knew it needed to be quiet, secluded and just me and her. Christmas came slowly and my strategic, military, precision, operational sequence of events was now on. Ina got dropped off by military transport and I planned every little detail including getting my mother round to the house to give it the woman's touch.

It was great seeing Ina. We spent most of it away but in hindsight we should have spent more time at home in our own comfortable surroundings. Still, every morning we woke up together, but it was another day closer to her return to Afghanistan.

When the time came to drive her to the airport I was determined not to show the same emotion as I showed when she first left. I dropped her off and put my bravest face on. I was once again gutted and felt very empty. My life, my wife had been taken away from me, again. I drove home sick to the stomach and began another two months without her.

It was just as hard this time as before but, I had already completed nine months of the twelve-month hell. The worst feeling that you have having both being deployed on operations is that you know how your next of kin gets informed if there is injury or death. How my heart raced: as we live in a cul-de-sac you see an unusual car or even military vehicle pull up or turn around in the close. I have seen a car pull up outside the house with two men in suits. My heart stopped as I watched the car turn around and pull off. Did they know what they had just done? People driving around military quarters should not slow down past houses; they do not know what heartache they cause.

All this emotional pain but not once did I blame the Army or the Welsh Guards; I was grateful as it was the Army that got us together in the first place.'

Nicky Mott very generously gave me his perspective on a long and happy marriage, which has stood the test of time while coinciding with his Army career; he has been married to Karen for twenty-three years:

'When Karen and I were posted to Germany in 1987 I don't recall having a master plan of how to ensure life was going to be better for us both, I just assumed it would be better than the life we would have if I left the Army and moved back home. To start a marriage, as many of us do, away from immediate family members is not easy for anyone, to throw on top of that the constant deployments on exercises or operations certainly takes a special person to hold the mantle and be a wife of a soldier. Karen says that you have

no alternative when married in the Army, but to get on with it, but I have no doubt I wouldn't be the rank I am today without the love, dedication and support I've received from Karen over the past twenty-three years. I'm sure this sentiment would be echoed by many married servicemen across the services.

When we first moved to Germany we were so excited and at the same time, very nervous and anxious about what lay ahead. In the early days of our married life it wasn't all plain sailing and as many other couples have experienced in the past, we were not well off, and were about to start making many decisions which in the past had been done for us by family members, or in my case by the chain of command within the barracks. Other wives on the patch were great to Karen when we moved into our first quarter, they knew what issues we would be facing and offered their support if required; we were becoming part of a new family overnight.

As a professional soldier, it's extremely comforting to know that the wives have friends and support from each other back on the patch when we are deployed on exercises or operational deployments. The young, newly married girl two doors down, living in a strange environment with less money and a young baby will be supported by the more experienced wives on the patch who will keep her motivated, dedicated to support her family and keep it on the right track for the future. As a result, the newly married guardsman away on operations knowing that his wife is supported will be able to do his job more successfully. The support of the wives to one another is like no friendships on "Civilian Street"; you won't find a complete street, estate or community anywhere in the UK which faces the same issues as Army wives do on a daily basis.

When looking at the wife of a soldier we must look at the whole package, and what she's expected to be. Not only does she run the house, bring up the children and be strong for them (most of the time without the assistance of their other half), sort the DIY and pay the bills, but she also plays the part of dad for lengthy periods of time which includes taking the children to sport, hobbies, parents evenings or liaising with teachers, bankers, insurance companies; the list is endless. Then on the return of her husband she should be glamorous and ready for the Mess functions and act as if everything is in hand and nothing of significance requires his attention, because she's aware he's got his job on his mind and will be off again in the near future. Many women would bail out at the first innings.

Our side is easier and we have the best part. I'm convinced that without the support of our wives back home the success of the Army and its achievements would be hindered.

I've been extremely fortunate to have had a great career, which has been, and still is, exciting, challenging, very rewarding and with plenty of variety. My children Nathan and Charlotte are both a credit and make me extremely proud of their achievements. None of this has been achieved without sacrifice and a lot of hard work. I have one person in my life to thank for making these achievements happen and that's Karen, my wife; she's been the backbone of this family for the past twenty-three years and continues to be to this day. Soldiers are extremely fortunate to have wives who are prepared to support them in the way that they do. If anyone deserves a medal, it's the wife of the soldier.'

It is important, of course, for both partners in any relationship to be appreciated, but I found it particularly moving to hear such genuine feeling from these men, which they offered up with no thought for the macho or emotionally buttoned-up image of the soldier. They have a deep love of their own families and also a profound loyalty to their Regimental family.

Many people may say that being a soldier is not for a married man, but there would be a serious shortfall of experience if soldiers were to leave as soon as they married. The outlook on his career may change, but to carry on doing the job he started, it ultimately always involves total support from a partner – and indeed the whole family, children as well – and a great deal of understanding and acceptance. Having children changes priorities in any marriage but the separations involved in Army life may cause some men to change to a more static career.

Our children were born into this lifestyle; they know no different. Maybe one day they will step back from it and wonder if they could repeat the cycle themselves. Maybe they will yearn for a more settled existence. Whatever they do, I hope they will reflect and realise that, despite the upheavals and the many goodbyes, they will also have learned from having to be adaptable, self-confident and loyal to friends both old and new.

One of my mother-in-law's sayings, that 'you have to work at a marriage', has proved very true, especially when Richard has been away. These times have been tough, but there has to be a metaphorical carrot at the end of the stick to see us through, and for us this has been the knowledge that the times we do have together are quality times. I can look forward to a homecoming with the reassurance that he has never taken me for granted and that he understands. This understanding, though, comes with time. I would not go as far as to say that the separations and upheavals in Army life get any easier, but knowing what to expect reduces the fear of the unknown that all new wives and partners must face. I am incredibly grateful that I have had so many wonderful years with Richard, and have the prospect of many more, unlike other family members who have been denied the joys, frustrations and quiet satisfactions that Richard and I and others such as Nicky and Karen Mott are so lucky to have experienced.

10

The Last Post

Gathering material for this book has been an extremely humbling experience for me; it has been an immense privilege to be the one to bring these special stories together. This is not my book, it belongs to those who have contributed to it: to the 1st Battalion Welsh Guards, to the servicemen and -women of the Army, Navy and Air Force and to all their families and friends. They each have their own stories, all similar to those I have told, every one just as life changing and significant as the next. Above all, they contribute, as one massive team, to the vital role of supporting and maintaining their country's Armed Forces.

I have shed so many tears while listening to these stories, with both old friends and new. Within a few minutes of meeting people they have revealed to me their darkest moments. I feel honoured to have been entrusted with the task of telling their stories sensitively, yet as openly as possible, according to their wishes. In putting their words on paper, I have relived their stories, so that at times I would strain to see the page through my own tears. I have been left feeling wrung out after writing the most emotional of passages.

But I have also heard fond memories, laughed together over happy times shared and marvelled at the quirks of tradition that make Army life the enigma that it is. I have been moved by the spontaneous acts of kindness and compassion that have so frequently come to the fore, the camaraderie and lifelong friendships created out of adversity and a shared hardship. Pride, nostalgia and reminiscence would then bring a lump to our throats again. Laughter and tears; so closely related. I seem to have written this book through a fog of emotion and have emerged feeling so grateful to have been the one who happened to put it together.

For most of the contributors in *Don't Say Goodbye* life carried on as 'normal' once the Battalion returned from Afghanistan in the autumn of 2009. Most of the families have readjusted to everyday life; some were separated again when their husbands went on exercise to the Falkland Islands for three months from June to August 2010. This might seem easy in comparison with deployment to Afghanistan, and in terms of danger of course it was; but for some wives, it was psychologically difficult to adjust to being separated again so soon. In November 2010 the Battalion started their pre-tour training and preparation for the next deployment to Afghanistan, planned for the spring of 2012, when the 'goodbyes' must start again.

Some of the wounded have recovered physically enough to the point where they can return to regular duties, while some are still receiving rehabilitation at Headley Court in Surrey, or in St Athan in the Vale of Glamorgan. Others may be slowly recovering from PTSD or may not yet have discovered that they are suffering from it, but with the development of treatment, awareness and acceptance of this condition, their future looks so much brighter than that of their predecessors. Military charities have provided an increasingly vital service since the start of the Iraq and Afghanistan wars, and there are now at least ten charities devoted to British servicemen and -women, including ones that help those with specific injuries and conditions such as PTSD, lost limbs or for those who have been blinded in action.

I visited the wounded men again, to find out about their progress one year after sustaining their injuries. Their positive attitude, eagerness to regain their active lives and absolute determination came through every time. Modern advances in prosthetics mean that there are varieties of legs and arms for different occasions: prosthetic limbs suitable for everyday walking, running or cycling; even the party pieces that are reserved for making children feel at ease and for going to fancy dress parties as Long John Silver. There is talk from some of the wounded about their aim to enter the next Paralympics: a second chance to channel their enthusiasm, energy and determination into something that will bring its own immense reward.

Many men and women who have been injured find hidden reserves of strength and motivation to recover that they did not realise they had. In addition, their families, friends and the Regiment invariably provide a backbone of support, from the moment when families receive the 'knock on the door' through to helping them decide which prosthetic leg or arm is the best for them. For servicemen and -women who have no family support, perhaps even no family, the Regiment becomes their surrogate family and provides the encouragement, support and care that they may never before have had. In the end, the extra support, whether from actual family or the Regimental family, becomes the 'wind beneath their wings' for these men and women.

Among the men I talked to there have been some happy outcomes and some sad ones; some couples have become engaged, some have walked down the aisle and there are at least five new babies. Some relationships have failed, the stresses too much for a couple to bear; some men have left the Battalion, having decided that they are no longer prepared to miss out on seeing their children grow up. Above all, though, as with life in general, soldiers learn from their experiences, good and bad. They may have come away with a better understanding of another land and culture and the needs of its people, but having seen close friends killed or injured in action, they have also learned about themselves and their comrades. Their families, too, will have learned patience, and how to cope with the pain of worry and separation.

Geraint Hillard continued to have considerable complications and pain in his injured leg and made the decision in August 2010 to have a below-knee amputation. He hopes, and is determined, to do far more with a prosthetic leg than he would ever have done with the alternative, which would have been indefinite chronic pain and restricted movement. He and his girlfriend Jo realised just how strong their relationship had become after Geraint's injury.

Geraint took Jo to Paris on a Valentine's weekend, where they stayed in a hotel on the Champs Élysées and visited the Arc de Triomphe, Notre Dame and the Eiffel Tower. After this dose of romance, they had their first child, Taylor Jane, in November 2010. This is the start of a new life for Geraint and Jo as a couple and as a family, and although Geraint's career will be considerably affected, their relationship has been sealed by this turn of events.

Dale Leach separated from his fiancé Alex during the year following his injury. He does, however, see their baby, Mathew, at weekends. Eighteen months on he was still receiving therapy from Headley Court, but has adapted his lifestyle to accommodate his injuries. The ever-present, upbeat soldier's humour shows through in his choice of number plates for his new car: 'NO 10 LEG'.

Gareth Davies and Kayliegh also have a happy ending: when I rang Kayliegh she told me the news of their engagement. I was so pleased for them. It was another tear-in-the-eye moment, the fairytale ending to such a romantic beginning. From the night they met on Gareth's return to Treherbert their story has been one of support from Kayliegh, Gareth's family and his local community. Kayliegh updated me on the rest of his news:

> '*We plan to go to Mexico to get married; it is somewhere we have both always wanted to visit. And we are also expecting a baby in 2011. We are so excited about it and the news has helped Gareth focus on getting better more quickly.*'

Gareth is still receiving treatment for his arm at Selly Oak and there is a strong chance he will regain full movement in it. He was treated for PTSD successfully and has been discharged from counselling:

> '*I am so happy that Gareth has had the help he needs because he is a much happier person and he talks a lot more about his feelings with me which is good. I have always supported him and always will; he means so much to me. Gareth has signed out of the Army and will be out by May 2011. We are looking forward to our future together.*'

Jamie Evans, too, has had a happy outcome in his relationship with Donna:

> '*I have decided that as I am nearing thirty it is time to marry Donna so I proposed in July 2010 with plans to marry in 2012. I have taken up cycling as my running and rugby days are over. I am enjoying road cycling, and am looking at purchasing an off-road bike to tackle some more challenging routes. I think it's safer off-road with the drivers around today.*'

While Jamie's leg injury is improving, his hearing continues to be a problem:

'I am waiting for a consultation with a specialist, although the outcome is bleak as tinnitus gets worse not better. Tinnitus and hearing loss would be the major factor that would stop me from deploying again, not my leg injuries. This will influence my decision about whether or not I have a future in the Armed Forces. Maybe it is time to sample "Civvy Street". This is a very difficult decision for me as the Welsh Guards has been a major part of my life since I left school thirteen years ago. I am being given good advice by the Battalion which is very much onside and understands the situation that I find myself in.'

Donna looks back on her relationship with Jamie and the progress he has made:

'One year on from Jamie's horrific incident and although some things stay the same, a lot has changed. Jamie has recently run a half marathon in Kenya to raise awareness for charity. He was initially told by doctors that he should expect to always have a limp, and that he would never run again. His determination has proved them all wrong but he still feels lots of pain in his leg, and has good and bad days. However the accident hasn't faded into the background and has left me with a very different Jamie.

I love him dearly, but do not see the same man that left me to go to Afghanistan. Jamie is a quiet, private man and has always been that way, but now I see a painfully shy man who doesn't want to go out and see my friends and family. Who only wants to be with me in our house, and occasionally with lots of prompting will go out to see his close friends. He is deep and thinks a lot, and as much as I say I am here to talk to, Jamie will not burden me with his thoughts which I know torture him throughout the day and in his sleep of that horrific day his vehicle was blown up in the summer of 2009.

I expect a lot from Jamie as I see how he has physically

recovered but sometimes forget the healing that is needed mentally. We recently went to one of my best friend's weddings and it was a real struggle every step of the way to get Jamie to go to such a large social event. We had several attempts shopping for his suit; when he had to go into shops with loud music on he would lose his temper and say he wanted to go home. When we eventually bought it he started having second thoughts about going to the wedding.

I did manage to persuade him to go but he had flashbacks in the heat and while looking at the lights. He drove back to the hotel to be on his own. Again, this caused numerous arguments as I struggle to understand what is going on in his head.

We are muddling along together and keep busy on weekends as Jamie is best when he is active, but my concern is that the problems are being pushed away and not being dealt with properly. Jamie and I have had a lucky escape; we have a lovely house together, got engaged and plan to be married. We are looking forward to our lives together, hoping for our own family in time.

I am trying to adjust to our two-day relationship again since Jamie returned to the Battalion in Aldershot, only coming back to Wales at weekends. After having him home for a whole year (although under horrible circumstances) I now find myself in a kingsize bed sleeping in his pyjamas five nights a week waiting for Friday and then hoping Sunday comes slowly. Saying that though, I appreciate how lucky I am to have any time with him at all after everything he went through, and am acutely aware that some wives and girlfriends were not as lucky as I was and won't get to sleep next to their partners again.

Jamie has impressed and amazed me more than any one I have ever met. His sheer determination and mental strength has got him through this tragic incident. He has worked so hard to regain his weight and strength. He is a very special person who *is not bitter, has no regrets, and accepts his injury and counts himself very lucky. I also count myself very lucky to be his girlfriend. This has made me realise that he is everything to me and his safety and us being together means more to me than anything.*

I frequently talk to Jamie and beg him not to go back to Afghan, not to return to work and to get another job but he refuses to listen. He loves what he does; he is really good at it and has no fear of returning to Afghan if and when he is needed. I, and also his mother, will not be as strong as Jamie. The thought of him returning to Afghan fills me with anxiety and dread. I will miss him but love him and want him to be happy. He is my best friend and the time we spent together in our house while he has recovered has been so special. Unfortunately for me the Army is what makes him happy and as hard as that is for me I need to accept that.'

Tom Spencer-Smith's shoulder injuries from the blast from an IED are improving:

'I am back at work and although some people have an understanding of how I am recovering, others do not. This is mainly because I look fine. In addition, because I do not go into great detail about the treatment I am receiving I inevitably keep people in the dark, so of course the recognition is less than it might have been. My injury will take time to heal; I still can only do three or four press-ups and can't carry any weight through my shoulders. However my plan is still to have a career in the Army and I sincerely hope that this fairly minor injury doesn't prevent that from happening.'

Many of the other people who have shared their experiences with me have also made readjustments to everyday living within the Battalion. Stacey Merritt-Webb looks back:

'When Darren returned we promised ourselves some time each week/month to go out together and make time for ourselves as a couple. Unfortunately we haven't really stuck to that plan and fell back to the routine we had before very quickly. We should make more effort to have time alone.

I think this tour of Afghan has made us both re-evaluate life and what's important and not, those seven months were the hardest and most emotional of my life so far and I can't even imagine what my husband went through mentally and physically. It certainly put things into perspective for us both, the thought of having to do it again in 2012 fills me with dread – but I will because I love my soldier.'

Elizabeth Blackledge and Alannah McDonald told me that their relationships with their partners are now all the stronger for the experiences they went through during the six months the Battalion was in Afghanistan. Elizabeth brought me up to date with her news:

'Since Afghan things have begun to return to normal; with a few minor exceptions. Charlie is much better in the heat than he used to be, and this has facilitated some brilliant sunny holidays to Egypt and Mallorca, which are a little warmer than our previous trips to Cornwall. We have also both started reading about the history of Afghanistan and the surrounding region and it has now, somewhat bizarrely, become a comforting mutual pastime rather than a subject of fear and separation.

Overall, we are much stronger. Afghan serves as a stark reminder of how important we are to each other. It has been of great use in pulling us out of minor squabbles that accompany any long-term relationship, and for a month or two he definitely found a higher appreciation for my cooking.

When he returned I pieced together his experience, but only when parts of the jigsaw were freely offered. There will always *be things we will not divulge to each other about that time, but we understand each other much better, and I know that when he heads back out in 2012, I will be comforted by the familiarity of the experience and it will be a little easier.'*

Alannah told me that:

'Speedy and I are closer than ever. We have always had a good relationship but the emotions of that tour have definitely cemented a stronger bond between us. In my eyes if you can trust and support each other through something like Afghanistan then you will hopefully be able to survive anything as a couple. On reflection I am incredibly thankful and proud to have gone through the experience but my thoughts and prayers will never stray from the families who are presently living through a tour or to those families whose men were taken from them so suddenly.'

For the families who lost their loved ones the Army is no longer their life in the way it was, but they will always be considered part of the Welsh Guards' family and this family will always look out for them. This has already been proven in the way that the Welfare Office and the current Commanding Officer, Charlie Antelme, have kept in touch with them and put help in place where required. The Regimental Adjutant, Colonel (Retired) Tom Bonas, has been a godsend to all the bereaved, helping where necessary to relocate them out of quarters and into the homes of their choice, helping to look at schools for children and ensuring that all has been done to make their grieving as hassle-free as possible. All those who contributed the initial stories of their loss to this book have been good enough to dig deep again and look back at the ordeal they have been forced to undergo.

Tobie Fasfous's mother Anne was over in the UK to attend Tobie's inquest hearing when we met to talk about how she was getting on a year down the line. I had felt rather intrusive having to snatch time with her when she was in the country for such an emotionally draining event, but the hearing had run quickly and smoothly and she was relieved to be able to put it behind her. Nevertheless, it had inevitably 'opened the wounds' for her again and lunch was a combination of happy memories and sad reflections. We met at the hotel she was staying in just behind Wellington Barracks and talked, cried and laughed for three hours about Tobie and her life since he died. Living in Dubai, Anne has found that she has had the space to grieve and to try to reassemble her life again, but although she has been grieving from a distance she has still managed to support events to raise funds for military charities. She believes that, had the situation been reversed, Tobie would not have isolated himself and would have carried on with life as best he could, which gives her the strength to attempt the same:

> 'Sitting at home on the sofa feeling sorry for myself wasn't going to help and would only prolong the task of learning to live and function without Tobie as best I can. It is a learning process, and I'm not sure I'll ever get to the end of it. We have had all the "firsts" a year on: first Christmas without him, first anniversary of his birthday and his death. These you can semi-prepare yourself for. But it's the other things that pop up from nowhere: the panic when I wonder if I will forget what his voice sounded like, or his cheeky smile or what a hug felt like, and realising that there are so many "firsts" that will never happen for Tobie; these are the things that catch me unawares.
>
> My father was in the Army for a time; he was stationed in the Middle East and North Africa for several years and I grew up with his stories and artefacts from his postings around the house. He, Tobie and I were the three nomads of the family and we were all very much alike. In fact, Tobie used to describe me to his friends as being "a female version" of him.'

Working full-time as a human resources manager, and having younger son Alex in Dubai with her, has helped Anne to get back on her feet. She has also had a great deal of support from her friends:

'Living thousands of miles away from my immediate family was hard in the beginning but my friends and colleagues, many of whom had known Tobie since childhood, were invaluable in their support and understanding. Most of my colleagues are men but their caring side really came to the fore. From our head office in the UK to each of our local offices in the UAE, either by phone, email or in person they were all there for me. Jimmy and Eugene even went out and bought me a new mobile phone, the exact replica of my old broken one, and transferred the photo of Tobie that he had put there himself, along with a personalised ringtone and all the recent text messages between us, from the old one to the new. I'll never forget what the guys did for me just from knowing that something as simple as a phone was so important to me.

Tobie will always be a Welsh Guardsman so we will forever have a connection with the Battalion and continue to make return trips to the UK for significant "events". I have tried to keep life as normal as possible but I still can't bring myself to pack away all his things, or all the "memorabilia" we have collected since his death; it would feel as though I were packing Tobie himself away in boxes, and he's still very much a part of us and our lives.'

One year on and Margaret Evison has worked hard to set up the Mark Evison Foundation, which promotes the personal, mental and physical development of young people, particularly those who have less opportunity. It provides funds to enable these people to gain confidence, courage and self-reliance, as well as developing new skills.

Margaret felt that the Foundation would serve to perpetuate Mark's philosophy in life: he embraced personal challenge, self-development and teamwork. During his life he had opportunities to set himself challenges, such as running five hundred miles across the Pyrenees and two weeks trekking on the glaciers of Norway. He even had an ambition to be the youngest person to walk to the South Pole, although unfortunately lack of funding prevented him from doing so. A major part of the fun for him was in the planning of these adventures, and such experiences gave him the confidence and leadership skills that helped to make him the excellent soldier and the thoughtful, compassionate person that he was. It is very fitting that the Foundation, his legacy, encourages and promotes the values and experiences that Mark held in such high esteem.

Debby Morris told me how she was coping with life without her son Dane Elson:

'Almost a year on and it still seems like I am watching this happen to me, I am not part of it. I miss Dane so very very much but he is with me everywhere I go. I think and talk to him constantly as if he were with me. His things are still everywhere in the house. Everyone is still talking about him because he was loved by all who knew him and his beloved dog died two weeks ago so she is now with him, they will be rolling around together like he used to do when he came home for the weekends.

The Army have been very supportive and there have been numerous services and functions. I received the Elizabeth Cross from Prince Charles at Clarence House on Dane's behalf. There were five other families there on the day so it was nice to talk to them properly as when having met them before there were so many people that it wasn't possible. When Rupert Thorneloe's parents were leaving, his father came up to me and said "we now share a bond" which is so true. His wife and parents are so lovely.

His "bruvs" Paul and Smudge still keep in touch and still come down regularly to see us from Wigan and Birmingham with their partners. They are a huge support to me, and I to them. Whenever I turn the computer on there are messages from his many Army bruvs, too many to name, a lot of whom are now leaving the Army.

We now sponsor a rugby team called the Celtic Barbarians in honour and memory of Dane. The Lance Corporal Dane Elson Memorial Cup game starts on 23rd May and I will present the cup to the winning team in July. The shirts have "in memory of L Cpl Dane Elson" under the badge and the Welsh Guards' emblem on the sleeve and collar.

In many ways the last year has gone so fast and in others it seems like yesterday. It has been a very busy year with all the services and events and it still carries on. We now have a willow tree and a hardwood bench dedicated to Dane at the National Arboretum, in the Afghanistan section. It seems like everyone wants to keep remembering, which is how it should be.'

Stuart Elson told me that he was still struggling terribly to come to terms with Dane's death:

'People tell me that time is a great healer; well, it doesn't feel like it. The strength of my own feelings means sometimes it's hard to remember that I'm not the only one suffering. Losing Dane has had a profound effect on all our lives, and sometimes I overlook that his sisters have had to deal with the loss, too. One thing for sure is that I am immensely proud that Dane was in the Army and, just as important, was a Welsh Guard.

In June of 2007 we stood on Horse Guards Parade and watched our son take part in Trooping the Colour. No parents could have been prouder. Our son, such a naughty, rebellious, little ragamuffin taking part in one of the most prestigious military occasions in the world, we could never have expected so much.

Since Dane's death I have spoken to many of his colleagues, and while I expected most of them to be pleasant and say nice things about him, I am overwhelmed with the high regard in which Dane was held,

*particularly as a soldier. Knowing him as I did, I really shouldn't
have been surprised. He was always gutsy and would never give in,
probably what caused him to be in so much trouble but I also know
that he was extremely conscientious when people depended on him.*

*One thing I have found, is the need for contact with and
from the Regiment. It is a link to Dane like no other, probably
because of the fact he was killed in action, and to this end we
have been grateful for the visits we have had from a number of
Welsh Guards, particularly Lieutenant Colonel Charlie Antelme,
Captain Darren Pridmore and Padre Morgan. Also, Captain
Ian Moore from the Royal Welsh Regiment who was our Family
Liaison Officer and has remained a family friend; they really do
not realise how important their visits are.'*

When I heard from Carol Brackpool, she also wanted to stress
how much support she had received from the Army after her
son John died:

*'The Welsh Guards have given us so much support, they visit
often and are always there if I need any help. The Regimental
Adjutant, Tom Bonas, rings regularly and the new Commanding
Officer, Charlie Antelme, has visited me. Seeing as Johnny was
with them such a short time I wasn't really expecting this. They
have all been great. I'm not sure how I expected to feel ten months
down the line but the hurt is worse. I miss him more and more
as time goes by. We are coming up to the anniversaries of the last
time I saw him, the last time I spoke to him and of course a year
since I lost him. I really cannot see a light at the end of the tunnel
when my pain will ease. All I can do is take one day at a time and
hopefully one day I will wake up and instead of feeling sad I will
smile and think of my Johnny.'*

Carol was one of the original group of mothers, united by the
fact that each of their sons had been killed in Afghanistan.

They came together to set up the charity Afghan Heroes, which is dedicated to the welfare of those directly involved in the conflict. From providing short-break accommodation for the wounded, their families and families of the fallen, promoting an environment where they can be together and help each other through times of extreme pressure and anxiety, to sending a box of useful items to every British serviceman and -woman in Afghanistan, the charity has been a great success. Carol has done several fundraising events herself, including a parachute jump and driving along Route 66 in America on a Harley Davidson motorbike.

In the spring of 2010 John's sister Kim gave birth to a son called Henry John. John's father Alan said that the arrival of a new baby has given him reason to keep strong now and he sees Henry several times a week. John's family had a plaque laid for him at the Emirates Stadium, the home ground for Arsenal Football Club, of whom John was an avid fan, and on the anniversary of John's death, the war memorial in his home town was inscribed with his name; it will remain for ever alongside the names of other men from Crawley who have given their lives in past wars.

I feel it is vital to remember the work that these men, who gave their lives, were doing in Afghanistan. Often the media feeds us the statistics of those killed and sometimes those who were wounded, but rarely mentions what their sacrifices were for. Yes, they were in direct combat with the Taliban, but there was also work going on behind the scenes to clear the roads of IEDs so that the forces could gain access and help the Afghan people to rebuild their lives. There were schools to build and electricity projects to run, but in order to do this the troops also had to carefully build up and maintain the trust of the locals. Despite the differences in culture and religion, decent citizens the world over have a common aim; they want the best for their families, a healthy life and friends and neighbours who they can like and trust. The international troops out in Afghanistan are doing their best to share these common values at the same time as respecting local values that arise from cultural differences.

This can be seen in the work that Sean Birchall was doing before he was killed by a roadside bomb; the gratitude of the local people is reward in itself and also justifies British presence in Afghanistan.

Sean's legacy, his school and community project in Afghanistan, continues to prosper following subsequent involvement from ISAF (International Stabilisation Assistance Force) to provide the security necessary to enable local workers to renovate it. Thousands of dollars of investment led to improvements including new electrics, desks and paint, and the school re-opened five months after Sean's death. By the time the Grenadier Guards completed their subsequent tour in March 2010, between ninety and one hundred and fifty children were being taught there. The school can now accommodate over three hundred and seventy pupils.

Many of the children who now attend would previously have received no education, or were taught in mosque madrasas (religious schools) where only basic literacy and numeracy is taught; this renovated school, by contrast, now has a curriculum recognised by the Afghan government and the children will leave with useful qualifications.

Support projects from home, too, have provided the school with much needed educational supplies, including one project initiated by the secondary school in Guildford that Sean attended. This project was so successful that it extended to other nearby primary schools, the church and even the local old people's home.

Major Alex Corbet Burcher, who replaced Sean as IX Company Commander, said:

'On arrival in Basharan, under Sean's command, IX Company was clearing compounds of IEDs in a well-known insurgent stronghold. The locals were initially cautious about our presence but relations improved greatly and Sean began the process of developing an excellent relationship with the locals, who from then on came to checkpoints to warn us about Taliban activity. Relationships with them and with the Afghan National Security Forces continued to develop after his death and the Afghan National Army now patrol the area, reassuring the locals and establishing good relationships with the community for the first time.'

By the time the Welsh Guards handed over to the Grenadier Guards in October 2009, the repair and building of twenty wells was providing more running water for drinking and farming. Plans were in place for the installation of a hydroelectric power turbine to make full use of the fast-flowing river running through the village to bring electricity to two thousand homes. Also by this time the project had repaired numerous bridges, provided one hundred prayer mats, fifty copies of the Koran, and repaired a mosque damaged by small-arms fire.

What was a very unstable area, known as the 'Badlands' and on the Battalion's arrival dominated by insurgents, became, in Alex's words, 'a relatively benign and secure area' with a thriving community within the six months of the tour.

It is testimony to the gratitude and compassion of the Basharan people that after Sean's death his wife Jo received a letter of condolence, translated into English, from the village elder. He praised the work that Sean and his Company had done and the ongoing work that the present troops were doing, and thanked her for her support.

Christopher King's burial place is perfect for a man so well loved and so energetic, being in the centre of activity in his village. As the local post office has been closed, the church has become a significant local focal point, as it would have been historically. It is used as a post office twice a week for people to collect their pensions. The daily paper is delivered to the church door and it hosts an annual festival of music and arts. Judy tells of local youngsters who visited Christopher's grave on the anniversary of his death and on his birthday this year, when he would have been twenty-one: they left messages, photos and the odd unopened can of Guinness on his grave in memory of him.

A print of a painting by the artist Hugh Beattie now very appropriately hangs in the village church with a plaque of explanation underneath. It was dedicated to Christopher during the Remembrance Sunday Service in 2010. It depicts the altar in the Garrison Church in Aldershot on the occasion of the memorial service for the Welsh Guards on their return from Afghanistan. The altar is draped with the Welsh Guards' Colours, the Union Jack stands in the corner and the sun streams onto the scene through a beautiful stained-glass window. It is a very fitting tribute to Christopher and the six other men killed. Indeed, it represents all those hundreds of men and women from across the Armed Forces who have died in action in the past, and are continuing to do so.

Christopher's grandmother Judy has worked as a Samaritan for several years. Before Christopher went to Afghanistan she dealt with anxious calls from soldiers who were preparing to go on operations and building the mental wall around themselves to harden up before the event, and dealing with their concerns about the dreaded goodbye to their families. This gave her insight and helped her to understand what Christopher went through before he left. She has spoken to soldiers who have returned, and who may not be coping, which has also helped her to cope with his death. However, she takes the grief of those around her onto her own shoulders and finds the responsibility overwhelming at times:

'Time doesn't heal; it just helps you cope. As a grandma you don't expect to lose a grandchild. I always remember some words a friend once told me: "A mother is only ever as happy as her unhappiest child." It is so true; I have to cope with knowing my child is hurting because he's lost his child and a grandson who is hurting because he's lost his brother. The last thing you want is for your own son to lose his baby. It's not like rubbing knees better or taking splinters out; you can't fix it. I am grieving for them as well.

But they all cope so well and are all supportive of me, so I have nothing to complain about. Yes, I get weepy, but I am unutterably proud of Christopher, proud of my family, and so pleased I had the "déjà vu" to be able to help with the boys' upbringing, of doing it all again; I am glad I had that precious time.'

When I told Judy about the title 'Don't Say Goodbye', and the different 'goodbyes' in various parts of the book – the goodbyes to friends, to children starting boarding school, to a loved one going on exercise or an operational tour, and the ultimate goodbye when we never see them again – her reply was both thought-provoking and immensely poignant:

'Of course, none of the families who have lost their loved ones ever do say goodbye really because they are always there in our hearts.'

My friend Sally reflected on the year since Rupert's death.

'It took almost a year to formulate an initial plan and to lay the foundations for our new, unwanted life. In anticipation of our

eventual move from the Army quarter, my first priority was to plan the education for Hannah and Sophie and we have found a wonderful school, so this has been a great step forward.'

One of the last conversations Sally had with Rupert was about where they might consider sending the girls to school one day, and although he had an idea of where he thought they should go, neither he nor Sally had planned any further. So, when Sally had to make a move, she naturally wanted to honour Rupert's wish but was very careful to consider other places as well. In the end, his suggestion came up trumps

'not only because Rupert had suggested it, but I knew it was the best one for both of them. It was strange; as I came away from visiting it, I felt that Rupert was with me, confirming my decision. I just knew it was the right school.'

Sally was full of praise for the Welsh Guards' Regimental Adjutant, Tom Bonas, who 'really went the extra mile to help; he came to all the schools with me so I didn't get boggled, and was able to ask many relevant questions.' She also emphasised the ongoing support from the Army network in helping her to find a house; it was through the Grenadier Guards that she found a place to rent near the school of choice for Hannah and Sophie.

Shortly after Sally moved she had to call an electrician to repair a problem with the computer. He made the connection with Rupert straight away, as there were photos of him around the house. Not only had he been in the Army himself but he had also worked with Rupert in Iraq. Filling out his form, he turned to Sally and said, 'OK, this form says I have just been stuck in traffic for an hour. We all look after our own in this life, so what other jobs can I help you with?'

He spent the next hour hanging pictures and wiring up the

computer. It was a lovely spontaneous act of kindness in a world that can be so clinically 'by the book' at times.

Although Sally is making important decisions for the future, there are certain times of the day which can test her strength:

> '*What I dread the most is time on my own to think in the evenings; the days are generally not too bad because I am so busy, but the evenings are more difficult. My coping mechanism is simply to go to bed early, which is just as well as the girls are up at the crack of dawn every day.*
>
> *Some days it's like wading through treacle; people tell me I look well but I feel no different from the day before. I miss him so very much. I still can't believe that he is not coming back; I feel that he is just away. I have been told that grief is like a huge black hole: it's always there but in time, other colours gather around the edge and start to blur the sharp edges. But it doesn't go away, it's still there underneath. I will have to learn to cope with it because it is not something I can ever get over.*'

However, the time of day Sally looks forward to the most is picking the girls up from school, having them home and being there for them. Hannah is proving to be a very sensitive and thoughtful child; Sophie is the 'firecracker' and is frequently getting into mischief, but equally fun and adorable to be with. Hannah has very fond memories of Rupert and talks of him often, telling people that 'my Daddy taught me to swing on a swing'. Sadly, Sophie is too little to have such memories of her Daddy.

Sally now works hard to fill the beautiful memory boxes gifted to the girls for them to treasure in the future.

Since Rupert's death in 2009, some incredible initiatives have been taken, including the launch of the Radley Armed Forces Fund by Radley College, where Rupert and Lieutenant

Douglas Dalzell were educated. Douglas was tragically killed on operations six months after Rupert, while serving with the Coldstream Guards during their deployment to Afghanistan. This fund, set up in their memories, aims to educate the sons and daughters of forces personnel, whether they have Radley connections or not, who are killed or seriously wounded while serving their country.

In July 2010 Richard and I took Oliver and Annabel to a memorial polo match organised by Rupert's sister Jessica in Kirtlington, Oxfordshire where Rupert used to play polo frequently. On a wonderful, sunny day with a lovely family atmosphere, the Band of the Welsh Guards played music at the request of the children as it moved around the field asking families what they would like to hear. There was a parachute display, and an auction, following which the players battled it out on the field as hundreds of families looked on while eating their picnics and sharing wine and stories with old friends. Sally's girls took their turn on the climbing wall, which was manned by young Welsh Guardsmen, and joined the other children in stroking the polo ponies under the shade of large English oak trees. At the end of the match everybody joined in to flatten the turf back into place where it had been churned up by the ponies' hooves, a tradition in polo called 'treading the divots'. The Rupert Thorneloe Memorial Cup was presented to the winning team and the event raised an immense sum for the Welsh Guards Afghanistan Appeal.

The reasons for going to war have always been, and will always be, contentious. Saying to those whose loved ones have been killed or seriously injured that we should not have been there in the first place does not help their grieving process. The bereaved families need to know that their loved ones did not die in vain. The wounded need to know that that the injuries that will now prevent them from doing the job they lived for were suffered for a reason. The good that has come out of the situation in Afghanistan needs to be emphasised, whether or not we 'win' this war.

These sentiments were emphasised by the Welsh Guards' Padre, Deiniol Morgan, who gave the address at the memorial service for the Welsh Guards on their return from Afghanistan in October 2009. This was the first time the Battalion as a whole had had the chance to come together to mourn. I didn't attend as places were limited and I was conscious that there were many family members who deserved seats. Richard did go, though, and told me that it was a moving sight, as one family representative from each of the seven men who were killed walked up the aisle to place a candle with their loved one's name on it at the high altar, where they remained alight throughout the service. Padre Morgan's address was a moving yet down-to-earth and positive acclamation of these men's lives and what they stood for:

'The people of Helmand, the transformation of whose lives was at the heart of our main effort, are very much like you and me. Their appearance, customs, diets and lives differ from ours but beneath all that you would find people who loved kindness, loyalty, truthfulness and family just as much as we do. In being called to serve them, and to aid the process of their liberation from cruelty and barbarity, we needed to remember this. The victory to be sought was the victory for the people of Afghanistan.

In some people's eyes, the conflict in Afghanistan seems to have no end. And because of this our great fear is: did they die in vain?

These seven men were prepared to lay down their lives not knowing whether they had succeeded or not. Here is true courage – and it's one of the reasons that there is such a deep and *profound admiration for our soldiers throughout the country. The fact that they were willing to die, that they did die, serving the people of a distant and dangerous country is tribute enough to them.'*

Laughter, tears, happiness and sorrow have been spent in the writing of this book: by the many people who have contributed, and by myself in speaking for them. Singing the song of the families behind the scenes on the modern-day 'home front' started with an idea, grew into a necessity and ended with fulfilment. I have tried my best to do these people justice so that they may be understood and appreciated, not pitied or disregarded. And, most of all, I hope I have paid just tribute to those who have lost their lives and to their families who are left to carry on. I hope, too, that the book will serve to honour all those who have been killed from other Regiments and services, when these stories are echoed in the hearts of their families and friends.

I thought I knew the Army lifestyle well, but in hearing the stories of so many I realise that my experience is the tip of an iceberg. What lay beneath is the silent, unseen and often unheard story of the majority of those who go about their usual lives in unusual circumstances, and will continue to do so.

In a country such as Britain, where we enjoy the freedom that has been earned by the giving of so many lives for so many years, it is easy to take for granted the way we live. In a society that sees less community spirit than before, as families are spread around geographically, as neighbourhoods are fragmented and local businesses are lost, the need to belong remains as strong as ever. The lives of military families are lives of friendship, trust and loyalty, of community spirit and a genuine appreciation of each other.

Looking back on the sixteen months since the funerals of those seven Welsh Guardsmen in the summer of 2009 I realise that life does, has to, go on. It seems an age since the moment I witnessed the harsh reality of living on a knife-edge in the eyes of the grieving wives and families. They were helpless to shape the destiny of their loved ones, turning with dignity to prayer to provide hope and light. They will neither forget nor ever say goodbye but their experience in living the Army lifestyle, the resourcefulness they needed to adapt to ever-changing situations and the independence required to live apart for such long periods may, ironically, have prepared them for the challenges ahead. They are well equipped to find the inner strength to come through their grief and rebuild their lives. This is the age-old story: the story of the battle, the wounded and the fallen and, in turn, the personal battles of those left behind. It has not changed for centuries.

Don't Say Goodbye opened on the summit of a mountain and yet more mountains have been climbed since I started writing this book, both metaphorically and literally. Many of the wounded and bereaved are still climbing, but with the help of those close to them, we can only hope and pray that they reach the top.

Acknowledgements

During the course of writing *Don't Say Goodbye* I have felt rather like the Pied Piper, scooping up so many people en route that I was not sure how many there were until I stopped the music and looked back. I was astounded, on counting up the contributors, to find that there were over seventy in total. As well as individuals, this number has been condensed into a series of families and couples, but I was delighted to include them all as, without them, I would not have had such a strong representation of different stories and would not have had a book to write. I am grateful to each one, but in particular to the families of the seven men who were killed in action in the summer of 2009 with the Welsh Guards. My special thanks go to Sally Thorneloe, who shared her thoughts and troubles without hesitation, despite the anguish she must have suffered in the process. All the bereaved were so willing to share their memories and experiences, as a dedication to their loved ones. In the process, I have met some truly inspiring and courageous people. I hope I have done them justice.

My sincere thanks go to His Royal Highness The Prince of Wales who so kindly agreed to write a foreword which endorses the importance of telling this story and to Henry Finnegan, his Assistant Equerry, for his rapid response over my request to apply for permission.

My thanks also to Mark Mellars and Stacey Merritt-Webb for so generously offering me the use of their very personal journals, without which much of the raw emotion would have been lost.

I am so grateful to Nicky Mott who not only contributed but endured endless requests to put me in touch with relevant people and to Andy Campbell who trawled through forty CDs of Battalion photos to try to find a cover shot. Thank you to Robin Orange, the Athurton family, Susanna Stanford, Hugh Beattie, Stacey Merritt-Webb, Sarah Launders and Sally Thorneloe for generously allowing me to use their photos.

Then there are those behind the scenes; John Warburton-Lee for his 'how to get published pep talk'; the Welsh Guards Welfare Office, particularly Darren Pridmore, for spreading the word when the idea to write a book was first conceived; the Commanding Officer, Charlie Antelme, for letting me use the Officers' Mess to interview the Guardsmen; the men who were polite enough to allow me to pester them for final consent to publish while on exercise in Kenya and those who put up with constant phone calls and emails when picking over minutiae. I also thank the Regimental Adjutant Tom Bonas for his interest throughout and for spreading the word amongst the Battalion.

Of course, there would not be a book at all without help from those who gave me inspiration; my creative writing tutor, Jaci Harries, who encouraged me to believe that there is a book in all of us. When I realised that maybe she was right, I took the idea to Jane Mays, who helped me enormously in the early stages of trying to find a publisher, and to Fi Cotter-Craig, who suggested a list of potential agents; I am so grateful to them for putting me on the right track. I was incredibly lucky to be accepted by my agent Lizzy Kremer, of David Higham Associates, who believed in the idea and my ability to write from the start, and who found me a wonderful Senior Editor, Fenella Bates at Hodder and Stoughton. They guided me through my initiation into the world of publishing, a very steep learning curve for me, and managed to pull me through the other end with a book to show for it. Fenella's patience and calming influence saved me from the mania of the last few weeks and Lizzy's level head kept my feet firmly on the ground.

I am aware that there are so many behind the scenes at Hodder as well, without whose team work this would not have happened, but in particular my thanks go to the Assistant Editor Ciara Foley for her superb job in contacting the contributors for consent, to Helen Coyle for her structural edit and to Jim Caunter for his proof reading. My thanks also to the Publicity Director, Karen Geary and her publicist Lucy Zilberkweit. I also thank Lizzy's assistant Laura West at David Higham.

Thank you especially to my family for their interest, encouragement and support and for their tolerance and understanding; my brother Simon and sister Kate and my brother-in-law Edward and sister-in-law Rebecca. In particular, I thank my father, The Lord Dear, and my step-mother Alison, for their fascination in the project and to my in-laws Jane and Rodney Stanford for their grammatical advice.

But most of all, thank you to Oliver and Annabel for your patience, for understanding when I missed the occasional sports match and for always asking how the book was coming along. And to Richard, for your total belief in me. I once described you as a 'determined, bloody minded and persistent man who is not one to give in or give up', some of which seems to have rubbed off! But without you I would not have this story to tell, so thank you for your unconditional support, your encouragement in the idea, its planning and its execution, and for getting me into the Army life in the first place. You never talk shop when you come home; I offloaded my entire warehouse every day. You always believed I could see it through which, in turn, made me all the more determined to make it happen.

Index